The Heatons of Deane

The varying fortunes of a Lancashire family over 850 years.

by
Edmund R. Heaton

Front Cover:
Arms of Heton of Heton-in-Lonsdale, C13th. Bishop Heton's Tomb, Ely Cathedral, 1609.
Lostock Junction Mills, Bolton, 1900.

This book is dedicated to all those women,
born a Heaton or married to a Heaton,
who have played their part in this story,
and to whom I am conscious of
not having done full justice.

© E. R. Heaton, 2000,
author & publisher,
Berllan Ber, Abermagwr,
Aberystwyth, Ceredigion,
SY23 4AR, UK.

All rights reserved.
No reproduction permitted in whole or in part,
in any medium, without the prior written approval
of the author & publisher.

ISBN 0-9538247-0-5

Printed by Cambrian Printers Ltd, Aberystwyth, Wales

Contents

		Page
Acknowledgements.		4
Introduction.		6
Chapter 1	Early Origins	9
Chapter 2	Two Hundred Years in Lonsdale	16
Chapter 3	The Move to South Lancashire	36
Chapter 4	Years of Progress & Prosperity	42
Chapter 5	A Family Divided	66
Chapter 6	New Landlords	84
Chapter 7	Gentlemen, Yeomen, and Husbandmen	95
Chapter 8	Towards the Industrial Revolution	115
Chapter 9	The Ravenhurst Branch	131
Chapter 10	Trade and Industry	144
Chapter 11	The 20th Century	163
Chapter 12	Heatons Elsewhere - USA; Wales; Yorkshire	176
Conclusions		196
Appendix 1	Ramification	199
Appendix 2	Heaton Heraldry	202
Appendix 3	Heaton burials at St. Mary's Church, Deane	206
Appendix 4	Did they come with Canute?	209
Index		210

Acknowledgements

Firstly I have to acknowledge the very considerable debt that I owe to a man who died 85 years ago. It would have been impossible for me to have written this book at this time without access to the work of John Heaton Partington (1838-1915), completed in 1903, and whose papers are deposited in Bolton Central Library and Chetham Library, Manchester. For some years around the turn of the century Partington diligently researched the history of this Heton/Heaton family in Lancashire, meticulously searching out the references and documents which he required. The financial backing and encouragement he received from William Heaton of Lostock enabled him to engage the services of Hardy & Page, a firm of professional genealogical researchers to assist him, but always under his strict direction as surviving letters make clear. This made it possible for him to extend his investigations in a degree of detail which would be difficult even now when communications are so much faster and data so much more accessible than was the position 100 years ago.

I have to say that I do not always reach the same conclusions as Partington from the facts he revealed but have few doubts as to the accuracy of the latter. Wherever possible the references given by Partington have been checked and in numerous instances more recent publications and references have been consulted. However time and distance has prevented a number of the older references from being examined and in these cases the information given by Partington has been accepted at face value.

I am greatly indebted to Mr Ron Smith of Bolton for his provision of advice and information applicable to the Heaton family generally and the research he himself has undertaken in relation to various branches of the family. Mr Colin Wood of Oldham was extremely helpful in enabling me to track down a number of 19th century Heatons in the Greater Manchester area as also was Mr Frank Stirrup of Cumbria. I am grateful to Mr Tom Arkwright of Chorley for his masterly legal analysis of the transactions and litigation which took place in the 16th century between the Heaton and Anderton families. To Mr Richard Heaton of Plas Heaton, Denbighshire, I express my grateful thanks for the information he supplied with regard to his family and to Mr Richard Heaton of High Wycombe goes the credit for discovering documents in the Public Record Office which throw much more light on Heaton relationships in the early 17th century. Mr James Heaton of Lancaster was a considerable help with the information he provided about his own family. I am grateful to the family of the late John Heaton of Keighley for allowing me to refer to his research and to Mrs Hazel Holmes and Mr Robin Greenwood for arranging this. The information supplied by Mrs Julia Heaton Krutilla of West Virginia, USA has been invaluable in relation to the spread of her family in America and I thank her warmly. I am fortunate that I have been able to make reference to the findings of a recent archaeological survey of Heaton Old Hall,

Bolton, carried out by Manchester University Archaeological Unit and I am grateful to Dr Michael Nevell for making their report available to me. Heraldic artwork was supplied by Messrs Baz Manning and David Hopkinson and their skill is impressive.

Members of the staffs of Lancashire Record Office, Bolton Archives, Bolton Environment Dept., Lancaster City Museum, the National Library of Wales, Royal Commission for Historic Monuments in England (RCHME), and Royal Commission for Ancient & Historic Monuments in Wales (RCAHMW) have all been most cooperative in helping me to obtain access to the material I required and I thank them all. Any misinterpretation of the data with which I have been provided by anyone is, of course, entirely my fault.

Every effort has been made to trace the copyright holders of any illustrations used and specific permission obtained. If, on occasions, these efforts have been unsuccessful I hope my use of these illustrations will be excused.

Eddie Heaton
Aberystwyth, 2000.

Introduction

The start of the Third Millenium A.D. would seem to be an opportune time to publish the history of a family which can be traced back through nearly nine centuries of the Second Millenium and indeed, if the conclusions of one particular researcher can be accepted, over 1000 years back, into the First Millenium also. Over this period they spread through the whole of Lancashire society except the aristocracy; being successively, lords of the manor, knights of the realm, clergy, lawyers, merchants, yeomen farmers, successful industrial tycoons, managers and operatives, as well as sometimes becoming failed entrepreneurs, debtors, paupers and the occasional murder victim. Their undoubted prolificacy has ensured that hundreds of people in south Lancashire now bear the name Heaton or are related in some way to this extensive family. Understandably, the number of family branches which can be followed in a work of this nature is limited but it has been possible to trace the main line over more than 25 generations.

Members of this family first come to our notice around the year 1140, during the reign of King Stephen. Most of the earliest written records relate to land which they owned, land transactions into which they entered, and land disputes in which they were involved. In some instances the holding of a public appointment by an individual is a matter of surviving written record but the normal household activities of a family of no particular note were very rarely recorded. In more recent times we find more documents relating to disputes and agreements between individual members of the family and the similarity between their problems and our own becomes more marked, as also does the genuine family affection which existed in relationships which were often initially formal and a matter of family arrangement in connection with marriage.

The family can be identified as living firstly by the estuary of the River Lune, near Lancaster, where they owned the manor of Heton-in-Lonsdale from which they took their name, spelt in this way until the late 16th century. They enlarged their holdings over the next 250 years in this area of north Lancashire, holding various public appointments, and in the 13th century two successive generations of the head of the family were of sufficient substance to receive knighthoods. Thereafter the estate was dispersed amongst several sons and no member of the family in Lancashire subsequently held a title. Finally, on the death of the head of the family in 1387 most of the lands in north Lancashire were inherited by his two daughters and, on their marriages, passed out of the hands of the Heton family.

However, two generations earlier in 1309, a younger son had been granted the manor of Heton-under-Horwich in south Lancashire by the Baron of Manchester. This manor, which had been been carved out of the former forest of Horwich, was a township in the parish of Deane near Bolton, Lancs. and together with the remnants of the Heton lands in Lonsdale formed the estate which the family were to hold for the next 260 years, and became the area in which their various descendants settled and multiplied up to the present time.

From the early 14th century until the middle of the 16th century the Hetons prospered on their lands between Bolton and Horwich, increasing their holdings by a marriage in 1398 to a Billinge heiress, which brought the manor of Birchley near Wigan into Heton ownership. Other members of the family became merchants, churchmen and servants of the king. In the 1500s a long series of disputes and litigation between various members of the family was exploited by an unscrupulous neighbour who, by playing off members of the family against one another, was able eventually to acquire the bulk of the Heaton freehold estates from the young heir in 1570.

When the freehold land passed into the hands of other families, many Heatons who had previously farmed their land as tenants, found their situation little changed and continued for many generations to occupy their lands as lessees. From the late 16th century, these yeoman farmers worked to increase the productivity of their land and conduct their domestic textile businesses. From 1790 onwards the Industrial Revolution was launched in Lancashire by these men, some of whom succeeded and others failed. For 150 years Heaton entrepreneurs were engaged in the cotton industry in Bolton and other towns and a few are still very much involved in textile manufacture today.

Although the concentration is undoubtedly still in south-east Lancashire, members of the family have moved away in small numbers throughout the whole of their history and they can now be found in many parts of the UK and abroad. Their recent enthusiasm, during the 20th century, for trying to re-establish their connections has enabled a chapter to be included in this book which gives details of Heaton families now living elsewhere than in Lancashire.

E.R.H.
Aberystwyth
March 2000

18th century map of Lancaster and the Lune estuary, probably little changed from five centuries earlier.

Chapter One

Early Origins

In the early years of the 12th century, what is now north Lancashire was considered to be either part of Northumberland, because it had been within the old kingdom of Northumbria, or an extension of Yorkshire, because ecclesiastically it was within the province of York. Less than 100 years had elapsed since the Norman Conquest had brought William I to the throne of England in the year 1066, and the area with which we are concerned had gradually become known as Lonsdale, derived from the name of its main river, the Lon or Lune. William had given these lands to his kinsman Roger of Poitou who had made Loncastre or Lancaster his headquarters and established his new castle there. By 1102, however, Roger had forfeited his lands to the Crown, following his unsuccessful opposition to Henry I., and thereafter they were always in royal hands. On Henry's death in 1135 they passed to Stephen and then to Henry II. Stephen's reign, 1135-1154, was notable for virtually continuous strife between factions supporting the king and those supporting the other claimant to the throne, the Empress Matilda.

Living through those turbulent times, at Ulverston in Furness, was a family whose head was a thane named Waldef, the first known ancestor of the family which is the subject of this book. He had three sons, Augustine, William, and Adam and one daughter, whose name is not recorded, but who married Norman de Redman.[1] By him she had a son, Henry de Redman, who is recorded as entering into a charter in 1190 to pay 3 shillings a year to provide lights for St. Mary's Church, Furness. In this charter he names his uncles, William, son of Waldef, and Adam.[2], thereby providing documentary evidence of the existence of the first members of the family which was to become the Heatons of Deane.

Henry held the office of Seneschal to Gilbert fitz Reinfred, Baron of Kendal, and as such was responsible for and would have been entitled to live in his lord's castles, manorhouses and other residences. In 1195 Henry de Redman is recorded as being fined 120 marks (£80), a very considerable sum at that time, for joining in the rebellion of Prince John against his brother Richard I, whilst the king was away at the Crusades. Henry was a character who could have come straight out of the pages of Sir Walter Scott's "Ivanhoe", albeit on the unpopular side, that of Prince John. However, given the circumstances of the time his attitude is perhaps understandable. John was wellknown in Lonsdale, whereas Richard spent only six months in England during his 10-year reign, due to his commitments to the Crusade in Palestine and his lands in France. John, on the other hand, as Count of Mortain and later as king, proved to be a beneficent and generous overlord to the land which became

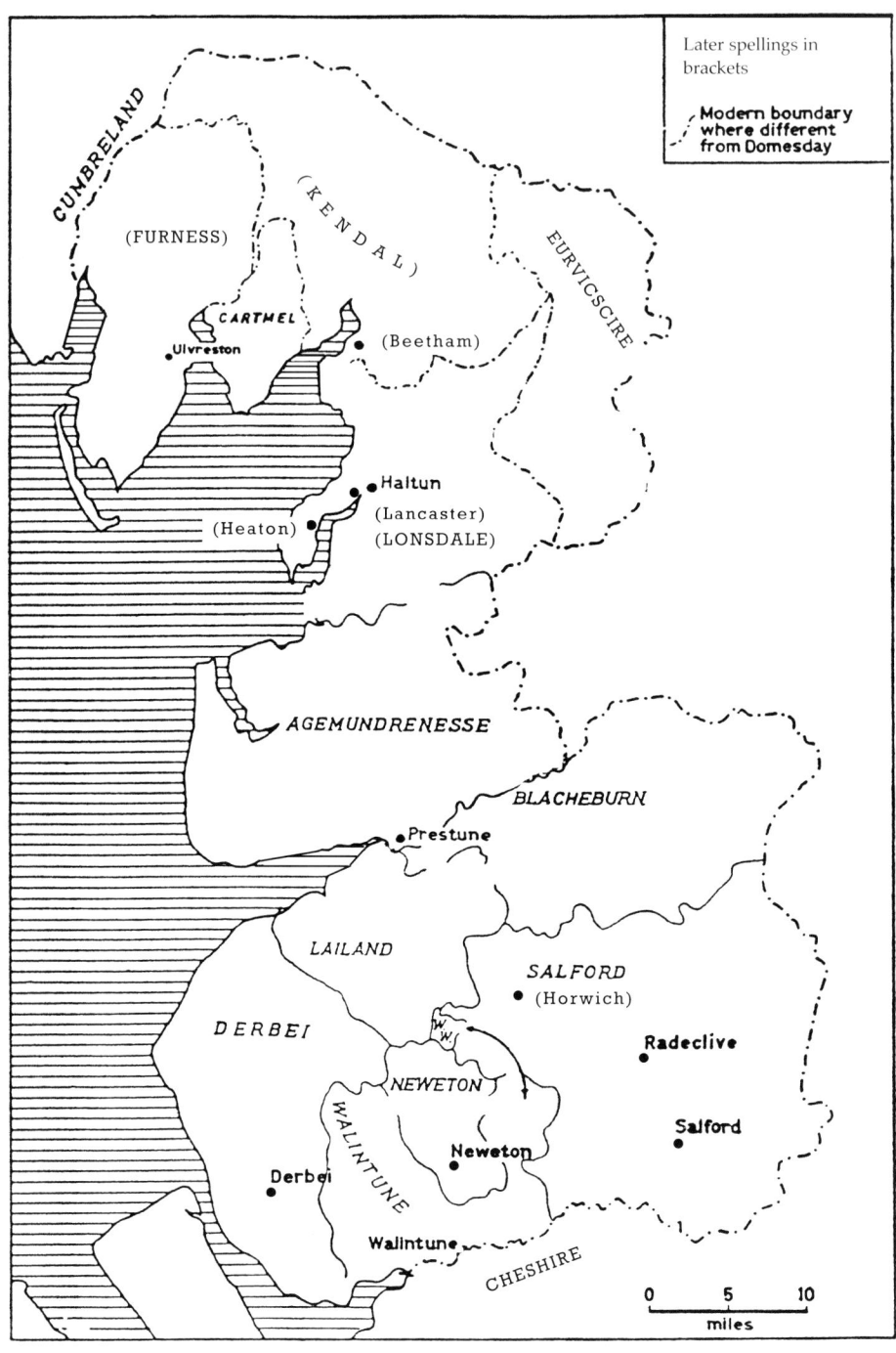

Map of the Hundred divisions of the county at the time of the Domesday Survey.

Early Origins

Lancashire, carrying out much building work and granting a charter to the burgesses of Lancaster on terms advantageous to them. Henry is recorded as still owing £4 of his fine when John came to the throne in 1199[3] and one presumes he was then excused payment of the amount outstanding.

First Land Acquisitions

Augustine, Waldef's eldest son, acquired land of half a carucate in Torver in Ulverston, from William de Lancaster, 2nd Baron of Kendal (1170-1184).[4] A carucate was a largely fiscal measurement used for taxation purposes and is difficult to equate to acres but it was basically the same as a hide or ploughland and was the area of land which could be ploughed in a year by one eight-ox plough team. It equalled from 60-180 acres depending on the nature of the terrain and the soil. For this land Augustine pledged service to William as his lord amounting to one-forty-eighth part of a knight's fee, very probably commuted to a money payment. William reserved for himself and his heirs hunting rights for "buck and doe, wild boar and sow, goat and goshawk". This land and a water-mill standing on it was, in 1246, the subject of a dispute between the descendants of Augustine and William which will be referred to later.

At about the same time Augustine took the first steps to establish the family's interest in the lands from which they subsequently took their name. He acquired a moiety or half part of the vill and manor of Heton-in-Lonsdale from Roger, son of Orm, who had himself, not long previously, obtained the estate from Roger, son of Ranulph de Marsey.[5] Augustine acquired the other half of the manor of Heton from Adam de Hoghton by a charter[6] executed during the reign of Richard I (1189-1199) at the court of the Barons of Penwortham, the original superior lords of the entire manor of Heton-in-Lonsdale.

This manor had been split when Warin Bussel II, a former Baron of Penwortham, had given half each to two daughters on their marriages. Augustine acquired the two halves from their descendants separately[7] and the manor continued to be held as two separate estates throughout its history even though both these estates were in the same hands.

Further land acquired by the descendants of Waldef around this time included a carucate in Brune (Bourn) with "appurtenances" i.e. buildings, being a one-third part of the township of Thornton in the parish of Poulton. This was obtained direct from King John by Augustine's son Roger in 1199 for a payment of 15 marks (£10).[8] Roger had previously obtained other pieces of land over the previous ten years; in 1189, half a carucate in Grimsargh from John when Count of Mortain[9] and four covates (perhaps 80 acres) in Wesham also in 1189, and a further carucate in Wesham in 1194, the latter for a payment of 4s.0d (20p) a year.[10] Transfers of land also took place within the family, all serving to increase the size of Roger's estate. On 21 November 1202 he purchased half a carucate of land in Torver from his uncle William for 10 marks (£6.66).[11] Two days later he acquired four oxgangs (half a carucate) in

Urswick from Alexander, son of Ulf of Hyton, for a payment of 10 marks plus 5s.4d (27p) per year in perpetuity.[12]

Thus the foundation of what was to become the Heton estate in Lonsdale was laid down and this was added to from time to time, until it passed out of the family's hands in the late 14th century.

The Land

The manor of Heton-in-Lonsdale appears in Domesday Book as Hietune, extending to four carucates or perhaps 700 acres, and being under the control of the important manor of Halton. Before the Norman Conquest, Halton was owned by the Saxon Earl Tostig, who challenged his brother, Harold, for the kingship, and was killed at the battle of Stamford Bridge in 1066. When Roger of Poitou was given control of Lonsdale by King William I he made Lancaster his headquarters and Halton declined in importance. There is little detail given in the Domesday Survey about the various manors under the control of Halton, other than their overall areas, whereas in other parts of the country the usual Domesday entry would give tenants' names, the extent of arable, pasture and meadow land, fisheries, number of ploughs, etc. This lack of information may well mean that Lonsdale had been ravaged by William's devastation of the north of England in 1069 and even twenty years later had hardly recovered from this experience.

Heton is situated approximately 2 miles from Lancaster on the western side of the tidal estuary of the River Lune. The land is flat except for the slightly raised ground which was the site of the vill of Heton and on which the presentday hamlet of Heaton stands, about 50 feet (15 metres) above the land around. The name Heton is derived from the Old English "heah + tun", meaning "high farmstead". Heaton is a not uncommon placename in the north of England but almost always it is associated with a location which is notably at a higher altitude than is the case at Heaton-in-Lonsdale. Presumably, before the Domesday Survey, the location of the vill of Heton was of such significance in relation to the surrounding land alongside the estuary that the local inhabitants considered it appropriate to call the place a high farm even though the difference in altitude is only a few feet.

Land Tenure

Introduced initially by the later Saxon kings and applied in its final strict form after the Norman Conquest, the feudal system constituted the main control over the Anglo-Norman social structure and method of land tenure for 600 years until it was abolished in the 17th century. It was based on the concept that the King owned all the land of England and that all the great landholders were his tenants-in-chief who themselves sublet (subinfeudated) parts of their lands to their tenants. Notwithstanding that land might be held in feu or freehold nevertheless the landowner was in fact a tenant holding land from his immediate lord in perpetuity and in certain circumstances, e.g.

treason against the king, lack of an heir or intestacy, failure to meet his obligations of service to his lord, he could be deprived of his land.

Every freeholder was required to swear oaths of homage and fealty to their superior lord and take livery of seisin, a symbolic piece of the land, to indicate the taking of possession. The consideration for the holding of land by a free man was the performance of honourable services (knightservice) or the payment of a sum of money or goods. This procedure took place in front of several witnesses who would subsequently be available to confirm the fact. However, in the absence of a documentary record of this ceremony it was common practice to bring a fictitious legal action (a fine or quit-claim) to ensure that the new tenant's entitlement to possession was recorded in the court rolls. These quit-claim records, with Wills, charters, and other documents form the major part of the evidence of landholding and feudal relationships in the Middle Ages.

Introduction of Surnames

At this period surnames were uncommon amongst all classes of society in England. Only the most important landowners of Norman origin had started to use a surname, normally locative in character, i.e. associated with the names of their main estates.[13] Most people were identified by a patronymic name, their personal name being associated with their father's name to distinguish them from other people with the same personal name. If confusion was still likely to arise, the name of a grandfather would be used as well. It was not until the end of the 12th century that the practice of using a hereditary locative surname began to be adopted amongst the lesser landholders. This was a practice the lords of the manor of Heton began to adopt around that time and the first occasion when the name de Heton appears is in a charter of 1199 whereby King John conveyed to Roger de Heton a carucate of land in Brune in the parish of Poulton. The Heaton form of spelling was not adopted until the early 17th century.

Extract from Domesday Book showing the entry for Heton (Hietune) on the third line with only an indication of the area as iiii carucates.

Resettlement

We have seen that the Domesday Survey of 1087 contains no details about the manor of Hietune other than its area and we surmised that this was because it had been devastated by William the Conqueror's campaign in the North of England in 1069. Even a hundred years later, when the land was acquired by Augustine, the charters refer to the bare land only with no indication of cultivated farmland and buildings. It is conceivable, therefore, that only a small proportion of the four carucates of perhaps 700 acres, comprising the nucleus of the manor, was being cultivated. The land above high water mark, alongside the estuary, although potentially fertile, would have needed drainage and much cultivation to convert it into good farmland. The rising land behind the estuarial strip was woodland or moorland which would also require a lot of work if it was ever to be anything more than rough grazing. The fishing and wildfowling in the estuary needed exploitation by construction of traps, flight pools and other devices.

It is unlikely that the new lord of the manor of Heton-in-Lonsdale would have moved to live there immediately, probably preferring to stay in the greater comforts of his father's manor in Ulverston, and he would have needed to appoint a steward to establish the village, and arrange for all the necessary work to be started on the land. The first requirement was to attract tenants to occupy the land and in order to do this some of them would have had to be offered certain inducements. Some of the new occupiers might have been bonded tenants of Augustine's father in Ulverston who could have been directed to move themselves and their families to Heton but some would have been freemen and they might require some persuading.

In addition to the grant of land made to each tenant, for which he returned customary labour services on the lord's land, and/or a money payment, it was frequently accepted that it was the lord's responsibility to make available to his tenant certain initial stock with which to start up his holding[14]. This was customarily 2 oxen, 1 cow and 6 sheep (ewes). The cost of such animals around the year 1200 was 4 shillings for an ox, 3s.6d for a cow and 6d for each sheep. Within the next hundred years prices increased markedly and by 1300 the cost of these animals had increased by a factor of three to 12s., 10s. and 2s. respectively.[15] The tenant was expected to provide his own pigs and hens which were the other livestock on which the peasants relied.

The resettlement of Heton-in-Lonsdale and its rebuilding into a prosperous, thriving manor would, therefore, have probably required land to be made available on fairly concessionary terms and for the tenants to be set up by the lord with basic livestock as their initial capital. Those bringing special skills as fishermen or wildfowlers would, in addition, need assurances that they would have the opportunities to employ these skills to their advantage, and indirectly for the benefit of their fellow-villagers. All these arrangements would have been recorded in the manorial rolls that constituted the official records of the contracts between the lord of the manor and his tenants. Only

Early Origins

rarely have such records from this early date survived and this, alas, is not the case for Heton-in-Lonsdale.

Notes & References

1. Pipe Rolls -Dodsworth's MSS vol.4,p.61 . Norman de Redman was Bailiff (Dapifer) to Warin, Master of Sancti Hospitali, Jerusalem. He died in 1150. [JHP]
2. Coucher- Book of Furness, p.509. [JHP]
3. Pipe Rolls- Dodsworth's MSS vol 4, p.65. [JHP]
4. "Lancs. Pipe Rolls", Wm Farrer, 1902, p. 402.
5. Ibid. p.406.
6. Ibid. p.409
7. Ibid. p.411.
   Lancs. & Ches. Record Soc. "Final Concords", pp83/4.
8. Charter Rolls in the Tower of London. P90. [JHP] . Now in the PRO.
9. Victoria County History of Lancashire, vol.7, p.108.
10. Papers of J H Partington, 1903, Pt.1,p.5. Bolton Central Library, ref. B920B.HEA.
11. "Final Concords" by W. Farrer. Pub. by Lancs. & Cheshire Rec. Soc., vol. 39, p. 17. [JHP]
12. Ibid. vol. 39, p. 22.
13. R.A.McKinley " Surnames of Lancashire", chap 1.Leopards Head Press,London,1981.
14. "Agrarian History of England & Wales", vol.II,1042-1350. Sally Harvey, p. 121.
15. Ibid., p. 746.

Chapter Two

Two Hundred Years in Lonsdale

We have seen that a good deal of hard work on the land would have been required to re-establish the productive capacity of the manor of Heton-in-Lonsdale following the devastation of this area by William the Conqueror. However there was another hazard which the villagers also had to face in their attempts to make a future for themselves and obtain a living from their farming activities. The north of England was under constant threat of invasion by the Scots at this period and the site of Heton is not a very good defensive position, particularly if the original manorhouse was located in the same position as the present 18th century Heaton Hall. Although the manor house would probably have been surrounded by a moat and a strong wooden palisade within which the villagers could retreat in times of danger, nevertheless it is unlikely it could have resisted a determined enemy for very long and in case of attack reliance would probably have been placed on help coming quickly from Lancaster Castle, just over two miles away, and to which a messenger would have been sent post-haste as soon as danger threatened from Scots raiding parties or Irish Sea pirates. Indeed the villagers probably hoped fervently that the close presence of the castle garrison would deter raiders from coming anywhere near.

A large part of the agricultural land in the North of England consisted of small fields reclaimed from the infertile hill country by individual freeholders, but, in the case of Heton, we know from 13th century charters that not all the tenants were freemen as there are references to villeins and bonded families attached to the manor[1]. Notwithstanding that there were saltmarshes along the river estuary, the flatter alluvial land around the site of the village was naturally fertile and once the initial drainage and clearance work had been carried out the manor would, very possibly, have been managed by Augustine or his steward in a way similar to other such lowland holdings at this period. Instances of this three-field system of cultivation being operated in the North are rare but those which did exist were located on the more productive land alongside estuaries[2]. The configuration of the present-day hamlet, the obviously fertile nature of the land, and what we know of the early social structure of the manor suggests that Heton-in-Lonsdale was managed on this basis.

The Village

It appears that the medieval village would have been somewhat larger than the present-day hamlet. Heaton Hall, built in the early 18th century, is at the end of a long straight drive which may once have been the main street of the village and still has houses along part of its length. There is no church but there was once a chapel in the village which no longer exists. The nearby small church of Overton with its distinctive Norman architectural features can be dated to a period coincidental with the re-establishment of Heton-in-Lonsdale. The villagers' houses would have been of somewhat crude construction with each dwelling set in its own plot or croft, of a size dependant on the amount of land available, but normally about an acre.[3] Within these crofts the tenants could grow fruit and vegetables and pen up their own animals. There was usually a boundary fence or ditch between these plots and the open fields. At one end of the village street, a little away from the village houses, would have been the priest's house, probably close to the lord's manor house within its defensive enclosure. On the low hill behind was the manor's wooden post mill, first erected at a very early date and shown on maps and charts up to the 19th century, and with Mill Cottage still occupying the site.

Under the three-field system, cultivable land of the manor outside the village would be divided into three large enclosures which themselves would be divided into strips shared amongst the lord and his tenants in accordance with manorial custom. Two fields would be worked in alternate years for arable crops followed by a year of fallow, during which the animals of the manor would be turned on to the stubble to graze and manure the land. The third field would be the important meadow from which hay would be cut to provide winter fodder, with the animals allowed to graze the aftermath after the hay harvest had been collected. The woodland and waste of the manor which was not suitable for cropping would be grazed as common by the livestock of the lord and his tenants. Certain rights in accordance with custom would accrue to the tenants of the manor in relation to the common or waste land including collection of wood for fuel (estovers); turning out pigs to forage (pannage); cutting peat for fuel (turbary). It seems very likely that grazing stock on the saltmarshes was a right the villagers also enjoyed and this is an activity which has been carried on right up to the present day.

It was considered that an average peasant family of five required about 12 acres to sustain them.[4] It is probable that only a proportion of this would be of cultivated land around the village, surveys in Lancashire in 1323 and 1346 showing that the great majority of holdings in the county were under 10 acres. The balance would be made up of assarts, i.e. reclaimed land from woodland, moor and marsh. Additional food would be obtained from the produce of fishing and wildfowling.[5]

The lord of the manor retained a proportion of the arable land under his direct control as his demesne, the church was allocated certain glebe lands, and the remainder was distributed amongst the villagers. In return for the right to occupy their land the lord's tenants would be required to perform menial services by working a certain number of days in the year on the lord's land without payment. The lord would build his own mill at which his ten-

14th century farming activities from the Luttrell Psalter. The mill shown is of the post-mill type likely to have been erected at Heton in Lonsdale.

ants would be required to have their corn ground, for which service the lord would take a proportion of the grain. Valuable fishing rights in the River Lune were almost certainly attached to the manor of Heton as these are referred to in one of the charters under which Augustine acquired the lordship.

The Dwelling-houses

The village of Heton-in-Lonsdale was located on the alluvial land alongside the estuary of the River Lune and there was no source of good building stone within a convenient distance. It is very likely therefore that all the buildings in the village were constructed of a timber frame to which were fixed panels of interwoven hazel sticks plastered with mud, a method termed "wattle and daub".

The largest house in the village would have been the manor house, occupied by the lord of the manor. At that period it was usual for minor landowners to live at their principal manor in a hall-house with outbuildings close by which provided accommodation for cooking, washing, housing animals, storing corn, brewing and other activities. A hall-house was a building of two or more bays, a bay being about 12 feet wide x 16 feet deep (3.6m x 4.8m). It was occupied by the landowner and his family, together with his servants, and gave very little privacy to anyone. The owner would have his private apart-

Cattle grazing the saltmarshes alongside the Lune estuary. With a different breed of cattle this same activity could have been seen a thousand years ago.

ment to which he and his family could retire and for sleeping, but everyone else lived and slept communally. A two-bay hallhouse was a building occupied by someone rather low on the social scale and it is probable that the lord of Heton-in-Lonsdale would have been able to provide himself with something rather better than this. A three- to five-bay building would have been more likely, one end bay of which would have been screened off to provide private accommodation for the lord and his family, with a floor inserted above to give a first-floor solar or additional accommodation for the owner.

The constructional frame of the house would have been of substantial oak timbers, adzed to shape and very possibly of cruck form, pairs of matching frames, reaching from the ground to the ridge of the roof, being cut from a single tree. Alternatively, the house would be built of straight timbers, beams and roof trusses. The hall-house, except for the solar, was open from floor to thatched roof and these crucks, beams and trusses would be very visible inside the building. The degree of decoration on them in the form of chamfering and carving would be an indication of the social status of the owner of the house in his attempts to outdo his neighbours in the quality of his dwelling. The wattle and daub panels filling the spaces between the structural frames would be plastered or rendered both inside and out with many coats of limewash applied. Interior decoration could consist of pictures painted on the plastered panels. Windows were just open panels in the walls protected by shutters. The hall was heated by an open fire on a hearth in the centre of the hall and the smoke had to find its way out through a hole in the roof. Smoke-blackened timbers in the roof of an old house are an indication that it was originally a hall house.

Furniture was sparse, only the lord of the manor, his lady, and any special guests having chairs and everyone else making use of benches and stools. Food was eaten off trestle tables which were taken down when not required, to provide sleeping space. The landowner with his family and guests ate at a table set across the hall on a low dais backing on to the screen dividing off his private apartment into which he could retire at will. Everyone else sat at tables down the length of the hall. The food was cooked in a separate building and had to be brought from there into the hall, obviously losing heat in the process. A major advance at a slighter later date was the provision of a stone chimney with flues and fireplaces built on to the gable of the house abutting the lord's private accommodation.

The houses of the villagers were much more primitive. In the 13th century they probably consisted of single room dwellings which may sometimes have been lengthened by the addition of a byre for housing cattle at the lower end, when they would be termed a longhouse. It is unlikely that the villagers could have afforded properly squared timbers and their houses and animal shelters are likely to have been built of straight poles cut from the forest and erected to form a basic A-frame to which horizontal poles would be lashed or pegged. Wattle and daub or turf would have been used to clad the outside of the building and the roof would be thatched or covered in turf. Windows were just small holes in the walls covered with rough cloth or shutters. Again, the only source of heat was a fire in the centre of the floor with a hole in the roof to let the smoke escape. These houses were just temporary dwellings which probably had to be replaced every generation and their constructional materials were such that no complete examples have survived, the main evidence of their existence being the postholes which they left, or their stone foundations.

The Wardship

Augustine had been succeeded as lord of the manor of Heton-in-Lonsdale by his son Roger and we have seen in the previous chapter how Roger had added to the land holdings which his father had acquired. By 1202 he held land in Ulverston, Torver, Heton, Grimsargh, Wesham, Brune and Urswick. The locations of these holdings are significant, since even when the bulk of the Heton lands in Lonsdale passed to other famillies by marriage in the late 14th century it appears that land in Ulverston, Brune and Urswick was still held by the descendants of those members of the family who moved to south Lancashire at the beginning of the 14th century.

Roger married Sabina, by whom he had two sons, Roger and Adam. However he then died at a young age in 1204[6] and Sabina was left a widow. In 1206 Sabina appeared personally before King John at Lancaster where she paid half a mark to have it confirmed that the revenues from land at Wesham and Brune should constitute her widow's portion or jointure.[7] She subsequently married Ralph de Hole as her second husband and was still living in

Typical cruck-built, timber-framed hallhouse as constructed in England and Wales from the 12th century onwards.
(Crown Copyright. Reproduced by permission of RCAHMW).

1246 when she and her husband Ralph brought an action against the Abbot of Dieulacresse, which they subsequently withdrew.[8]

Roger de Heton had held lands as tenant-in-chief of the king and therefore, on his death, King John exercised his right to the wardship of his infant son and heir Roger II. However, in the year 1206, Sir Henry de Redman, a cousin of Roger senior, purchased the wardship and marriage of the infant Roger from the king for the sum of 40 marks.[9] This gave Sir Henry control over the administration of Roger's estate until he attained his majority at 21 or married, retaining the revenues and allowing his ward only what he needed for his maintenance. Sir Henry could also control the arrangements for the marriage of his ward and, as happened in so many cases of wardship, this resulted in Roger marrying Agnes, the daughter of Sir Henry de Redman. They had a son and heir, William, and other children.[10]

In the year 1234/5 Roger obtained a confirmation from Adam de Hoghton of his rights in that half of the manor of Heton which he held from the Hoghton family, acknowledging his obligation to give one-ninth of a knight's fee for this holding.[11]

An Argument with an Abbot

Roger de Heton's land in Broune was adjoined on the west by the manor of Rossal which was part of the large estate owned by the Abbey and Convent of Dieulacresse. Arguments over the exact location of the boundary between the Heton lands and those of the Abbot constituted a longrunning dispute between the two parties which went on for many years. The first instance of a legal action being brought was in 1216 when, on 28 August in that year, the Court ordered the Sheriff of Lancashire, Ranulph de Blondeville, earl of Chester, to ensure that a pasture at Rossal was handed over to the Abbot by Roger de Heton.[12]

The dispute was again revived in 1222 when, on 30 October, Brian de Insula as Sheriff was told by the Court that following diligent enquiries it had concluded that the pasture land in dispute rightly belonged to the Abbot and that a quit-claim to that effect should be entered into by the parties, which was duly done.[13]

Notwithstanding this apparent resolution of the argument the dispute broke out again in 1238, in the 21st year of the reign of King Henry III., when four local gentlemen were ordered to hold an assize of "novel disseisin" which again appears to have confirmed the Rossal pasture in the ownership of the Abbey and Convent of Dieulacresse.[14]

A Pair of White Gloves and a Sparrowhawk

In the year 1235 Roger de Heton sold land in Bolton-le-Sands to Richard de Copland and in accordance with the usual practice and to ensure that a written record of the transaction was kept in the court records, a fictitious action was brought before the court at Lancaster on 13 May of that year. Richard de Copland was the plaintiff and Roger de Heton and Agnes his wife were the impedients (defendants). The land in question was four oxgangs (perhaps 40 acres) with appurtenances (buildings) at Bolton. Roger and Agnes acknowledged the land to be rightfully Richard's, having been given by them to him and his heirs for ever. The rent he was to pay for the land was a pair of white gloves or one penny yearly at Christmas and in consideration for Roger and Agnes' acknowledgment he gave them one sparrow hawk.[15] There may already have been a further monetary payment made by Richard in addition to the rent of a pair of gloves or one penny but it was unnecessary for this to be mentioned in the action as adequate consideration was evident to bind the parties.

Title to a Mill

In the previous chapter we referred to one of the first acquisitions by Augustine, son of Waldef, of some land with a mill upon it at Torver in Ulverston. In 1246 this land and mill became the subject of a dispute as to title between Roger de Heton and William de Lancaster, 3rd Baron Kendal.

William apparently tried to claim from Roger performance of certain customs and services termed "suit of mill" in respect of the land. This service would have required Roger to submit to paying to William a proportion of his corn ground at the mill, whereas Roger claimed that no such service was due from him. Roger brought an action at Lancaster Assizes in 1246 requiring

William to state on what grounds he claimed the customs and services. William based his claim on his assertion that William, his grandfather, was entitled to Augustine's suit as was William's daughter Hawise, from whom he inherited. Roger disputed this and produced the original charter in evidence showing that the only service required was one-fortyeighth part of a knight's fee, calling in support of this the testimony of Gilbert fitz Reinfred, an original witness.

Roger appealed to the Grand Assize which involved the Sheriff naming four knights of the shire to elect a jury of twelve to hear the case. In the event the parties apparently reached agreement, termed a concord, and Roger paid 1 mark (66p) for licence to settle the case by concord. The concord was recorded at Lancaster on 20 October 1246 by a Fine[16] (a fictitious action) wherein Roger complained that "William threw down the water corn mill in Thorfergh to the injury of his free tenants in that vil." It was stated that Roger and his heirs should have liberty to erect and maintain the mill without objection from William or his heirs. Afterwards William quit-claimed (released) Roger and his heirs from all claims of suit of mill from him or his heirs. In consideration of this release Roger gave William 2 marks (£1.33).

Knighthood

In 1256, for the first time, Roger de Heton was referred to in documents as Sir Roger de Heton knight, "Dominus Rogerus de Heton, miles". He is named in this way on a quitclaim document of that year between Roger de Heysham and the Prior of Lancaster, where he appears as a witness. There are a number of other documents recorded where his name appears in a similar capacity.[17] Presumably he was required to accept the style and title of Knight when the value of the lands he owned exceeded £15 per annum. Whilst ostensibly an honour, nevertheless acceptance of knighthood brought a man certain obligations which as a mere esquire he was not subject to. If called upon to do so, he was required to serve the king in a military capacity in England for 40 days a year at his own expense, with horse, arms and armour, appropriate to his status, which also meant that he would have to suitably equip a number of his servants as troopers to accompany him. Sir Roger only had another six years to live in 1256 and was then probably over sixty years of age, so active service himself was hardly a practical proposition. In these circumstances it seems very likely that his son would serve in his place, together with a suitable number of servants, or that his obligation would be commuted to a money payment. In the Welsh wars 20 years later the fee in lieu of 40 days active service for a single specific knight was set at 40 shillings[18].

A Prosperous Manor

Sir Roger de Heton died in 1262, having been lord of the manor of Heton-in-Lonsdale for 58 years since his father's death in 1204. During that period it appears that the productivity of the manor increased considerably and it became notable for the crops of corn which were raised on the fertile soil there, although the yield was probably little more than half a ton per acre as against three tonnes plus with modern wheat varieties at the present day. It is significant that Sir Roger adopted the device on his coat-of-arms of three golden wheatsheaves on a green background (in heraldic terms "vert three garbs or"), emphasising the fact that his manor was noted for its production of corn.

Six hundred and fifty years later in 1914 the Victoria County History of Lancashire was still confirming the parish of Heaton-with-Oxcliffe as having a higher proportion of arable land than any other parish in the Hundred of Lonsdale. The modern acreage of Heaton alone is stated as being 1319 in total, of which 90 acres are saltmarsh, the remainder being arable and grassland. The total acreage of arable land in the parish in 1914 was 478 of which the bulk was in Heaton rather than Oxcliffe. The position at the present time remains much the same so the area of cultivated land in the 20th century is still somewhat similar to that which existed in the 13th century.

Heton-in-Lonsdale was exceptional in having such a high level of corn (wheat and oats) production but the other farming enterprises from which the tenants of the manor and its lord derived revenues were their flocks and herds of sheep and cattle. Sheep were kept primarily for their wool with meat a secondary product. They grazed the rough moorland and waste of the manor and the cows foraged the stubble, aftermath and saltmarsh, being given some hay in the winter. The productivity of the animals was an improvement on the period before resettlement but even so it was poor compared with later achievements. The ratio of lambs born to ewes was about 8 lambs to every 10 ewes, compared to modern figures achieved where many flocks average 16 lambs from 10 ewes. Calves born to cattle averaged not more than 3 calves to 4 cows per year, whereas modern targets are for every cow to calve every year.. A high proportion of ewes died each year (12-20%)[19] and the milk yield from the cows was low. Fish and wildfowl were required to supplement the villagers' diet.

The farmers of Heton were fortunate that a market had been established at Lancaster only two miles away at which they could sell their surplus produce and buy their requirements. With the cereal production of the manor as high as it was, an early essential was the erection of a mill for grinding the corn. One of the first windmills in the district was erected on the hill above the village, probably in the early 13th century. This would have been a timber structure of the post mill type and a mill existed on that site until the 19th century. It almost certainly belonged to the lord of the manor although there were instances of communally owned mills. The lord would take a proportion of the grain, anything from 1/25 to 1/12 of that brought to the mill[20], yielding him a substantial profit after paying the miller and maintaining the mill.

Great Events

During the lifetime of Sir Roger de Heton a number of events took place which were to have a far-reaching effect on the people of England in their progress to nationhood. In 1215, at Runnymede on the River Thames, King John signed Magna Carta (The Great Charter), which was originally intended principally as a measure to safeguard the barons from oppression by the king but in which there are important clauses relating to no taxation without the authority of the Great Council and its successor, Parliament, and no imprisonment without conviction by a free person's peers or by the law of the land, which eventually benefitted the whole population of England as they all became free men and women.

In 1216, as a boy of nine, King Henry III came to the throne which he was to occupy for 56 years until 1272. He was fortunate that during his minority he was served by competent, loyal Englishmen but his subjects, later in his reign, became discontented with the manner in which foreigners, principally French, acquired excessive influence over the king and held offices of state which gave them very considerable power and the ability to spend large sums of money raised by taxation. This discontent culminated in the 1250s in open dispute between the English barons and gentry, led by Simon de Montfort, Earl of Leicester, and the king and his foreign advisers. In 1258 a general council took place at Oxford where certain provisions, regulating the making of various key state appointments, were agreed between the barons and the king.

However, King Henry subsequently renounced the provisions agreed at Oxford and civil war broke out between the king supported by his son Prince Edward with the foreign magnates, and Simon de Montfort, backed largely by the lesser barons and knights. De Montfort summoned his own council which was, for the first time, called a Parliament, and included not only the barons who supported him but also the lesser knights of the shires and burgesses from the important towns. In the war Simon was initially successful, winning the battle of Lewes in 1264, where he captured the king and the prince. However Edward later escaped and raised an army with which he trapped Simon's forces in 1265 at Evesham, where de Montfort was defeated and killed.

The main significance of this episode was the fact that foreign interference in the government of England was removed for ever and for the first time a parliament had been summoned which included representatives of commoners of lower status than the great barons. This innovation began to be repeated in later years until it became the general practice and laid the foundations for a Parliament which includes representatives of all the people.

The King's Coroner

When Sir Roger de Heton died in 1262 he was succeeded by his son, Sir William. It is unlikely that Sir Roger was embroiled in the king's dispute with the barons and knights under Simon de Montfort as this did not reach a climax in the battles at Lewes and Evesham until after his death. Although Sir William de Heton, his son, had feudal obligations of knightservice as a tenant-in-chief of the king for land at Ulverston and elsewhere, it seems unlikely that he was called upon to present himself for active service against De Montfort. It was not royal policy to withdraw military forces from the north of England to form an army in the south due to the ever-present threat of invasion by the Scots and Heton-in-Lonsdale could be regarded as a frontline location. Evidently Sir William did not support the rebellious Simon de Montfort as there is no record of any penalties being inflicted on him, but nor does he seem to have benefitted substantially from any particularly notable acts for the king during the civil war.

William had married Christiana, daughter of Adam de Houghton, and they had several children, all given family names of William, Roger, Adam and others. Christiana brought as her dowry an estate of one carucate in Middleton, given to William by Hamo, Christiana's brother, in consideration of the marriage.[21]

Sir William held public office during his lifetime and it appears he was a man well-respected by his neighbours and the authorities. In 1269 there is evi-

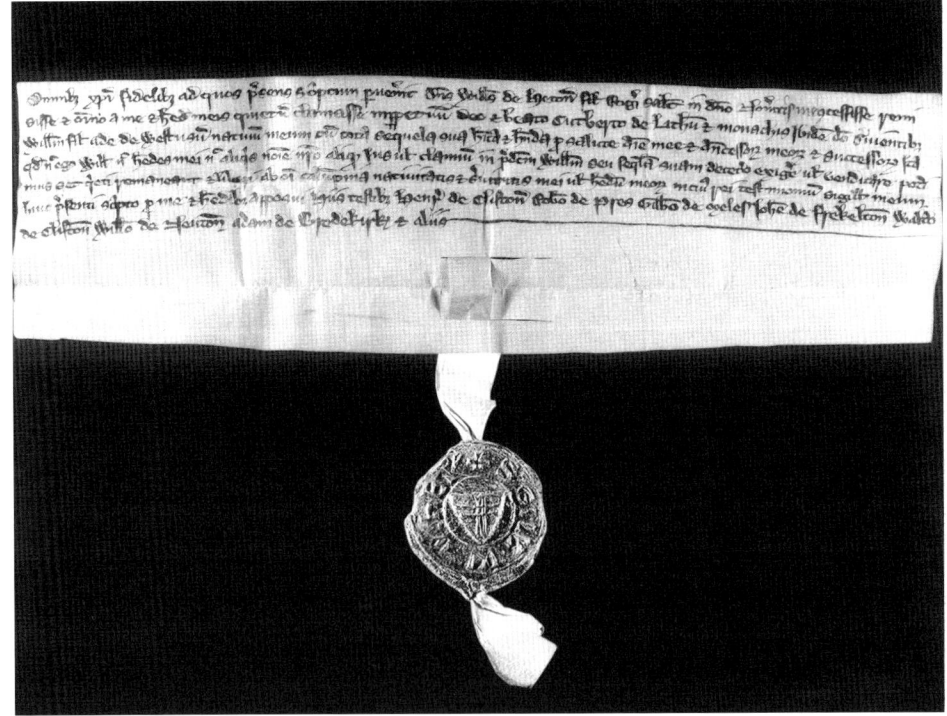

Charter and seal of Sir William de Heton (died 1292).
(Illustration by courtesy of the Dean and Chapter of Durham Cathedral)

dence that he held the office of King's Coroner for Lancaster, being given that designation in a document dated August of that year between Thomas de Coupmanwra and the Abbot and monks of Furness, where he is named as a witness.[22]

At about the same time a dispute between Sir William de Heton and John de Oxcliffe, the lord of the adjoining manor was settled by a compromise in relation to the boundaries between the two manors wherein pieces of water known as the Merepool near the River Lune and Sithpool and a location called the Moss are mentioned.[23]

Heton-in-Lonsdale never had a proper church but there was a chapel dedicated to St. Cuthbert and a priest's house in the village which came under the jurisdiction of the Priory of St. Mary's in Lancaster. Apparently there was some dissatisfaction on the part of the Prior with regard to his legal title to the site so that in 1269 Sir William confirmed the boundaries of the plot which was to be owned by the Priory in perpetuity, and ensured adequate access to it.[24].

Probably around this time, Sir William sold land he owned in Bolton-le-Sands to Thomas de Coupmanwra for which the fee was twelve pence per annum[25].

The Wars in Wales

King Henry III died in 1272 and his son acceded to the throne as Edward I. For several years previously there had been sporadic conflict between Prince Edward and Llewelyn ap Gruffudd, native Prince of Gwynedd in North Wales. Llewelyn had allied himself with Simon de Montfort in his dispute with the king of England and had sent troops to help De Montfort at Lewes. His proposed marriage to the daughter of Simon de Montfort proved to be the last straw for King Edward who saw this as a threat to re-establish a Montfortian party amongst the English barons, with whom Llewelyn would ally himself. Edward took action by preventing Simon's daughter from travelling to Wales, and made preparations for a fullscale war, which finally broke out in 1276, continuing into 1277, when peace was made, only for fighting to flare up again in 1282/3, resulting in the death of Llewelyn, the annexation of his lands in Gwynedd by King Edward and the building of the famous castles at Caernarfon, Conwy, Beaumaris, Rhuddlan, Aberystwyth, Harlech, Denbigh, and elsewhere to ensure that the Welsh remained subjugated.[26]

There is no record of Sir William de Heton participating in this conflict, the king's policy again being to draw troops from the Welsh marches and the midlands and south of England, rather than from near the border with Scotland. However, Henry de Lacy, Earl of Lincoln, who was the superior lord of several parts of Lancashire, including the Honour of Clitheroe, Lordship of Penwortham, and Barony of Manchester, took a large contingent of mounted troops to help the king in Wales, in performance of his feudal duties.[27] It is probable that amongst his retinue were members of the de Heton family who subsequently settled in the vicinity of Denbigh, of which de Lacy was granted the lordship in 1282. The subsequent fortunes of these North Wales Hetons will be considered in a later chapter.

In 1294 a general rising of the Welsh took place, including an attack by the local Welsh against the Earl of Lincoln's forces at Denbigh, in the defence of which we may be sure that Hetons took part. The rising was eventually suppressed and the king set to work to rebuild those castles which had been damaged and destroyed in the fighting.

Sir William's Succession Problems

The early death of Roger, second son of Sir William, who died before his father, and the childlessness of William, the eldest son, complicated the succession to the lands held by Sir William and he was obliged to make various settlements to ensure that his grandchildren were adequately provided for. Several documents were entered into to give effect to Sir William's intentions.

At Shrewsbury on 8 May 1283, by a fine (fictitious legal action), William III, son of Roger de Heton and grandson of Sir William, acknowledges that the manors of Heton-in-Lonsdale and Broune-in-Amunderness (to the south of the Lune) are in the right of William II, son of Sir William de Heton, with remainder to William III, son of Roger, on the death of William II, his uncle. This was presumably to give effect to a settlement made by Sir William. For this acknowledgement William III received one goshawk. Christiana, Roger's daughter, also put in her claim in respect of Broune which she maintained had been granted to her by Sir William, her grandfather[28] and this was subsequently accepted. Sir William de Heton died in the 20th year of the reign of King Edward I, i.e. 1292, and was succeeded in the ownership of his estates by his eldest son William and his grandson, William son of Roger. Other grandchildren were Christiana and John, daughter and younger son of Roger.

John, Son of Roger

John plays an important part in our story for it is very likely that it was he who obtained a grant of the manor of Heton-under-Horwich in Salford Hundred in 1309 and continued the Heaton story in south Lancashire, although during his lifetime he appears to have been an absentee landlord, continuing to live in Lonsdale. The Heton move south is dealt with in more detail in the next chapter. John was a "doomsman" of Bolton le Sands, an official of the manor whose responsibility it was to ensure that accused persons were present at the court when their cases were to be heard. On 5 February 1325 he was fined 6d because he did not have William, son of Alexander, before the manor court and again on 5 March 1325 he and another man were fined 12d because they did not have Simon de Bolton before the court. His duties appeared to extend also to the Hundred court, a higher authority, since on 26 November 1325 he was fined 2d because he did not have Benedict, son of Alan, before the Hundred (Wapentake) court at Lancaster. The office of doomsman seems to have been an appointment which the junior members of the gentry were willing to accept. It must have carried some kudos, although on the face of it, it appears to have brought little advantage to the holder.

Grandchildren Inherit

Following the death of Sir William de Heton in 1292, his childless eldest son William II succeeded to lands in Heton-in-Lonsdale, Ulverston, Rosset, Thorver, Wesham and elsewhere with his nephew William III, son of Roger, having an interest as remainderman with the right to inherit on the death of William II. It seems William III immediately inherited lands in Heton and Broune from his grandfather and his sister Christiana also inherited an immediate interest entitling her to an income from lands at Broune.

William II was apparently still alive in 1300 when an "Inquisition ad quod Dampnum", held at Lancaster before the King's Escheator found that William held a moiety (half) of the manor of Bolton (le Sands) for a pair of white gloves or one penny for all services. The whole manor at the time was assessed at 10 marks (£6.66)[29]. In 1302 the sum of 40 shillings for every knight's service was levied for the marriage of the king's eldest daughter and in the assessment for the Hundred of Lonsdale it is stated that William de Heton held land in fee of the Earl of Lincoln for one-fourteenth part of a knight's fee and a part fee in Heton for 2 shillings per annum. This appears to be the last certain reference to William II and it may be assumed he died not long afterwards.

The distribution of Sir William de Heton's estates amongst his son and grandchildren meant that no one heir held land worth in excess of £15 per annum and therefore this resulted in a loss of knightservice to the king. An Inquest Quo Warranto was held to determine the cause of this loss. This enquiry took place before Sir Henry de Cressingham and other justices at Lancaster in 1302. Efforts by the King's Attorney to claim possession of the manor of Broune for the king against William de Heton III were unsuccessful and he retained possession.

Just William

The last five generations of Hetons to hold the lordship of the manor of Heton-in-Lonsdale were named William and this, on occasions, causes some confusion. Following the death of Sir William in 1292 the succession passed to his son, William II for a few years until c. 1302 and on his death his nephew William III, son of Roger, succeeded to the estate. There was at least one other son, Adam de Heton of Little Pulton, known to be living in 1293, but of whom little else is known.

It is recorded [30] that in 1307 Sir Richard de Hoghton, son of Sir Adam, who exercised overlordship over certain lands in Heton which were subinfeudated (sublet in perpetuity)) to William de Heton , transferred this overlordship to his own son, Richard de Hoghton. A fee of nineteen and a half pence per annum appears to have been paid by William III for this land[31].

The Hetons of Heton-in-Lonsdale - c.1140 - 1387.

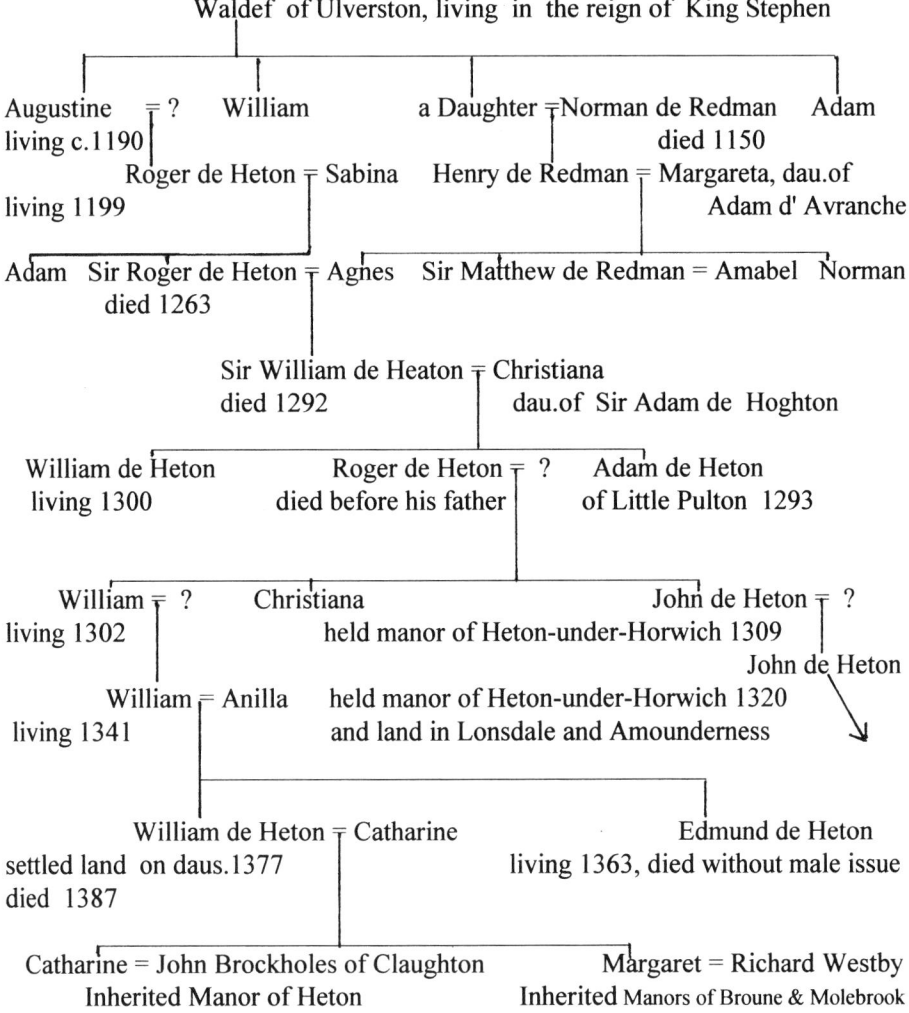

In 1283 Sir William de Heton and his son William II had entered into a settlement whereby, after 40 years, lands in Heton and Broune would revert to William III, son of Roger. In 1323, William III had to pay relief to the Sheriff of Lancaster to inherit the land from his grandfather's and uncle's trustees. The exact date of William III's death is not precisely know but could well have been within a year or two of that date.

William IV, son of William III, had married Anilla and they had two sons, William V and Edmund. In 1323 William and Anilla proceeded to confirm their ownership of certain lands.[32] On 27 Oct. of that year, by a fine passed at York, Ranulph Gentil confirmed the manor of Heton and three oxgangs of land at Great Urswick as being granted to William and Anilla and their heirs. On 17 April 1328 another fine was passed at York, confirming William and Anilla's ownership of the manor of Moulebreck, granted to them by William de Caton, son of Roger.

Keeper of the Peace

In 1361 King Edward III made the first appointments of Justices of the Peace, a now well-respected public office, the holders of which exercise many functions including trying many types of minor offences. However the predecessors of the JPs were the Keepers of the Peace, first appointed in 1277, whose function was to make sure that offenders were apprehended and brought before the manor or Hundred courts but who did not try cases themselves. Initially four men per county were given this responsibility and the fact that William de Heton III was so appointed by the king at Halton on 2 November 1323[33] is a measure of the high regard in which he was apparently held in the county. It seems probable that when acting as doomsman, John de Heton, son of Roger, was in fact responsible to his relative for bringing before the courts men whom the Keepers had indicted.

Summoned to the Great Council

Reference has been made previously to the fact that the rebellion of Simon de Monfort and his followers, although put down by the king and his son, nevertheless had far-reaching repercussions. The provisions of the Oxford Council which the king had largely accepted, and the fact that de Montfort summoned a council or Parliament to which members of the lesser gentry were invited, as well as the great magnates, set a precedent which was followed to an increasing extent in later years. On 9 May 1324 the king at Westminster issued a writ to the Sheriff of the County of Lancaster to name appropriate gentlemen of the county to attend a meeting of the Great Council of the Realm at Westminster. The qualification for inclusion in this number was to hold freehold land with a value greater than £15 per annum and it seems that William de Heton III met this qualification as he was named by the Sheriff as one of those who were to attend the meeting of the Great Council.[34] Although this was an indication of his position of importance in the county it is an honour which he might prefer to have avoided, involving as it did a long journey to and from London, risking all the hazards which beset 14th-century travellers from robbers, poor roads, disease, and absence from home for a long period.

National Events

The long reigns of king Henry III, 1216-1272, and king Edward I, 1272-1307, were followed by that of the eccentric, ineffectual, unpopular king Edward II. In 1314 an English army, on its way to relieve the beseiged castle and town of Stirling, was heavily defeated and routed by the Scots at Bannockburn, under the command of their King Robert the Bruce. This ensured no further interference by England in the affairs of Scotland and for a long time left the whole of the North of England vulnerable to frequent incursions by Scots from over the border. Once again the people of Heton-in-Lonsdale were no doubt profoundly thankful for the presence of Lancaster castle nearby. The garrison, even though possibly depleted by the losses suffered at Bannockburn, was still a strong deterrent to Scottish raiding parties.

Edward II died in 1327, murdered by Roger Mortimer, the lover of Edward's Queen Isabella. His son Edward III commenced his 50-year reign by executing Roger Mortimer and imprisoning his mother Isabella in relative comfort for the rest of her life. His military ability and strong attitude towards Scotland restored order along the border and in the northern counties.

Edward III's claim to the French throne precipitated the Hundred Years War, which may be said to have broken out in 1337. As far as can be determined the Hetons in Lonsdale were not directly affected by the call to arms but they would certainly have experienced the demands made by the king for additional taxation in order to prosecute the war. In 1341 William de Heton IV was appointed one of the Assessors for the Wapentake (Hundred) of Lonsdale by a Commission issued by the king on 26 January[35]. Their responsibility was to levy a ninth of the production of corn, wool and lambs, parish by parish. The Assessors put the parishioners upon oath to answer correctly as to the true value of the production of corn, wool and lambs in the parish. It seems that many of the parishioners in these northern counties pleaded that much of their land had been laid waste by the Scots following the English defeat at Bannockburn and their production had been drastically reduced.[36]

The Black Death

In June 1348 ships sailed into port in Dorset bringing on board a cargo which was to make drastic changes to the social structure and systems of land-holding throughout the country. These ships from the Mediterranean carried bubonic plague borne by fleas on the black rats living in the holds of the ships. Once the rats got ashore the plague, known as the Black Death because of the appearance of the symptoms, spread rapidly through the country and in 20 months had affected most of Britain, killing between 1/3rd and

2/3rds of the population. Even when this first onset subsided pockets were left which flared up from time to time and caused the plague to become endemic for centuries.

The deaths from plague in 1348/9 caused a severe shortage of labour, and laws were hurriedly passed in an attempt to prevent peasants leaving their home villages and the service of their lords, to obtain better wages elsewhere. These measures were only partially succesful and landowners, desperate to obtain labour to work the land, competed with one another by paying higher wages for the services of labourers and craftsmen. Because of the labour shortage many menial labour services for land were converted to a money payment with which to hire labour elsewhere. This was intended only as a temporary measure but in practice, in many instances, it became permanent and brought about a substantial change in the form of feudal services.

With much land left without tenants, holdings were amalgamated and this led to the emergence of the larger tenant farmer, eventually to become the yeoman. We do not know exactly how the Hetons of Lonsdale and Amoundernesse were affected, but as they appeared to be dependent, at least to some extent, on serf and villein labour (see note 1) then, no doubt, they experienced the same problems as landowners throughout the country and probably had to make a number of concessions to their tenants in terms of rent, wages, nature of services, amalgamation of holdings,etc. Production of crops and livestock was obviously very badly affected by the shortage of agricultural labour and it took many years to restore the position to anything like that which prevailed before the Black Death. In some respects it was never restored.

The Final Years

On the death of William de Heton IV, Edmund, his younger son, inherited the lands in Heton which the Hetons held from Sir Richard de Hoghton for one-fourteenth of a knight's fee plus a payment of nineteen-and-a-half pence per annum. His presence is recorded at Preston as a juror at an inquisition on 25 July 1356 and at Lancaster for a similar purpose on 28 April 1361[37]. In 1364 Edmund is on record as having leased a burgage plot in Lancaster with appurtenances, i.e. a plot with a street frontage and a building upon it, to one John for 20 years at a rent of 14 shillings payable at Easter and on 1 November in each year.[38]

Edmund de Heton died childless and his estate passed to his niece Catharine, the elder daughter of his brother William.

William de Heton V succeeded to the possession of the manors of Heton-in-Lonsdale, Brune, and Molebreck on the death of his father, together with half the manor of Rosset and land in Thornton. He and his wife Catharine had no sons, only two daughters, Catharine and Margaret. Catharine married John Brockholes and Margaret married Richard Westby.

In 1377 William made a settlement whereby he appointed Ralph de Ipre and

Peter de Bolrom as trustees (feoffees) to hold the manor of Heton for the use of his daughter Catharine, and the manors of Brune and Molebreck to the use of Margaret. By 1387 William had died and his settlements took effect. The former Heton lands passed to his daughters and into the control of the Brockholes and Westby families by whom they were owned for many generations.

The only lands in Lonsdale and Amoundernesse remaining in Heton ownership were those which at an earlier date had passed into the possession of John de Heton, son of Roger, or possibly Adam de Heton, son of Sir William and uncle of John.

Notes & References

[1] Lytham Charter 4.2.4.Ebor, Durham Cathedral Archives, Durham University Library. This reads in translation:-
"To all faithful in Christ to whom this present writing pertains I, William de Heton, son of Roger, give eternal greeting in the Lord. Know that I have yielded, remised and entirely quitclaimed for myself and my heirs forever, to God and blessed Cuthbert of Latham and the monks serving God there, William, son of Adam of Wesham, my villein, with all the family he has or will have, for the salvation of my soul and those of my ancestors and descendants, so that neither I, William, nor my heirs, nor anyone else of our name will be able to lay claim against the aforesaid William and his family and that they remain free from every villein dispute and service of me and my heirs. In witness whereof, etc., etc." The date is uncertain but must be between 1262 and 1292.

[2] "Agrarian History of England & Wales", vol. II, Edward Miller, p.399.
[3] "Lords of Holderness", B. English. Oxford, 1979.
[4] "Agrarian History of England & Wales" vol. II, H.E.Hallam, p. 966.
[5] Ibid. pp. 990/1, 995.
[6] Victoria County History of Lancashire, vol. 7, p.154.
[7] Ibid.
[8] Papers of J H Partington 1903, part 1, p.7 and notes to p. 6. Bolton Central Library, ref. B920B. HEA.
[9] Ibid. Notes to page 7.
[10] Ibid.p.7.
[11] Christopher Townley's MSS, p.582. Chetham Library, Manchester [JHP].
[12] Partington Papers, op. cit.. Pt 1, p.8 and notes to p.8.
[13] Ibid.
[14] "History of Poulton-le-Fylde", H. Fishwick. Chetham Soc. ,vol. 8 new series, p.124. [JHP]
[15] "Lancashire Fines,etc." W. Farrer. Lancs. & Chester Record Soc., vol. 39, p. 67 [JHP]
[16] Ibid.vol.39, p. 97. [JHP]
[17] "History of the Church of Lancaster" W. O. Roper , Chetham Soc., new series,vol. 31, p.287.
[18] "Welsh Wars of Edward I", J.E.Morris. OUP, 1901. P.43.
[19] "Agrarian History of England & Wales", vol.II, E. Miller,pp 410/411.
[20] Ibid. p. 693.
[21] Coucher Book of Furness, p. 72. [JHP]

22. Partington, op. cit. Pt. 1, notes to p.17.
23. Ibid. p. 17.
24. Ibid. p. 18.
25. Ibid. p. 19
26. J E Morris " Welsh Wars of Edward I", op. cit.
27. Ibid.
28. Partington, op.cit. p.20-22.
29. "Lancs.Inquests, etc.". Lancs. & Cheshire Record Society, vol.48, p.302.
30. Dodsworth's MSS vol.9, p.285 [JHP]
31. Ibid. p. 263.
32. "Final Concords, etc." William Farrer. Lancs. & Ches. Record Society, vol. 46, pp 55,78.
33. Parliamentary Writs, vol.43, p.1006.
34. Dodsworth's MSS, vol.8, pp.158/9. [JHP]
35. Papers of J H Partington - op.cit. Pt.1, pp. 28/29 & notes.
36. Ibid. P.29
37. Dodsworth's MSS, vol. 8, p.184. [JHP]
38. Christopher Townley's MSS, p. 582. [JHP]

Chapter Three

The Move to South Lancashire

The manor of Heton-under Horwich which was to come into the hands of the Hetons was part of or adjoining the Forest of Horwich which had been held by the Grelley family, Barons of Manchester, since soon after the Norman Conquest. Its exact boundaries are not known but in a survey of 1322 it is described as 16 miles around and worth a total of 220 marks (£146.66p) per annum from grazing, falcon breeding, honey, minerals, charcoal and timber[1]. The fact that a Heton was to become lord of a manor and township named Heton in the Hundred of Salford was a pure coincidence and neither gave the name to the other. The manor of Heton had this name from the 12th century and the Hetons had taken their name from their manor of Heton-in-Lonsdale.

The Forest
The Grelleys were of a very privileged status to have their own hunting forest, as the majority of land suitable for the chase in England was subject to the King's Forest Laws, which excluded everyone but the king and those to whom he gave permission from hunting there. The laws applied not only to the deep woods where the deer lived but also to considerable areas of agricultural land on their fringes where the deer might wander, irrespective of the ownership of the land. In the late 12th century the royal forests were estimated to cover one-third of the land of England with the Crown controlling 86 forests of various sizes throughout the country.[2] The peak might be said to have been reached in 1184 when The Assize of the Forest was held at Woodstock in Oxfordshire, and the strict forest laws were codified.

The principal quarry was either the native red and roe deer or the fallow deer, introduced in the 12th century by the returning Crusaders. Not only was the royal court very enthusiastic about the chase but venison formed a valuable source of food as the king and his retinue made their frequent progresses through the country. The Forest Laws were very strict and were stringently applied, the penalties laid down for anyone breaking them by killing or disturbing the king's deer being drastic in the extreme - blinding, mutilation and even death, as well as heavy fines and imprisonment for lesser offences.

Gradually the strict control exercised by the Crown began to be somewhat slackened and by the mid-13th century private forests were becoming fashionable and an increasing number of forests and parks were being established by the great magnates and lesser landowners. In contrast, however, many landowners whose land had been largely sterilised by being made subject to the Forest Laws in the past, were combining to buy out the royal restrictions and obtain freedom to manage their land as they wished.[3]

The Move to South Lancashire

In 1282 Robert de Grelley, Baron of Manchester died and the Grelleys ceased to use the forest exclusively for the hunt. Various people seem to have had interests in parts of the forest during the late 13th century as tenants or licencees of the Grelleys; principally hunters and users of cleared sites (assarts) which were let as "vaccaries" for grazing. There were no longer good reasons for the Grelleys to retain exclusive possession and parts of the forest were subinfeudated or sublet. At this time three foresters were appointed to be responsible for the management and control of the forest and they were to be maintained from 40 oxgangs of land (perhaps 500 acres) distributed between Lostock, Rumworth, Heton, Halliwell, Sharples, Longworth, and Anderton, all manors within the barony of Manchester[4]. The manor of Heton was first granted to Richard de Hulton who is recorded as holding for a service of one-tenth of a knight's fee in 1303.

The last de Grelley to be Baron of Manchester was Thomas who remained unmarried and had only one sister, Joan. In May 1301 he granted a charter to the inhabitants of his town of Manchester (Mamecestre), creating it a borough and granting the burgesses certain privileges and encouragements to trade.[5] In March 1309 Thomas de Grelley made a transfer of his manor of Manchester, including the forest of Horwich, to his brother-in-law Sir John la Warre and his sister Joan, subject to a yearly payment of 100 marks (£66.66) to himself for life. He survived until 1313 and was aged 35 when he died.[6]

Absentee Landlords

The evidence that John de Heton, son of Roger, was responsible for the Heton family's move to South Lancashire is to some extent circumstantial but nevertheless is positive and convincing. John was named as the son of Roger de Heton when he was fined 2d by the court of the Hundred of Lonsdale on 26 November 1325 for failing in his duty as a doomsman of Bolton-le-Sands,[7] in not bringing an accused person before the court. Although he remained an absentee landlord all his life and never actually lived there for any length of time, it seems he was granted the manor of Heton-under-Horwich in 1309, the same year as the transfer of the barony of Manchester from the Grelleys to the la Warres. In 1309 the Grelleys were mesne (intermediate) lords of land in Lonsdale which included the manor of Heton and their overlord both there and at Manchester and Horwich was Henry de Lacy, Earl of Lincoln. Members of the Heton family had served with de Lacy during the war in Wales in 1281-1294 and he must have known them fairly well. It is conceivable that these connections between the various families were used to obtain the grant of the manor of Heton-under-Horwich to John de Heton after Richard de Hulton's death in 1307, the same year in which king Edward I died and his son Edward II succeeded him.

John, son of John, the second Heton to hold the manor of Heton-under-Horwich still appears to have functioned largely as an absentee landlord, even though there was more involvement with affairs relating to the Hundred

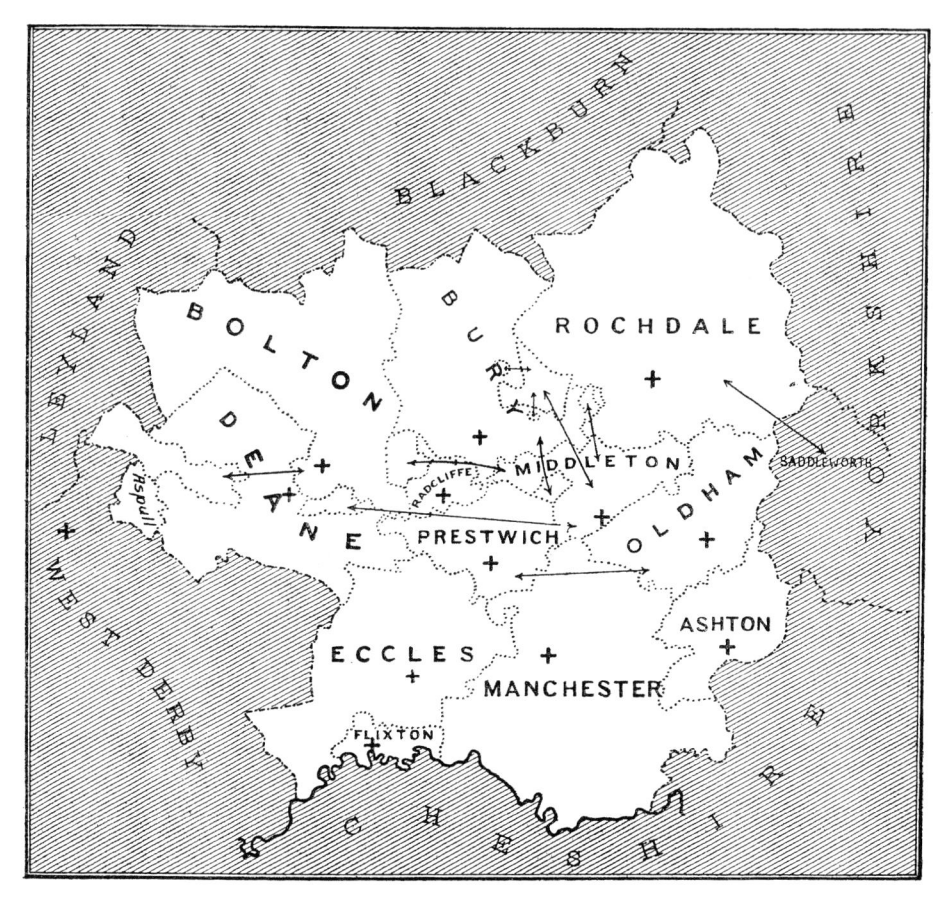

The Hundred of Salford in the 14th century.
(With acknowledgements to Victoria County History).

of Salford. In a survey of the whole barony of Manchester, carried out in 1320, John de Heton is recorded as holding the manor of Heton-by-the-Forest for one-tenth of a knight's fee and paying " for sake 8d, for [castle]ward 12d, and putary of the sergeant (foreman) and the foresters".[8] This was confirmed in a further survey carried out in 1322, which mentions the knight's service only, i.e. the same as that for which Richard de Hulton had previously held the manor. Apart from these records of his tenure there is no evidence that John was very much involved directly with the manor of Heton-under-Horwich One of his few links with the area was the appearance of his name as a witness to a grant of land sealed at Farnworth on 24 June 1321[9].

In 1332 John, son of John de Heton, was apparently living on the Heton family estate at Broune in Thornton since he was assessed at 13d (6p) on goods there for the Subsidy (a form of taxation) in that year.[10] This is significant as emphasising the links between the Heton family in Lonsdale and

Herding swine in the forest. Treefelling and clearing land for cultivation. Luttrell Psalter.

Amounderness and that at Horwich. A further longstanding connection was the fact that in the 16th century Hetons at Heton-under-Horwich still owned land at Ulverston, Rosset, Furness and Urswick, very probably the residue of the lands which the Hetons in Lonsdale owned and which passed down to those at Horwich.

The Manor

When John de Heton took over the manor of Heton-under-Horwich in the first decade of the 14th century he was faced with many of the same problems as those which had confronted Augustine in Lonsdale, 120 years earlier. However the land with which he had to work was rather different to that at Heton-in-Lonsdale. It was by no means as fertile, it was at a much higher altitude, and lent itself much more to rearing livestock than growing corn crops. Its previous use as hunting forest meant that, apart from the few areas which had already been cleared for grazing, it consisted of scrub and heathland with a scattering of large trees and some dense thickets. Its altitude is between 100 and 300 metres (300 -1000 ft) above sea level, with the one saving factor that most of it is south-facing. A later document describes the manor of Heton as being 1200 acres of land but it is probable that when John took over initially it was about 700 acres in extent. Rather more clearance of trees and scrub is likely to have been necessary than was the case in Lonsdale and the first John de Heton seems to have taken his time in proceeding with clearance and cultivation of his new manor as there is no evidence that he lived there during his lifetime.

Whereas the manor of Heton-in-Lonsdale appears to have been managed on the large field system with villein labour, it seems likely that there were rather more free tenants at Heton-under-Horwich to whom areas of land were let, and who were made responsible for clearance and initial cultivation, so that the land was never divided into large fields and strip-cultivated as in Lonsdale. It probably took one or two generations before the land was completely cleared and its full potential could be realised. Apart from appointing a steward to collect rents and ensure that tenants were performing their obligations the first two generations of Heton lords of the manor seem to have had little to do with the land directly, being still resident on the family estate in Lonsdale.

A Rebellion

In 1311 the old Earl of Lincoln, Henry de Lacy, a loyal supporter of Edward I throughout his Welsh and Scottish wars, and overlord of the Hetons in Lonsdale and at Horwich, died. His sole heiress was his daughter Alice, married to Thomas Earl of Lancaster and when de Lacy died Lancaster was able to add his extensive estates to his own and become one of the most powerful men in the kingdom. Lancaster incurred the enmity of King Edward II two years later when he was principally responsible for the execution of Piers Gaveston, Edward's favourite. In 1314 when called upon by the king to send men for the army being raised to invade Scotland, Lancaster sent the minimum number for whom he was legally liable under his feudal obligations. His father-in-law de Lacy had always fought in Wales and Scotland himself without pay and brought far more men than he was strictly obliged to, amongst whom were members of the Heton family.

Lancaster built up a private army of his own based at Pontefract where he was joined by numbers of northern gentry. For some years the king and Lancaster with his supporters were at loggerheads and the possibility of civil war constantly simmered only just beneath the surface. Then in 1321, suddenly and unexpectedly, Edward's fortunes improved. Several magnates rallied to his support with their forces, following an insult to his Queen Isabella by a Lancaster supporter, and with a strong army the king felt able to move against his enemies. For some weeks the two armies manoevoured until they finally faced one another at Boroughbridge, north of York on 17 March 1322. Edward was victorious; Lancaster was captured, tried, and executed by beheading within a few days. His estates were confiscated and retained by the king or distributed amongst his supporters. After the battle, eighteen other important individuals were executed and suffered confiscation of their estates.

The aftermath of this rebellion had some effect on the Hetons, implying that they had given some support to Lancaster who was their overlord. However the penalties inflicted on them were not particularly severe, indicating perhaps that they had only played a minor role in the rebellion. In the accounts off the Sheriff of Lancaster for 1324 there is noted the receipt of 5 marks (£3.33) from John, son of John de Heton "as a fine for his transgressions, by way of guarantors"[11]. This is only a small amount and is possibly the final instalment of a rather larger fine imposed for participating in the rebellion but which has otherwise been paid, only this final payment having to be obtained from John's bondsmen. He seems to have been let off fairly lightly for treasonable activities which resulted in others losing their heads and their lands. Also on record is the grant of a letter of pardon on 22 April 1322 to a William de Heton, otherwise unknown, but described as "an adherent of Thomas, late Earl of Lancaster"[12]. He too appears to have been rather fortunate.

Notes & References.

1. "Mamecestre", vol. II, p.390. Chetham Society, 1861
2. "The Norman Heritage", T. Rowley, 1977, p. 150
3. Ibid. p. 148.
4. "Mamecestre", op. cit. vol.2, p. 401.
5. Ibid, p. 246.
6. Ibid. p. 252.
7. "Lancaster Court Rolls", Lancs. & Ches. Record Soc., vol.41, p. 134. [JHP]
8. " Mamecestre" op. cit. vol.II, p.341.
9. Picciope's MSS, vol.3, p.8. Chetham Library [JHP].
10. Lancs. & Cheshire Record Society; vol.31, 70 [JHP].
11. Dodsworth's MSS, vol.4, p. 117. Chetham Library. [JHP]
12. Calender of Chancery Rolls, Various 1277-1326.

Chapter Four

Years of Progress and Prosperity

The assessment for the one-fifteenth tax of 1332 shows that John, second Heton lord of the manor of Heton-under-Horwich, was actually an absentee landlord, living on the family's estate in Lonsdale, and it also provides evidence to show that Robert, fourth son of John de Heton II, was living at his father's manor at Horwich at the time, this apparently being the first generation of Hetons to do so. The assessment for "Heton cum Haliwelle" shows Robert charged 12d (5p) for the tax[1].

The Family of John de Heton II
In the same year, John de Heton II made a settlement of his estate[2] at Heton in which he appointed Richard de Gildenale as his trustee (feoffee) and stipulated that the land should be held for his own use until his death and then pass to his son and heir, John III. If John III died without heirs then the land was to pass to the second son, Adam, and then, in similar circumstances, down through the various siblings in the order of Roger, Robert, Richard, Joan and finally Agnes, the youngest daughter. In the event that she died without heirs then the land should pass to the "right heirs" of John II, wherever they are to be found. It is clear that in exceptional circumstances the estate could pass out of the hands of the Hetons and over to any family into which Joan or Agnes or any sole heiress might marry, as there is no stipulation that the land should pass in the male line only.

John II died c. 1334 and his eldest son, John III inherited the estate. Robert de Huyton, lord of Billinge, had no sons but four daughters who became his co-heiresses. John de Heton III apparently married one of the daughters and her share of her father's estate, the manor of Birchley near Wigan, passed to the Hetons.[3]

There are no surviving records referring to John's second son Adam, and we know nothing about him. We have seen that Robert, the fourth son was resident in Heton and presumably playing his part in converting the land from forest into some arable but primarily grassland, erecting dwellinghouses and farm buildings. Richard, the fifth son, was a priest and from 2 April 1358 he was incumbent at the chantry of Holy Trinity Church, the parish church of Winwick[4]. This was a wealthy incumbency and provided Richard with a very good living.

Joan, the elder daughter of John II married Richard, son of Robert de Pilkington and on their marriage on 25 March 1336 Robert granted to them land in Rivington which was to revert to other members of the Pilkington family if Richard and Joan were to die without heirs[5]. Agnes the younger daughter probably married an Entwistle.[6]

However, it is the third son, Roger de Heton, who became the most prominent member of the family at that time and about whom most is known, because it was he who, in his chosen occupation of surgeon, served King Edward III personally for over 20 years, and even possibly his father Edward II before him.

The King's Surgeon[7]

We do not know where Roger de Heton trained as a surgeon. He may have studied as a clerk and obtained his knowledge from manuscripts to which he had access or he may have attended one of the medical schools which had been established at Oxford and on the Continent.

The first record of Roger was in 1328, the second year of Edward III's reign. He was then, at the request of the king's uncle Edmund, Earl of Kent, granted a life interest in the town of Pennanthlu, Merionshire, North Wales. He is there described as the "king's surgeon" and the implication might be that he had also been surgeon to Edward II and was known to some important people. He was obviously in favour with the king as in 1331 he also received a grant for life of a property at Aberffraw, a previously important place on the island of Anglesey from which the former Princes of Gwynedd had administered their principality until the conquest by Edward I in 1282. Roger paid the king a rent of £39 p.a. for his property at Aberffraw, subsequently reduced to £29 for his continuous service at the King's side. In 1342 Roger was given permission to hold a market there every Thursday and two fairs a year.

North Wales was not a convenient place from which to perform his duties to the King so in 1333 Edward asked the Abbott of St. Albans to provide Roger with accommodation and maintenance. However, in 1337 Roger's establishment near London was greatly improved by the grant to him "in fee", i.e. freehold, of a house close to the entrance to the Palace of Westminster, which he held of the king for a service of 2d (1p) per annum.

Roger died on 13 May 1349 and after an inquisition his heirs were confirmed as his widow Isabel and his two daughters, Alice and Isabel, aged 19 and 18 respectively, who became the owners of the Westminster property. It appears that some years later they sold the property back to the king for the sum of £20.

Roger would have accompanied the king on all his expeditions against the Scots and the French including the battles of Halidon Hill in 1333, the invasion of France in 1338, the naval battle of Sluys in 1340, very probably the battle of Crecy in 1346 and the seige of Calais in 1347. He was held in high regard by the king and was well rewarded for his long and faithful service.

Hetons in Residence

By 1334, when John de Heton III succeeded his father as lord of the manors of Heton-under-Horwich and Birchley, the Heton estates had enlarged notably. With Birchley, the total Heton holdings could have been around 1200

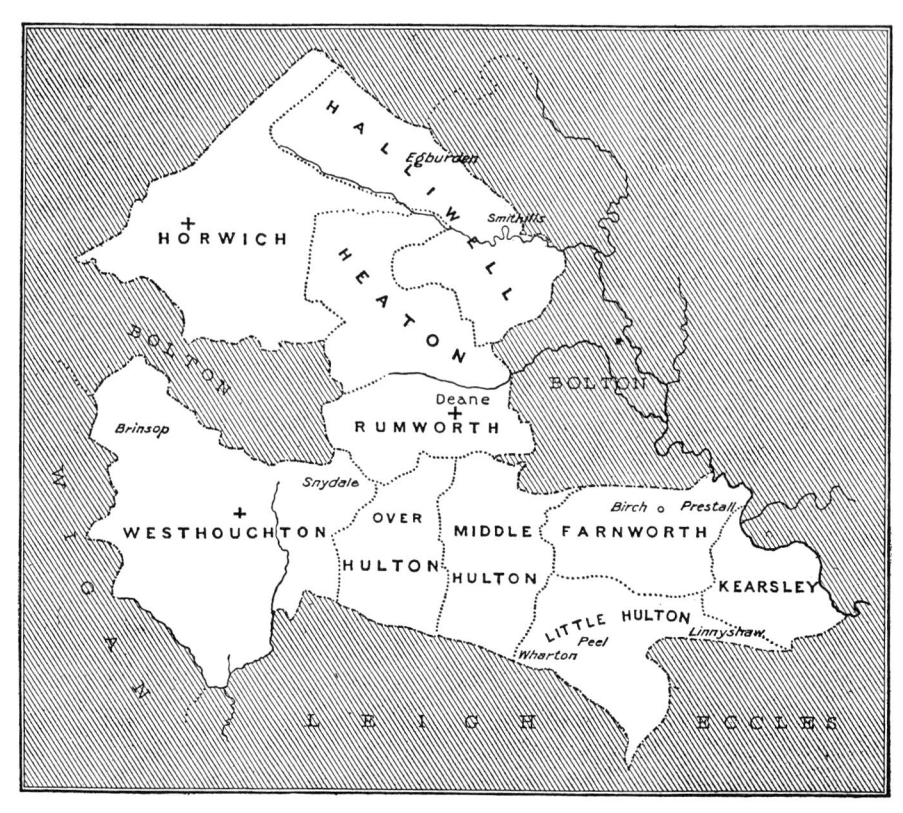

The Parish of Deane showing the townships into which the parish was divided. (With acknowledgements to Victoria County History).

acres, and as the land became increasingly productive, with the ability to earn greater income from it, the degree of management required to realise its full potential encouraged the members of the family to give up their residence in Lonsdale and move to Horwich.

The name of John de Heton, the head of the family, appears on several documents at this time as a witness to various transactions being completed in the Hundred of Salford of which the manor of Heton was a part. On 21 September 1334 at Ordeshall he witnessed the transfer of rights in land from Richard de Hulton of Ordeshall to John, son of Henry de Hulton of Farnworth[8]. On 28 October 1334 in the same place he witnessed a conveyance of further rights between the same parties.[9] Obviously he appears to have been fairly intimate with Richard de Hulton and it is possible that they were in some way related. The following year, on 15 April, at Hulton Park he witnessed a conveyance by William Radcliffe, the trustee of the Hulton settled estates, of the Park, Manor and Mill of Hulton with other land in Westhoughton, Rumworth, Denton and Manchester to Adam de Hulton for life[10], reverting to his heirs after his death.

In 1343 a marriage of John de Heton to Alice, widow of Orm Travers, son of Thomas Travers is recorded[11], and this would appear to be John's second marriage. He also appears as a witness to two documents sealed in 1347. John was still alive in 1361 as on 3 May in that year he witnessed a grant of land in Wrightington and Perbold in consideration of the marriage of his daughter Alyne to Thomas, son of Roger Banastre[12].

Anti-Social Behaviour

It would seem that a member of the family may have been somehow involved in the death of a neighbour because it is on record[13] that on 10 March 1340 John, son of John de Heton was granted a pardon for his part in the death of Henry Moldesson of Halum on condition that he went overseas in the king's service and stayed there. This is unlikely to have been the head of the family and presumably was a younger son about whom we otherwise know nothing.

In 1341 John de Heton was appointed to a Jury for the Hundred of Salford who were responsible for assessing the one-fifteenth taxes payable on the annual value of moveable goods belonging to merchants and others, together with the ninth of every sheaf of corn, lamb and fleece of wool.[14] These taxes were granted by Parliament to King Edward III to meet the costs of the war in France and in the County of Lancaster it was the Abbot of Furness and other Commissioners who delegated their responsibilities for the collection of the tax to the Hundred Jury of which John de Heton was a member.

John and his fellow-jurors produced an assessment which showed Westhoughton, with a much smaller area of land, as being liable to tax at a much higher figure than that assessed on Heton-with-Halliwell-and-Horwich and Over, Little, and Middle Hulton. These findings were rejected by the Abbot and the other Commissioners as being grossly unfair and presumably influenced by friendship, family connections and other considerations. The assessments were referred to the king and his Council for review, although we do not know the ultimate outcome[15].

Other offences also seem to have taken place for on 6 July 1345 John de Heton, with a number of other Lancashire men, was pardoned all "felonies and trespasses in England before 16 June" at the request of Henry of Lancaster, Earl of Derby, on condition that they went, when summoned, to Gascony in France on the kings service, and stayed there for a year at their own expense. In the following year the king issued letters patent to various men including John de Heton whereby the penalty previously imposed of service overseas was revoked in consideration of their each paying the sum of 50 marks (£33.33) into the king's chancery[16].

Agriculture

As already stated the manor of Heton-under-Horwich was agriculturally most suited to the rearing of livestock, principally cattle and sheep, with only a little corn grown on the best land for the farmers' own sustenance and as supplementary feed for cattle during the winter. As the land was gradually cleared and put down to pasture the pattern of husbandry followed that which had applied in Salford Hundred generally for many years and which was to continue largely unchanged until the gradual improvements in agriculture which gathered pace in the 18th and 19th centuries. In Lancashire it was difficult to fully fatten animals on the meagre pastures available and both cattle and sheep were mainly sold as stores for fattening in the Midlands. Prolificacy was low, the lamb crop reared being about 80% of ewe numbers and calves being 50-75% of cows per year.[17] Heton manor went up to 1000ft. (300 m) altitude and in their attempts to carry more stock, farmers reclaimed more higher land as summer pastures, leaving lower grassland ungrazed to make hay for winter fodder, and grazing the aftermath only, after the hay had been cut.

Lancashire was a county of nearly 1900 sq. miles and it had an average of two markets per 100 sq. miles by 1350[18]. The farmers of Heton were fortunate that they were within two miles of Bolton where a notable market and twice-yearly fair was held at which the Earl of Lincoln habitually sold much stock off his demesne lands.[19] Most fairs were held in the early summer and autumn, probably July and September. The summer fair was to buy and sell spring-born young stock or sheep after shearing or as barren stock if they had failed to lamb. The autumn fair was to sell store cattle and sheep to drovers and graziers to be moved south for fattening. After the calves had been taken off their mothers the cows' milk was largely used for the making of cheese.

The area was devastated by the Black Death in 1348/9, as was the rest of the country, with up to two-thirds of the population dying of bubonic plague. This resulted in a steep rise in wages but this proved to be temporary and by 1370 the position had stabilised again. By that date most holdings in livestock breeding areas were let at money rents with the family providing the labour to work the farm. With the rents he received the lord of the manor would hire labourers to work his demesne lands. Wages paid were of the order of 10s.-12s. (50-60p) p.annum for a carter or a shepherd, 7s.-8s (35-40p). for a ploughman. In addition each man could expect to receive 28 lbs of grain every 10 weeks[20].

By 1350 landowners themselves found their relationship to their overlords changed as the old feudal services became defunct and were almost universally replaced by money payments. The lord of the manor had probably reduced his area of demesne land, which he farmed himself, owing to difficulties in obtaining labour, and such land was let to tenants who were able to increase the size of their holdings in this way and by taking over, on fairly easy terms, the farms of their neighbours killed by the plague. In return tenants had to take over responsibilities for repairs to houses, barns and fences which previously had been undertaken by the landlord. By 1400 farm leases were being granted for 15 or 20 years and for the first time leases for a life or lives were introduced[21], a form of tenure which we shall come across to an increasing extent for the next four centuries as the Heaton story unfolds.

Years of Progress and Prosperity

Wars against the French and the Scots

In 1330 Edward III took over full kingship at the age of 18 and firstly turned his attention to Scotland in an attempt to stabilise the border and remove the threat of Scottish raids and invasion which occasionally reached as far as south Lancashire. An English army was formed under Edward's command with levies from all the northern counties. Very probably members of the Heton family and their servants and tenants served with this force and Roger de Heton, as surgeon to the king, was certainly present at headquarters, attending his master.

In 1333 the English army marched and engaged the Scots at the battle of Halidon Hill on 13 July. The Scots suffered a heavy defeat, the border fortress town of Berwick-on-Tweed was captured by the English and the north of England was cleared of Scots for the first time in the 20 years since the battle of Bannockburn. The Scottish king fled to France and the "auld alliance" between France and Scotland was revived.

When the French king, Charles IV, died in 1328 the claimants to the French throne were Edward III of England and Phillip de Valois, cousin of the last French king. Phillip seized the initiative by having himself crowned Phillip VI of France in 1328 but legal argument continued for some years between the English and French as to the true succession.

By 1337 the negotiations between France and England over the succession had failed and both sides prepared to fight what became known as the Hundred Years War. The English army was recruited largely from the midlands and south of the country and from Wales. Troops were not withdrawn from the northern counties because of the still-present threat of raids from Scotland. The system of raising an army by calling on the performance of knightservice or paying scutage money in lieu had been largely abandoned by this time and a mainly professional army was hired and paid on a contractual basis with money raised from taxes, frequently the one-fifteenth levy on all produce, authorised by Parliament and collected on a county basis. The army consisted largely of armoured men-at-arms who often fought on foot, and highly-skilled archers, frequently from Wales or Cheshire, who with their longbows could shoot 12 arrows a minute over a range of 400 yards.

The Hetons of Heton-under-Horwich and Heton-in-Lonsdale, like the population of the north of England generally, were not directly affected by the war in France, due to the continuing policy of not drawing troops from that area in case of an invasion by the Scots. The war began with the invasion of France by an English army under the command of Edward III in 1338. Roger de Heton was again in attendance on the king. Edward wished to engage the French in a pitched battle and inflict a positive defeat but the French avoided this.

French ships conducted raids against English south coast towns until an English fleet under Edward won a decisive victory over a combined French and Genoese armada at the naval battle of Sluys in 1340. Once again Roger de

Heton would have been on board. Following this battle a truce was signed in 1340 and hostilities ceased for the time being. The war was a constant succession of fighting and uneasy truces and in practice the armies only engaged in conflict for about one-third of the time.

In August 1346 the two armies met, almost accidentally, at Crecy where the battle resulted in a massive defeat of the much larger French force owing to superior tactics by the English whose casualties were very few. Many French noblemen were captured, bringing large ransoms to their captors. The King of Bohemia, an ally of France, was killed and his emblem of three ostrich feathers and his motto "Ich Dien" (I Serve) was adopted by the Prince of Wales and his successors. Roger de Heton was in attendance on the king but his ill-health was becoming more serious and his period of service with the king was coming to an end.

In 1347, after a long seige, the English captured Calais, a strategic port and gateway to the continent, which they were to hold for the next 200 years. King Edward commanded the army so once again Roger de Heton was present, probably the last time he was able to attend the king whom he had served faithfully for over 20 years, as his health was now failing.

After his defeat at Crecy, Phillip of France persuaded King David of Scotland to mount an invasion of northern England. The Scots mistakenly believed that the northern counties had been largely denuded of troops taken to fight in France but this was not the case.[22] The usual policy of ensuring adequate forces were left in the north had applied and an army was assembled at York which, under the Archbishop, William de la Zouche, marched north to Durham and met the Scots in battle at Neville's Cross. The result was a complete defeat of the Scots who lost many men killed and captured. Amongst the prisoners was King David of Scotland. Soldiers for the army were recruited from all over the north of England and it is quite conceivable that it included members of the Heton family, their servants and tenants.

In 1355 Edward, the Black Prince, took a new army to France with the intention of linking up with another army under the Duke of Lancaster. This manoeuvre failed and Edward, with only 6000 troops, found himself facing the new French king John II with 20,000 men near Poitiers on 17 September 1356. Superior English morale and tactics prevailed and the Prince won a resounding victory. King John was captured and taken to England pending payment of his £500,000 ransom, an unimaginable sum at the time. The Treaty of Bretigny in 1360 brought a temporary peace but hostilities soon resumed.

A claimant to the throne of castile, Pedro the Cruel, appealed to his ally, the Black Prince, for help and Edward took an English army to Spain in 1367. However, although the campaign was successful, many of the English fell sick with fever, including the Prince whose health was permanently ruined in consequence. He died in 1376 leaving his son Richard, aged 9, as heir to the throne.

King Edward's decline hastened after the death of Queen Philippa in 1369.

In 1374 his fourth son, John of Gaunt, took an army of 10,000 men through France from Calais to Bordeaux but by the time they arrived their numbers were reduced to 6000 and they were near-starving. When Edward III died in 1377 all that was left to England of the vast lands of Aquitaine which it had ruled at the start of his reign was Calais and a coastal strip between Bordeaux and Bayonne.

Hostilities continued desultorily during the following reign of Richard II, who was not really interested in seriously pursuing a claim for the French throne. The king's uncles took charge of the armies in France and hostilities continued with little being achieved. By their victory over the English at Otterburn in 1388 the Scots restored the former balance of power in the border lands. Finally the French war was wound up by a truce in 1393 which was intended to last twentyeight years and the king, now a widower, married Isabella, a young daughter of the French king.

The Duchy and County Palatine of Lancashire

In 1351 Henry de Grosmount, Earl of Lancaster, a close friend and companion of Edward III was made Duke of Lancaster, owning all the estates of the traitor Thomas and the old Earl of Lincoln, Henry de Lacy. In addition Henry was given palatine powers over the whole of Lancashire by the king, for life These powers meant that Henry could administer his Duchy as if he were king and it was completely independent of the rest of the country, subject only to continuing to pay the taxes upon which the king relied.

The 4th son of king Edward, John of Gaunt (Ghent) named after the town in which he was born, had married Blanche, daughter and heiress of Duke Henry and when her father died in 1361 she inherited the Duchy of Lancaster and the Earldoms of Leicester, Lincoln, and Derby, which were then transferred to her husband, but not her father's palatine powers . When Blanche herself died aged only 22, John of Gaunt became Duke of Lancaster and owner of vast possessions, making him the richest man in the kingdom. Amongst the lands of which he was overlord as successor to Henry, Earl of Lincoln, were the two Heton manors in Lonsdale and Horwich. In 1377, the year he died, king Edward granted palatine powers to John of Gaunt for life and in 1390, despite his general unpopularity, he persuaded his nephew the young king Richard II to make his palatine powers permanent and capable of being inherited by his male heirs.

John of Gaunt died in 1399 and his son and heir Henry, who had been banished from the country by Richard II was denied the right to inherit his father's estates by the king. This denial of the normal laws of inheritance caused general outrage; Henry returned against the king's order, gathered considerable support and was able to imprison Richard and take the throne himself as Henry IV. As well as becoming king Henry also retained his title of Duke of Lancaster and this is an arrangement which has applied ever since, every English monarch subsequently being also Duke of Lancaster and administering the Duchy and County Palatine with its separate chancery, exchequer and judiciary. Although his powers were reduced in the 19th century there is still a Chancellor of the Duchy who now holds what is largely a political office.

Further Generations of Hetons

John de Heton III had succeeded his father, probably in 1334, and is known to have been still alive in 1361, shortly after which he died. His family consisted of William his eldest son; Richard, Robert and John, styled John de Horewych, younger sons; and two daughters Alyne and Joan.

William succeeded his father as head of the family[23] but apparently for a short time only as he appears to have left no record behind him. Presumably he died soon after his father and it seems was followed as lord of the manor by his younger brother Richard de Heton.

Richard's wife was named Isolda[24] but we do not know from where she came and all we know of their family is that they had two sons, William the eldest, and John who became a priest and was appointed a chaplain or Fellow of Manchester Collegiate Church. John was appointed a trustee of a settlement as dowry for Elizabeth, daughter of Sir Edmund Trafford on the occasion of her marriage to Sir John de Pilkington on 20 April 1436.[25] He appears also as a trustee of a settlement by Sir John de Pilkington dated 14 June of the same year.[26]

The first record of Richard de Heton is on the Sunday before the Feast of the Conversion of St. Paul (25 January) 1369 when he appears as a witness to a document between William de Hulton and John de Lever relating to a farm at Great Lever[27]. Again we see the continuing association between the Hetons and the Hultons. The next recorded transaction[28] in which Richard was involved was at Easter 1371 when, in relation to a marriage contract between Richard, son of John de Radclif and Margaret, daughter of Henry de Trafford, he was bound as a bondsman, with five other gentlemen, in the sum of 100 marks (£66.66) to Henry de Trafford to ensure the fulfillment of the contract before the next Christmas Day. This is a substantial sum, probably about £100,000 in modern money, although it is virtually impossible to make a precise conversion as a number of economic factors have to be taken into consideration.

His two younger brothers, Robert and John are recorded as being witnesses in 1388 to a document conveying the manor of Worsley from Richard de Workeslegh to Robert de Workeslegh.[29]

It seems evident that Richard de Heton played an active part in local administration in his County and Hundred The next document in which his name appears is dated 7th December in the "seventh year of the Regality of John, Duke of Lancaster", an obvious reference to the grant of palatine powers to John of Gaunt in 1377 and hence dating the document 1384. It is a commission to Richard and others to act in the matter of the collection of a one-fifteenth tax on produce, granted for the defence of the realm.

Years of Progress and Prosperity

In the following year 1385 Sir Roger de Pilkington, Sir John de Ashton, James de Radclif, Robert de Holand, and Richard de Heton, esquires, were appointed Justices of the Peace for the Hundred of Salford,[30] a recognition of the fact that these gentlemen were generally accepted as people of some standing in the locality.

Other functions which Richard performed were as a member of Juries formed to hold Inquisitions post mortem in the cases of Richard de Radclif on 14 August 1380 at Lancaster, Richard le Byrun on 15 August 1397 at Manchester, and William de Chorley in the same year and probably in Manchester also.[31] The purpose of these Inquisitions was to determine what lands and other possessions were held by the deceased when he died, and often who was entitled to inherit.

A Corrody

The Hetons were the owners of a Corrody in the Priory of St. Helen at Marresay in Nottinghamshire. Originally a corrody was an obligation upon an ecclesiastical establishment to provide shelter and food for the incumbent when called upon to do so, but such obligations were often converted subsequently to a monetary payment in lieu. The entitlement to the corrody was in the gift of the lord of the manor of Heton-under-Horwich and we know that Richard first granted it to his cousin William Entwistle for life and then on his death to another cousin, Oliver Entwistle. The right to this corrody subsequently passed into the hands of Robert, younger brother of Richard de Heton, who was granted it by his nephew, William, who inherited on the death of his father, in the final years of the 14th century. When Robert died, the Prior of Marresay reached an agreement with the then lord of the manor of Heton, William II, Richard's grandson, that the corrody should be discontinued during William's lifetime.[32]

A New Lord of the Manor

William de Heton had married Johan, daughter of Gilbert de Billinge in 1398, probably the year in which his father died. Because his grandfather had married a member of the same family,

A 14th century knight and his lady in informal dress.

William and Johan were sufficiently closely related for the Church to hold that they came within the "degrees of consanguinity" which could prevent their marriage. It was necessary for them to apply for a dispensation to enable them to marry and this was granted by the Bishop of Lichfield and Coventry in 1398.[33] Their family consisted of Nicholas, the eldest, William their second son, another son George and probably others. They also had at least two daughters, Katherine and another whose name we do not know. It seems probable that when Johan died many years later William married again to Elizabeth, a widow, in 1442.

William de Heton began very quickly to play his part as a person of prominence in the district by being selected in 1398 as one of a Jury to hear a dispute between Matilda, widow of Robert de Barton and Richard de Holland as to the ownership of land at Barton in Salford Hundred. The jury included Sir Thomas Gerard, Knt; Sir William Atherton, Knt; James de Radcliffe; William de Heton, esquires, and others. For William to be described in this way would seem to indicate that by that date his father was dead and he had inherited the title of lord of the manors of Heton-under-Horwich and Birchley.[34]

The Roos Connection

Partington wrote at some length[35], maintaining that William de Heton entered the service of William, Lord Roos of Belvoir and Hamelake, and was entrusted by him with increasing responsibility in relation to Roos family affairs culminating in his appointment as Steward to William de Roos' son John (1397-1423) and as Receiver to the extensive Roos estates for a brief period during the minority of Thomas, John's younger brother. The first mention of William de Heton in this connection occurs in the Will of William, Lord Roos in 1414 when he was bequeathed a silver goblet. When William de Roos' son John went abroad in 1421 to fight the French, de Heton was appointed Steward to manage his estates. John de Roos was killed in 1423, his heir being his younger brother Thomas, a minor. The Crown claimed the wardship and William de Heton was appointed Receiver. This appointment did not last long as Thomas paid 1000 marks (£666) to king Henry VI in the following year, when he was then aged 18, to be allowed to marry and manage his lands himself. Thomas died in 1431 and William de Heton was one of his executors.

It has to be acknowledged, however, that a person of the same name, William de Heton of a Heton family in Yorkshire, a contemporary of William de Heton of Heton-under-Horwich has an equally valid and perhaps better claim to be the William de Heton in question. This Yorkshire family, which may have been connected with the Lancashire Hetons at a very early date, was researched in depth by the late Mr John Heaton of Keighley[36] who died in 1993. The possibility of a link between the Yorkshire and Lancashire Hetons will be explored in a later chapter. The fact that an identical name occurred in Lancashire and Yorkshire at the same time makes it very difficult to distinguish between the two men. For the moment we cannot state with certainty

Years of Progress and Prosperity 53

that William de Heton of Heton-under-Horwich had the close connection with the affairs of the de Roos family which Partington claimed. Indeed it seems perhaps more likely that the William in question was a Yorkshireman rather than a man from Lancashire.

However we do know that in 1410 William de Heton was a witness to a grant of land in Turton by Sir Henry de Torboke to his son John and Clemence his wife. It is stated in the document that a part of the land was once held by Thomas de Heton.[37]

An Early Legal Document in English

Wiliam de Heton and his cousin Elys de Entwissle were involved in a long-running dispute between Richard de Radclyf and Nicholas de Risley con-

The Hetons of Heton-under-Horwich, c. 1300 - 1500.

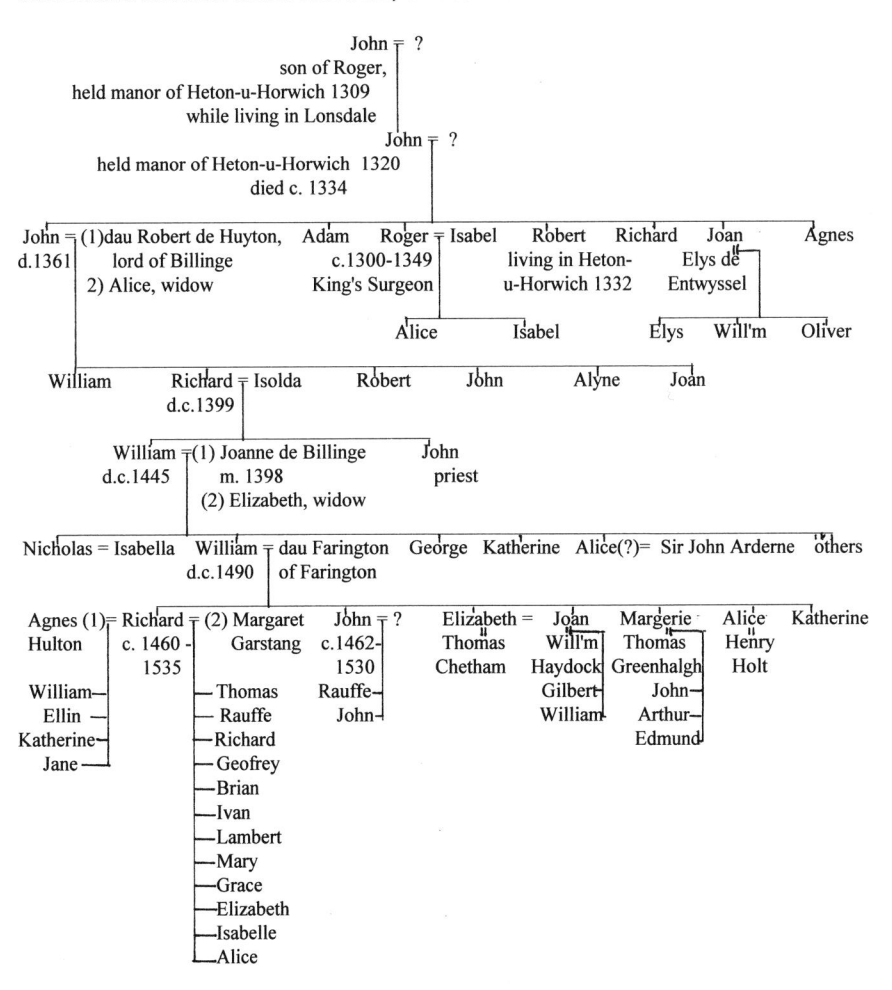

```
                              John ╤ ?
                           son of Roger,
              held manor of Heton-u-Horwich 1309
                      while living in Lonsdale
                                      │
                                   John ╤ ?
                     held manor of Heton-u-Horwich 1320
                               died c. 1334
    ┌─────────────┬──────────┬──────────────┬──────────────┬─────────┬────────┐
John ╤(1)dau Robert de Huyton,  Adam    Roger ╤ Isabel   Robert    Richard   Joan       Agnes
d.1361   lord of Billinge              c.1300-1349       living in Heton-   Elys de
      2) Alice, widow              King's Surgeon       u-Horwich 1332     Entwyssel
                                          │                                   │
                                    ┌─────┴─────┐                     ┌───────┼────────┐
                                  Alice       Isabel                 Elys   Will'm   Oliver
  ┌────────┬──────────────┬────────┬─────────┬─────────┐
William   Richard ╤ Isolda   Robert      John      Alyne      Joan
          d.c.1399
             │
          William ╤(1) Joanne de Billinge    John
          d.c.1445    m. 1398              priest
                  (2) Elizabeth, widow
  ┌────────────┬──────────────────┬────────┬─────────┬──────────────┬──────────┐
Nicholas = Isabella  William ╤ dau Farington  George  Katherine  Alice(?)= Sir John Arderne  others
                    d.c.1490  of Farington
  ┌────────┬──────────────┬──────────┬──────────────┬──────────┬──────────────┬──────────┐
Agnes (1)╤ Richard ╤ (2) Margaret   John ╤ ?      Elizabeth =  Joan      Margerie    Alice    Katherine
Hulton    c. 1460 -   Garstang    c.1462-        Thomas       Will'm     Thomas      Henry
            1535                   1530          Chetham      Haydock   Greenhalgh   Holt
William┤    ├ Thomas              Rauffe┤                     Gilbert┤   John┤
Ellin  ┤    ├ Rauffe              John ┤                      William┤   Arthur┤
Katherine┤  ├ Richard                                                    Edmund┤
Jane   ┘    ├ Geoffrey
            ├ Brian
            ├ Ivan
            ├ Lambert
            ├ Mary
            ├ Grace
            ├ Elizabeth
            ├ Isabelle
            └ Alice
```

cerning pasture at Redshagh Moss, Culceth. Elys de Entwissle had been ordered by the Bishop of Durham, who was to hear the case, to take evidence from the parties in lieu of their bringing actions against each other, and the parties agreed to submit themselves to the decision of an arbitration panel of four of their neighbours. In 1418 the parties entered into a Bond,[38] which unusually for such an early date was in English. It seems that William de Heton stood guarantor on this occasion for Richard of Radclif. It was not until five years later in 1423 that the dispute was finally resolved and Richard de Radclif was granted rights by Nicholas de Risley in the pasture of Redeshagh for his lifetime.[39]

Social Advancement and Estate Expansion

In 1417/18 William de Heton, together with ten other knights and gentlemen of the county, was appointed a Justice of the Peace of the County of Lancaster. Around 1420 the Heton estate was extended by several hundred acres in Horwich following the acquisition by William of an area of land named Ridley Wood from Thomas de la Warre, Baron of Manchester. This land, consisting of 3 messuages (farms) and a large area of land probably requiring improvement, was held by socage tenure for a payment of 20s (£1.00) per annum, and immediately adjoined the original manorial lands in the township of Heton.

Heaton Old Hall

When the family took up residence in the manor of Heton-under-Horwich this necessitated the building of a principal manor-house and also some houses for other members of the family. It seems probable that the first manor-house was erected on the site where Old Hall Farm, Heaton, Bolton now stands and was of a style similar to the hall-house described in chapter 2 as likely to have been built at Heton-in-Lonsdale in the 13/14th centuries. The more elaborate late medieval manor house which eventually replaced the hall-house at Horwich was, in its heyday, called Heaton Hall, and still exists in part as a farmhouse, the Heatons having lived there from the time it was built until well into the 19th century, either as owners or tenants. The house stands on what is now Old Hall Lane, at an altitude of approximately 540 feet (165 metres). It is a building statutorily listed as of architectural or historic interest and the citation prepared when it was listed in 1974 describes it as of "... Medieval origin, extended and modified at different periods since, and incorporating an inscribed stone ' restored 1895' ..." The house had been badly damaged by fire in the previous year and several of the early features, particularly in the roof area, were lost, although some early 16th century kingpost roof trusses still survive. It was restored during Lady Beaumont's period of ownership.

A recent survey of the existing building and its site carried out by the University of Manchester Archaeological Unit has revealed some very interesting details. In their report[40] the UMAU state that the surviving building consists of a 3-storey structure built of rubble stone and various features of the building indicate an original construction date of late 15th, early 16th century, i.e. during the lifetimes of William Heton (c.1420-1490) and his son Richard Heton (1460-1535). There have been later additions and alterations during the 16th, 17th, 19th, and 20th centuries. The existence of a now blocked-up covered entranceway for carts, waggons or coaches through the building and also traces of masonry forming vertical bonds in the stone walls where projecting wings, now demolished, may once have been located, leads UMAU to conclude that the surviving building was probably the gatehouse range of a complex around a central open courtyard with buildings along each side and the manor house proper at the rear, opposite the gatehouse. They instance as comparable arrangements Lostock Hall and Little Hulton Hall. but state that the Heaton Old Hall structure is larger than these two surviving examples. The date of demolition of the other buildings on the site is not known.

UMAU suggest that archaeological evidence of any other buildings which formerly stood on the site should be available and recommend that, with the cooperation of the present owners, further survey work should be carried out around the site and particularly on a raised earth platform at the rear. This investigation would consist of a non-destructive geophysical survey to deter-

Old Hall Farm, Heaton at the present time, showing the southwestern "inner" elevation. This is the probable gatehouse range now used as a house. The principal manor house would formerly have stood opposite the waggon entrance with service buildings along each side, enclosing a courtyard. By courtesy of University of Manchester Archaeological Unit.

mine possible wall lines associated with the original buildings; followed by the excavation of a number of trial trenches in suitable locations to test for the physical presence of underground structures and deposits. This work could take years but holds out the exciting prospect of the rediscovery of one of Lancashire's lost medieval halls on this site.

Isabella the Recluse

Nicholas de Heton, William and Johan's eldest son died before his father and his widow Isabella, presumably devastated by the unexpected loss of her husband, expressed a wish to spend the rest of her life as a recluse in a nunnery or other similar establishment. In fact in 1438 she was granted the right by king Henry VI[41] to occupy a hermitage in the churchyard at Whalley Abbey which had been endowed in 1360 by Henry, 1st Duke of Lancaster, with sufficient land and property to enable a female recluse to live there in comfort with two servants, for the rest of her days. Her only obligation was to pray daily for the souls of the Duke and his descendants. However it would seem that Isabella, when her sorrow for her husband's death had abated somewhat, felt a desire to return to the world outside and enjoy a wider social circle for, before very long, she absconded from the hermitage and refused to continue living there, to the great concern of the monks of Whalley.[42]

It appears that Isabella was not the first of the occupiers of the hermitage to regret their undertaking to live a life of seclusion and after this latest example the monks petitioned the king to close the hermitage and discontinue the endowment, giving as their reasons a number of instances of misbehaviour on the part of the recluses and their servants, culminating in this latest outrage by Isabella de Heton which took place two years before their petition. The king agreed to their request and dissolved the whole establishment around 1442.

The Fighting Continues

Throughout almost the whole of the 15th century English soldiers were fighting either at home or abroad., with a consequent heavy burden of taxation on the general populace. The truce with France held for a number of years but Henry IV was not able to impose his will on Scotland. It was in Wales in 1400 that the most serious situation arose for Henry. A prominent Welsh landowner, Owain Glyndwr (Owen Glendower to the English), with wide family connections, enlarged his quarrel with a neighbouring English lord into a general rebellion against English rule, which gained him support throughout Wales and enabled him to declare himself prince of Wales with probably some genealogical accuracy. Owain's forces were successful and he was able to ally himself with a number of malcontents in England, principally the powerful Percy family, Earls of Northumberland, and the French king who sent some troops to Wales. The English army was drawn from the Welsh marches and the midlands and again the Hetons and their neighbours in the North-West were left to watch the border with Scotland. In 1405 Owain Glyndwr and his Percy allies were heavily defeated at Shrewsbury by Henry IV and the rebellion began to fizzle out; the French troops went home, and by 1410 Henry had regained his authority over Wales. Owain was never captured and when and where he died is not known, although Monnington, Herefordshire, the home of his daughter and son-in-law has been suggested. He remains a hero to the Welsh even though his rebellion caused devastation over large parts of the country.

Henry IV died in 1413 without achieving very much to advance his cause in France. When his son Henry V succeeded him the pressure on the French was stepped up. Henry made demands which the French king was unable to accept and in 1415 an English army landed and after quickly capturing Harfleur marched toward Calais. After crossing the River Somme the English found their way blocked by a much larger French army near the village of Agincourt. In the battle which took place on 25 October 1415 the classic English use of archers and men-at-arms on a narrow front with the flanks protected was supremely successful and the English were wholly victorious with very little loss, whereas the French lost an enormous number of noblemen and other soldiers. For a few years the English cause was in the ascendant and a number of castles and towns were recaptured. However, the death of Henry V in 1422 began a disastrous decline in the fortunes of the English.

The Hetons appear to have played very little direct part in the later French wars although Partington maintains that George, a younger son of William de Heton was a professional soldier in the army in France in the period following Agincourt, later becoming Sergeant of the Royal Lardary in 1454.[43]

The reign of Henry VI saw the English obliged to gradually retreat from all their lands in France, starting with the raising of the seige of Orleans by Joan of Arc in 1428 and ending in the loss of Normandy by 1450. Whilst the populace had been prepared to accept high levels of taxation and general economic stringency whilst English arms were victorious, as soon as the situation could be seen to be deteriorating unrest became more widespread and many began to wonder whether a change of dynasty and policy might not bring about improvements. The resulting attempts by the Yorkist faction to oust the Lancastrian dynasty which had reigned for 60 years brought about a conflict which was to last for thirty years from 1455 -1485 and which became known as the Wars of the Roses. Although the fighting was often vicious and brutal it affected mainly the greater magnates and their households, whose frequent changes in support were often the principal factors in determining the winner in a particular round of hostilities, culminating in the eleventh-hour decision by Thomas, Lord Stanley to support Henry Tudor at the battle of Bosworth in 1485.

William, 2nd Son, Succeeds

William de Heton died about 1445 and was succeeded by his second son, William II; the eldest son Nicholas having by then died. In a survey of the barony of Manchester made 1 May 1475, the 13th year of the reign of king Edward IV, William de Heton is recorded as holding Heton-under-the-Forest (of Horwich) for the old feudal obligations of one-tenth part of a knight's fee plus "puture" (maintenance of the foresters), rent 8d (3p) and castleward 12d (5p). In addition he held the land of Ridley Wood by socage tenure for a rent of 20s (£1).

Partington suggests that William II married a daughter of the Farington family of Farington, basing this contention on the fact that their eldest son Richard adopted as his coat-of-arms the arms of Heton quartered with the arms of Farington. Although this seems likely, we cannot actually say precisely who William II married. Richard's own eldest son, another William, also married a Farington, so this would seem to have been another instance of cousins marrying, as in the earlier case of Billinge, although in this later instance it brought no great inheritance to the Hetons. The family of William II consisted of two sons, Richard, born c.1460, and John, born 1462, together with five daughters, Elizabeth, Joan, Margerie, Alice, and Katherine.

Although William II lived to a ripe old age and was lord of the manors of Heton and Birchley for 45 years there is little recorded of his activities and he does not seem to have been very prominent in the county. This may have been because he failed to back the right side or was inactive in the Wars of the Roses. This perhaps meant that he was a Lancastrian whereas for most of his later life the Yorkists were in the ascendancy. We know that he was still alive in 1488 since he was, on 1 April of that year, excused all further service upon juries, assizes, etc. because of his age. He was then over 70 years old[44] and probably died soon afterwards.

Richard de Heton was William's eldest son and there will be a great deal to tell about him later. The second son, John married and settled in Heton. He is on record as giving a deposition (a witness statement), which appears to be largely hearsay, in relation to a dispute as to the ownership of a farm in Westhoughton on 6 November 1522, when he then stated that he was about 60 years of age.[45] He died in about 1530, leaving at least two children, Rauffe and John.

William II had five daughters whom he needed to see safely married and for whom he had to find dowries. He seems to have accomplished this well since they all married local gentlemen.[46] Elizabeth, the eldest, married Thomas Chetham in 1466 and she received as a marriage settlement certain farms in Crompton. Joan, the second daughter, married William Haydock of Cottam. They had two sons, Gilbert, and William. The latter became a monk at Whalley Abbey and was hanged on 12 March 1537 for joining in the Pilgrimage of Grace (q.v.later). Another daughter, Margerie, became the wife of Thomas Greenhalgh of Brandlesome and they had three sons, Arthur, John, and Edmund. The fourth daughter, Alice, married Henry Holt of Balderston and received a marriage settlement of lands and tenements called Kirkeholt in Balderston for her lifetime. We do not know whom the last daughter, Katherine, married but she too received a settlement of lands from the Vicar of Bolton, probably as a trustee, on 10 August 1486.

Richard Heton of Heton and Birchley
In 1483 the new king Richard III was trying very hard to win favour with the gentry of the North and was generous with his disbursements to try and achieve this. During the lifetime of his father, Richard Heton was awarded an annuity of 5 marks (£3.33) and was one of a long list of gentlemen to receive such payments from the king.[47] Others who received similar payments were his cousin, Edmund Greenhalgh of Horwich and many of his neighbours, including Sir William Farington, Roger Hulton, Thurstan Anderton, Roger Lever and many others who expressed support for King Richard. However, when the crunch came in 1485 and the Lancashire gentry had to decide whether to support Richard III or the other claimant to the throne, Henry Tudor, Earl of Richmond, the majority of them stayed at home, as did Richard Heton and his elderly father.

After the Battle of Bosworth on 22 August 1485, when Henry Tudor became king Henry VII, those local gentry who had actively supported Richard III were attainted as traitors and this meant that their lands were forfeited to the Crown. Their number included Sir Thomas Pilkington, Robert Hulton, and several others known to or connected with Richard Heton.[48] Henry Tudor's victory at Bosworth was largely due to the last minute intervention on his side of Thomas, Lord Stanley with his substantial forces. Thomas was rewarded with the Earldom of Derby and the grant of lands formerly held by the attainted traitors. This included the township of Halliwell,[49] immediately adjoining Heton, and formerly held by Robert Hulton, so Richard Heton acquired a powerful neighbour with whom it was very much in his interest to be on good terms, particularly in view of his previous tacit support for Richard III even though this did not go so far as to take up arms in his cause. Richard appears to have at least maintained good relations with the Earl for in 1515 he was appointed by him as one of the Assessors and Collectors of the Subsidy tax for the County of Lancashire, a recognition of his worth in the county.[50]

Richard Heton succeeded his father William about 1490 when he was thirty years of age. Whether he was the absolute owner of the Heton estates, i.e. he held them "in fee" or whether he was the tenant for life with the freehold in the hands of trustees and held by them for his use during his lifetime is a matter which was to be the subject of endless legal argument in the next century as the Hetons became embroiled in more and more litigation amongst themselves. Around this time the "de" in the names of many gentry families was being discontinued and Richard was commonly referrred to as Richard Heton esquire of Heton and Birchley. The name was sometimes spelt Heyton but it was not until the start of the 17th century that the Heaton form of spelling the name was introduced.

Richard's Family

Richard's first wife was Agnes a younger daughter of Roger Hulton of the Park. It would seem that they were betrothed as infants and their marriage took place circa 1480.[51] They had a son, William, and three daughters, Ellin, Katherine, and Jane. Agnes died at an early age and Richard married again to Margaret Garstang, of whose background we know nothing. She bore Richard another twelve children.[52] Their seven sons were Thomas, Rauffe, Richard, Geoffrey, Brian, Ivan, and Lambert. There were also five daughters, Mary, Grace, Elizabeth, Isabelle, and Alice.

From the first marriage, the only son, William married Jane, daughter of Sir William Farington and was to inherit his father's estate. Ellin married John Lever of Little Lever, gent. and they had three sons, Richard, Thomas and Ralph.[53] Richard inherited from his father and the other two distinguished themselves in academia and the Church, becoming respectively Master of St. John's College, Cambridge and Dean of Durham Cathedral. We know nothing more about Katherine but Jane married Henry Blundell esq.of Crosby, as his first wife.[54]

Of Richard's second family, two of the sons, Thomas and Geoffrey became clerks in holy orders. Geoffrey became a servant or secretary to Archbishop Cranmer and in 1533 prevailed upon his master to write a letter to a Church dignitary calling on him to pay to Thomas Heton an annuity which was due to him in accordance with the terms agreed so that " he need not further attempt the law in this behalf".[55] It would seem that this approach by the powerful Archbishop was successful and the money was paid regularly. Thomas, at the time, was holding an office at Exeter, to which it is probable he had been appointed following representations made by his kinsman Roger Heton to Bishop Oldham.

In December 1539 on the occasion of the arrival in England of Anne of Cleves, king Henry's intended fourth wife, Geoffrey Heton played his small part in a moment of history when he was entrusted with the carriage of £50 from Chancellor Thomas Cromwell to Archbishop Cranmer, to be given to Anne as a gift at her reception by Cranmer at Canterbury.[56] King Henry's disappointment with Anne was largely responsible for Cromwell's fall and execution.

The remaining sons of the second marriage are inextricably intertwined with the family machinations which took place after Richard's death and these will be described in the next chapter. The daughters, where we know the outcome, appear to have been well provided for. In the case of Mary, her father laid out £40 in the purchase of the wardship and marriage of Richard Tildesley of Garret Hall from Sir Thomas Butler, and in due course Richard and Mary were married.[57] Isabel married John, son and heir of Richard

Langtree, esq.[58] and they had a large family. She was still living in 1573, aged 63. Elizabeth married John Chetham, gent. at Middleton parish church on 21 Jan. 1549/50. Of Grace and Alice we know nothing more.

St. Mary's Church, Deane

St. Mary's, the Parish Church of Deane, was the Heaton's church. For centuries their baptisms, marriages and burials were performed there; first in the small medieval chapel and then in the enlarged 15th century church. When, for lack of space, they could no longer be buried in the church itself they were buried in the churchyard and a number of memorials still exist and have been recorded by the Bolton Family History Society and others. The registers of other parish churches and chapels in the area all have their quota of Heaton baptisms, marriages and burials but those at St. Mary's are undoubtedly the most numerous. Unfortunately the parish registers there have not survived fully before 1637, nor do the Bishop's Transcripts, a source of similar information, exist for an earlier period.

The township of Heton and the parish of Deane was, until 1541, part of the large parish of Eccles but for the convenience of the inhabitants of this northern part of the parish a small chapel had existed since at least the 13th century on the site of the present church. The original chapel with its tower built in the 14th century was incorporated in an enlargement of the church which took place in the 15th century when the nave was extended and later two aisles were provided;[59] the one on the south side being paid for by Roger Hulton of the Park, Richard Heton's brother-in-law, with the cost of the one on the north side being met by Richard Heton and William Hulton of Farnworth jointly.

In the north aisle Heton and Hulton each provided a private chapel for the use of their own families but it appears that the elaborate embellishments and carved images in the Heton chapel, dedicated to St. Anne, were a source of offence to a number of local people whose preference was towards greater austerity in places of public worship. The action they took to express their feelings was described by Richard Heton in his subsequent pleadings before the Duchy Court as follows:-

"On the 24th August, 14th Henry VIII (1522), in the night time, about three o'clock in the morning, Edmund Greenhalgh, Oliver Lockwood, Gilbert Greenhalgh, Edmund Turner, Roger Makinson, Nicholas Mather, Nicholas Kershaw, William Kershaw, Arthur Bradshaw, Thomas Greehalgh, and Robert Greenhalgh, with 26 others, to them associate, arrayed in the manner of war, came to the said church of Dene, and pulled and cut down, as well all the timber work of the said Chapel, as also the altar and posts whereupon the images of the Holy Trinity and St. Anne stood, within the said Chapel...; the said riotous persons then cut the said timber in pieces and cast it out of the said Church and Churchyard..."[60]

Four of the defendants, Edmund, Thomas and Gilbert Greenhalgh and

St. Mary's Church, Deane.

Years of Progress and Prosperity 63

Roger Makinson were ordered by the Court to appear in the Duchy Chamber at Westminster on the 15th day of the next Hilary Law Term to answer to the writ but no record of the outcome of the case seems to have been preserved. It emphasises, however, the extent to which Richard Heton was a staunch adherent to the old Catholic faith, which may have influenced his actions with regard to the disposal of his estate later in his life.

Manchester Grammar School

This well-known educational establishment was endowed by Hugh Oldham, Bishop of Exeter, c. 1510 and on 16 April 1524 Hugh Bexwyke and Joan Bexwyke, widow, the surviving trustees of Bishop Oldham's Gift executed a charter known as the Foundation Charter of Manchester Grammar School. One of the witnesses to this charter was "Richard Heyton Esquire"and in the charter Hugh and Joan nominated Roger Heyton, gentleman, and John Bexwyke, chaplain, to act for them them as trustees in the capacity of "our true and lawful attorneys" In fact Roger only held this appointment for four years as he died in 1528 aged 55.

Roger Heton, born 1473, was probably a first cousin to Richard Heton. He was a successful lawyer practising in London and was named by Bishop Oldham as one of the executors of his Will made 16 December 1518. Roger acted as legal adviser to the other executors, most of whom were churchmen. He was one of the Gentlemen of the Chapel to Cardinal Wolsey and accompanied the statesman on his journey to Calais on the 11 July 1527.[61] In his Will, proved on 15 October 1528 in the Prerogative Court of Canterbury he asked to be buried in the Temple Church in Fleet Street, London and named James Heton, priest, and John Harmon his executors and made bequests to his brother Richard, sister Joan Harmon and her husband John. He would seem to have had no children of his own.

The Pilgrimage of Grace

Richard Heton died in 1535 aged 75 and for some years previously it had been known that king Henry VIII was looking for a way to divorce his wife Catherine of Aragon and marry again, to improve his prospects of producing a male heir. In 1533 a Bill was passed in Parliament pronouncing the king's marriage to Catherine invalid and leaving the way open for him to marry Ann Boleyn, a member of a Protestant family. The following year another Bill, creating Henry head of the Church in England and therefore vesting all Church property in him, was passed. This enabled the process known as the Dissolution of the Monasteries to begin, solving Henry's money problems at a stroke, as innumerable monastic properties were sold off to lay people. These two measures, the divorce and the dissolution, were anathema to devout Catholics such as Richard and may have hardened his resolve to see his estate pass to those of his family who adhered to the old faith, i.e. the children and grandchildren of his first marriage.

Feelings against the treatment of Catherine and the dissolution of the monasteries were particularly high in the North of England and in 1536 they were expressed in the Pilgrimage of Grace, a mild form of rebellion which was widespread throughout the northern counties but was fairly quickly suppressed with some of the ringleaders and the heads of some of the larger monasteries being executed.

The nearest the effect of the suppression of the Pilgrimage of Grace came to Heton-under-Horwich was at the Abbey of Whalley where the abbot was accused of sheltering rebels and was hanged with some of his monks, including William Heton, a nephew of Richard. The Abbey was taken over by the King's men and was dismantled. It is ironic that for at least the last 10 years of his life Richard "farmed" the tithes of Horwich under a grant to him by the Abbot of Whalley. A lease[62] granted to some of his neighbours, effective on his death, shows them liable to pay the Abbey £4 p.a. for which payment they would receive the right to collect such corn tithes from Horwich as were due. It might be thought that this involvement could have provided Richard with the opportunity to acquire some of the assets of the monastery but the fact that he did not do so could be attributed to his extreme age, his objections to dissolution in principle, more forceful neighbours, or lack of funds. For whatever reasons, none of the Hetons were involved in the acquisition of monastic lands.

Notes & References

[1] Lancs. & Cheshire Record Soc. vol.31, p.36.
[2] J H Partington (Bolton Central Library, ref. B920B.HEA, pt. 2, note 18, p. 6) notes that this document was found by his agents Hardy & Page in Feet of Fines, Lancaster 4-7 Edward III, no. 49, Case 120, file 25.
[3] Ibid. pt.2, p.11.
[4] Calendar of Patent Rolls 1327-1330, p. 252.
"History of the Chantries"p. 72. Chetham Society.
[5] "History of the Township of Rivington", W F Irvine, 1904, p.12.
[6] Partington states that Joan's nephew Richard de Heton called William and Oliver Entwistle his cousins.
[7] "Essays on the History of Medicine", Prof. G. Gask, Butterworths, London, 1950.
[8] Canon Raines' MSS, vol. 25, p.208. [JHP]
[9] Ibid. vol.29, p.209
[10] Piccope's MSS vol. 1, p.192 . Chetham Library, Manchester [JHP]
[11] Dodsworth's MSS, vol. 5, p. 94. [JHP]
[12] Piccope's MSS, vol. 3, p. 2[JHP]
[13] Calendar of Patent Rolls, vol. 1338-1340, pp. 454.
[14] Partington Papers op.cit. pt2, note 10 to p. 13.
[15] Partington op. cit. pt 2, p. 13.
[16] Calendar of Patent Rolls. 1345-46 p. 78.
[17] "Agrarian History of England & Wales", vol.3, pp. 191/2. Edward Miller.

18. Ibid. p. 331.D.L.Farmer.
19. Ibid. p.343. ditto.
20. Ibid. pp. 469-482. ditto.
21. Ibid. pp.596-600. Edward Miller.
22. Ibid. pp. 91-.93
23. Partington, op.cit.,pt. 2, p. 14.
24. Victoria County History of Lancs., 1911, vol.5, p.11.
25. "Fellows of Manchester College" Chetham Society, vol.21, new series, p.9.
26. Canon Raine's MSS, vol. 41. p.43. Chetham Library. [JHP]
27. Christopher Townley's MSS, p. 787. Chetham Library, Manchester. [JHP]
28. Canon Raines MSS, vol. 25, p.118. [JHP]
29. Croston's History of Lancs., vol. 3, p.255 [JHP]
30. Partington,op.cit., pt.2. note to p. 15.
    Victoria County History of Lancs., 1911, vol.5, p.10.
31. "Lancashire Inquisitions" Chetham Society. Pp. 8,65,68.
32. "Inventories of Churches & Chapels of Lancs." Chetham Society, vol.107,p.19.
33. Bishop's Registers, vol. 7-8, folio 128 [JHP].
    VCH of .Lancs.,vol 5, p.10 n.12.
34. Dodsworth's MSS, vol.4, p. 221 [JHP]
35. Partington,op.cit.,pt. 2 pp16-18 & notes.
36. Unpublished paper " Gamel's Saga", John Heaton ,Keighley, 1993.
37. Piccope's MSS, vol.3, 446. [JHP]
38. Trans. of Hist. Soc. of Lancs. & Ches., vol.3, p.107.
39. Canon Raines MSS, vol, 33, p. 262.
40. "Old Hall Farm, Heaton, Bolton" UMAU, March 2000.
41. Whitaker's "Whalley", 1872edn., vol.1, p.101. [JHP]
42. Partington op. cit.,pt 2, p. 22,n.26/27.
43. Acts of the Privy Council, vol.6, p.221.
44. Partington, op.cit. p.27, note 16.
45. Ibid. p. 25.
46. Ibid. pp. 26/27.
47. Harleian MSS no.433, art.249.
48. Partington, op. cit. p.29, note 7.
49. Dodsworth's MSS, vol.5 p.5 [JHP]
50. Ibid. vol. 8, p. 43.
51. Baines, op. cit. pedigree of Hulton of the Park. [JHP]
52. Visitation of Lancs. 1535. College of Arms.
53. Flowers Visitation of Lancs. p.8. College of Arms.
54. Ibid. p. 113.
55. "Works of Archbishop Cranmer", pt. 2, p. 266. Parker Society. [JHP]
56. Ibid. p.400.
57. Lancs. & Cheshire Record Soc. vol. 1, pp. 25- 26.
58. Norroy King of Arms, College of Arms, 1998.
59. Victoria Co. Hist. of Lancs. vol. 5, pp.1-2.
60. "Lancs. Pleadings in the Duchy Court" Lancs. & Ches. Record Soc. vol..32, p. 111.
61. Partington op. cit. pt. 2, notes to p. 33.
62. Canon Raine's MSS, vol. 6, p. 201.

Chapter Five

A Family Divided

> "A man esteemed worthy in Tudor times could do things that would exclude him from worthiness now. He could rob his neighbours by legal chicanery, take bribes in the performance of public duties, fawn and flatter with complete insincerity, burn his fellows for rejecting a creed, or hang them for necessities of state. The ethics of the age were not those approved today, and it is unfair to judge the actors too rigidly by our standards."
>
> *James A. Williamson 1953*[1]

This chapter attempts to explain the dissension and complex litigation which affected the Heaton family during the period 1529-1589 and which eventually enabled a wealthy neighbour to exploit the situation to the extent that he was able to acquire the bulk of the Heaton estates.[2]

Throughout the Middle Ages the principle of succession by male primogeniture had prevailed amongst gentry families and in many instances was strictly preserved by the system of entail which ensured that landed possessions passed to the nearest direct male heir on the death of the head of the family, who in effect was only a life tenant. On occasions the heir could be somewhat distantly related and the daughters of the current holder of the land might receive nothing. Even if the heir was the eldest son, all authority still vested in him and whether adequate provision was made for his sisters and younger brothers was at his entire discretion. Some landholders whose hands were tied by the provisions of a strict entail became discontented with this very restrictive arrangement and several efforts were made in the courts to loosen the bonds. By the end of the 15th century a measure of success in this direction had been achieved and methods whereby an entail could be broken were introduced, eventually, after much contradictory caselaw, to be clarified by the Statute of Uses in 1536 and the Statute of Wills in 1540, during the reign of Henry VIII.[3]

Nevertheless this greater freedom of disposal itself brought its own dangers and whilst a landowner might consider himself well capable of ordering the disposition of his estate he could exercise very little control over the activities of his heirs whose actions could result in the loss of an estate and the squandering of family assets through sale, debt, speculation, bad estate management, or the vesting of land in daughters in preference to more distant male relatives. Arrangements entered into with the best of intentions could, on occasions, rebound to the extreme detriment of the intended beneficiaries.

An Old Man's Dilemma

In the third decade of the 16th century Richard Heton was a very old man with a large family resulting from his two marriages and who were looking to their father to effect settlements of his estate which would satisfy their requirements. He was, very probably, torn between his natural affection for all his children and his wish to preserve the Heton lineage and lands intact, but perhaps swayed by his own profound attachment to the old Roman Catholic faith which was not followed by all the members of his family. The children and grandchildren of his first marriage were Catholics like himself but a number of the offspring of his second marriage were of the Protestant persuasion which was beginning to spread its influence through the country.[4]

His eldest son, William Heton of Birchley, had married Jane, daughter of Sir William Farington and had two daughters, Jane and Alice, but no son. William appears to have put a good deal of pressure on his father and in 1529 he succeeded in persuading him to make a settlement in anticipation of Jane's marriage to Miles Gerard, son and heir to Thomas Gerard of Ince, a member of a noted Catholic family. In this settlement Richard recited the lands he held as of fee, i.e. freehold, in Heton, Birchley, Rumworth, Lostock, Horwich and Ulverston-in-Furness, some of which lands were leased to his sons Richard, Bryan and Lambert. In consideration of Thomas Gerard giving to Jane an entitlement to a yearly income of 10 marks (£6.66) and undertaking to ensure that all his lands should be inherited by Miles and eventually by his male heirs by Jane, and in the event of William not having any male heirs, which was very likely, Richard was to settle half his lands on Jane and her male heirs by Miles Gerard.[5]

Under the provisions of this 1529 settlement half the Heaton lands as described would pass into the ownership of the Gerard family should William die without leaving a son to inherit, as seemed very likely. This settlement was obviously extremely detrimental to the interests of Richard's sons by his second wife, Margaret Garstang, the eldest of whom might have expected to inherit on the death of William Heton without male issue. It is not surprising therefore that they in turn brought influence and persuasion to bear on their father, no doubt with the support of their mother, to the extent that in the following year, 1530, the old man, who had then probably reached his seventieth year, is purported to have effected another settlement,[6] revoking in part that of the previous year insofar as it related to the manor of Heton and vesting that property in trustees for the use of his son Rauffe and on his death his son William.

However this second settlement did not assume that Richard Heton was himself the holder of the freehold interest in the manor of Heton, i.e. "seized in his demesne as of fee" as expressed in the 1529 settlement. Instead it was based on the premise that Richard was the tenant for life only, with the trustees named in the document holding the freehold for his use during his lifetime.

It is evident that the group of trustees named in the 1529 settlement were friends of William Heton, Richard's eldest son and heir, and the trustees in whom the freehold of the manor of Heton became vested by this 1530 document were friends of his sons by his second marriage. The Rauffe Heton mentioned in the document was a lawyer, son of Richard by his second wife, and half-brother to William of Birchley, and he seems to have used his best endeavours to ensure that the bulk of the estate passed eventually to Richard's family by his second wife.

Richard Heton was either badly advised, or at his advanced age failed to appreciate the full implications of the conflicting legal arrangements he was entering into, but difficulties which arose from the different constructions of these two settlements, and the complex nature of the relationships amongst Richard's family, resulted in longrunning and disastrous litigation between different members of the family whose interests were profoundly affected. In an extremely litigious age this ensured that the subsequent disputes continued for many years.

Some doubt was subsequently cast on the genuineness of this 1530 document. On his deathbed Bryan, a younger son of Richard by his second marriage, was alleged to have confessed that he persuaded his brother Rauffe, a lawyer, to draw up the 1530 Deed of Settlement and that it was a forgery. However in later litigation, after the death of William Heton of Birchley, between his widow and

Descendants of Richard Heton of Heton & Birchley by his first wife Agnes Hulton.

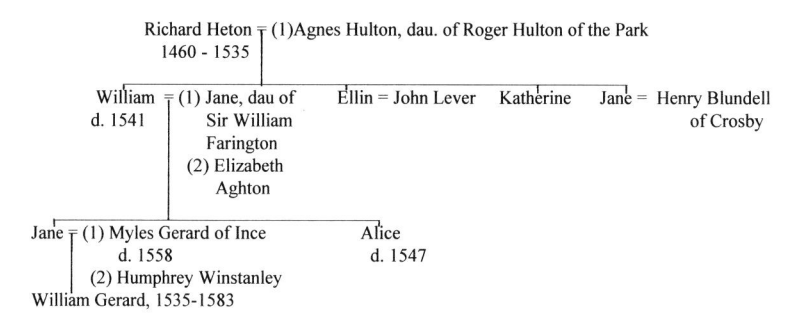

```
                    Richard Heton ⊤ (1)Agnes Hulton, dau. of Roger Hulton of the Park
                    1460 - 1535
        ┌─────────────────────┬──────────────────┬──────────────┐
    William ⊤ (1) Jane, dau of    Ellin = John Lever   Katherine   Jane = Henry Blundell
    d. 1541  │  Sir William                                              of Crosby
             │  Farington
             │  (2) Elizabeth
             │  Aghton
    ┌────────┴───────────────┐
 Jane ⊤ (1) Myles Gerard of Ince    Alice
      │         d. 1558              d. 1547
      │  (2) Humphrey Winstanley
  William Gerard, 1535-1583
```

Descendants of Richard Heton by his second wife Margaret Garstang.

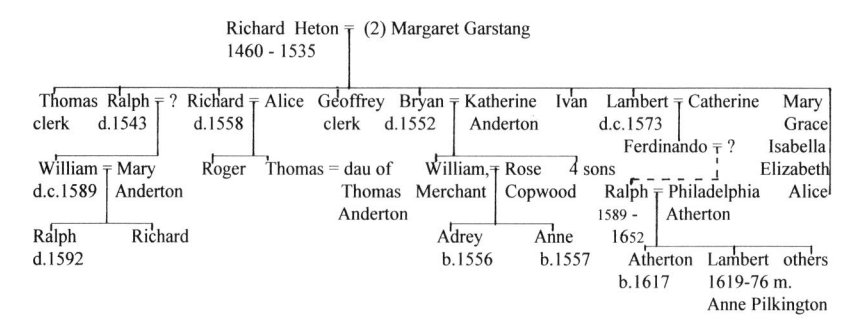

```
                        Richard Heton ⊤ (2) Margaret Garstang
                        1460 - 1535
 ┌──────┬──────┬───────┬──────┬─────────┬──────┬─────────┬──────┬──────────┬─────────┐
 Thomas Ralph⊤? Richard⊤Alice Geoffrey Bryan⊤Katherine Ivan Lambert⊤Catherine Mary
 clerk  d.1543  d.1558        clerk   d.1552 Anderton  d.c.1573                Grace
                                                           Ferdinando⊤?       Isabella
    William⊤Mary  Roger  Thomas = dau of  William,⊤Rose  4 sons               Elizabeth
    d.c.1589│Anderton           Thomas   Merchant│Copwood  Ralph⊤Philadelphia  Alice
            │                   Anderton                   1589 -│ Atherton
    ┌───────┴──┐                             ┌──────┐      1652  │
  Ralph    Richard                         Adrey    Anne    ┌────┴──────┐
  d.1592                                   b.1556   b.1557  Atherton Lambert others
                                                            b.1617   1619-76 m.
                                                                     Anne Pilkington
```

A Family Divided

William, son of Rauffe, neither party appears to have placed much reliance on the 1529 and 1530 documents and the case was eventually settled out of court in a manner to be described.

William of Birchley

Richard Heton died on 4th February 1534/5, but his wife lived on until at least 1541. His eldest son, William of Birchley, was the undoubted heir to his estates but the disputes which subsequently arose centred on whether William held the estates in fee simple, i.e. freehold, with the ability to dispose of them as he wished, or as tenant for life, bound by the provisions of previous settlements and the decisions of trustees. This succession of disputes and litigation was to last 35 years until eventually resolved to the detriment of the Heaton family, as shall be described.

Around 1500 William Heton had married Jane (aka Johanna), a daughter of Sir William Farington of Farington. This was a fortunate marriage for William, since his wife was of good family and brought with her a substantial dowry of 100 marks (£66).[7] After their marriage the couple moved to live at Birchley Hall, Billinge, where William lived for the rest of his life. It seems probable that Birchley was substantially improved and refurbished for their occupation and William was always described as "William Heton of Birchley ", and not "of Heton". Towards the end of the 16th century, when the property was owned by the Anderton family the Hall was largely rebuilt and it is now difficult to know whether any part of the older Heton house is incorporated in the present building.

William's daughter, Jane, married twice, both times to members of Catholic famillies, firstly to Myles Gerard Esq. of Ince and on his death in 1558 to Humphrey Winstanley Esq. The other daughter, Alice, never married and on her death, Jane became her father's sole heiress.

The estate which William inherited consisted of the manors of Heton and Birchley, together with land at Lostock, Horwich, Rumworth, Fosset, Sunderland, and Ulverston-in-Furness. These last three locations are close to the manor of Heton-in-Lonsdale and could conceivably constitute the remnant of the more extensive lands which the Hetons once owned in that area.

A Chance of a Male Child?

William Heton, for most of his life, appeared to be working diligently towards ensuring the succession of his estates to his daughters which would probably have resulted in the lands being lost to the Heton family. However, after the death of his wife Jane circa 1537, his attitude seems to have changed somewhat . Perhaps he saw the loss of a wife past child-bearing age as an opportunity to replace her with a younger version with whom he might hope to have a son who would inherit and retain the estate in the family.

In 1540, at the age of 60, he married 18 year-old Elizabeth, sister of John Aghton of North Meole[8]. Naturally this greatly displeased his daughter Jane and her husband Myles Gerard, who saw the possibility of losing their inheritance if a male child were born.

On his remarriage William entered into a settlement, the effect of which was to vest the Heton estates in Sir Robert Hesketh and John Aghton, as trustees, for the use of William and his wife Elizabeth and their male heirs and in default of a male heir the estate was to pass to William Heton, son of Rauffe the lawyer and halfbrother to William of Birchley.[9]

In the event William was disappointed in his endeavours to produce a male child and he died in 1541, only a year after his marriage, without his young wife becoming pregnant.

Young Widow v. Older Stepdaughter

Immediately after the death of William, his daughter Jane and her husband Myles Gerard brought an action in the Chancery Court of the Duchy of Lancaster, claiming possession of all the deceased's estates from his widow. They based their action on the 1529 settlement made by old Richard Heton which entitled William's daughters to succeed on his death. This settlement asserted that Richard held the estates in fee, i.e. freehold, but Mrs Elizabeth Heton, in her counterclaim, maintained that Richard Heton held a life interest only, the lands being vested in trustees, and consequently the provisions of the settlement were ultra vires and beyond Richard's power to make. It seems that the Gerard's arguments did not prevail and Elizabeth Heton continued in possession of Birchley Hall and the demesne lands around the house.

A year later in 1543 Elizabeth married John Bolde, second son of Sir John Bolde. Fierce legal disputes continued between Elizabeth and her stepdaughter Jane, but despite these the Boldes continued in possession of Birchley and its lands. It seems that the last settlement of the late William Heton in 1540 was held to take precedence over settlements made earlier. In a complaint of wrongful exclusion from Hough Wood which the Boldes brought against Evan and Lawrence Heton and others in 1541 they maintained that they held the Birchley lands as of fee, i.e. freehold,[10] but although this argument may have prevailed in this instance it was to be a different matter when tested in an action brought by someone who had a greater interest in disputing it.

Another Claimant Appears

In 1549 William Heton, son of Rauffe the lawyer, and nephew to William of Birchley, brought a complaint before the Chancellor of the Duchy,[11] claiming that the provisions of old Richard's second settlement in 1530 entitled him to possession of the Heton lands, following the death of William of Birchley in 1541 and of his own father in 1543. William denied that Elizabeth had any right to claim possession of Birchley as a widow's portion or jointure as her late husband had only a life interest and could not dispose of the property after his death.

Elizabeth and John Bolde's reply to this claim was to contend that the late

William Heton of Birchley held the estates in fee (i.e.freehold) and that when he married Elizabeth he executed a deed whereby he vested the estates in them both, and their male heirs, as her jointure. By virtue of this settlement, they claimed, William and Elizabeth enjoyed the property during his lifetime and on his death she and her new husband continued to enjoy the property as was her right.

This case appears to have dragged on for years and after two Commissions had sat and reported, the action was eventually settled "out of court" in 1552 and the agreement was embodied in an Indenture entered into by John & Elizabeth Bolde and William Heton.[12] As previously stated, in the event neither party appeared to rely on the precise wording of the 1529 and 1530 settlements; the Boldes never produced the 1529 document and William seems to have been happy to settle by negotiation; both parties may have been doubtful whether the documents would have helped their cause greatly. The nature of the agreement reached was that Elizabeth should have the use of the Birchley property for her life and it should then revert to William for 100 years, should he live that long, and then go to his son Rauffe, who became the remainderman. William appears to have obtained possession of the Heton demesne lands immediately since in an action brought by Richard Heton, son of Bryan, in 1553 against William Heton for trespass on his lands in Horwich and Heton. William responded that he had obtained title from John & Elizabeth Bolde and was entitled to occupy under that title.[13]

Financial Problems

By 1549 William Heton had established his right to hold the Heton estates in fee, subject only to Elizabeth's life interest in Birchley; leases granted by old Richard to his sons, Richard, Bryan and Lambert, and other tenancies; and with his son Rauffe (Ralph) entitled to inherit on his father's death. However William was not a rich man and the costs of maintaining the legal actions against the Boldes and others had been heavy. Elizabeth had a right to receive a substantial proportion of the rents from the estate,and he had to take further legal proceedings to compel some of the tenants to pay their rents to him, so his return from his estate was comparatively small.

In 1550 Elizabeth Bolde's brother, John Aghton, died and she and her husband eventually moved back to her family home at North Meoles.[14] It appears she disposed of her life interest in Birchley to Roger Wetherheld, a London moneylender, at that time.

After obtaining possession William struggled for five years with increasing financial problems and eventually found himself obliged to raise money to meet his heavy expenses. In order to do so he was obliged to mortgage his estates at Heton. Unfortunately he chose to do this with Edward Elmar and Roger Wetherheld, two London moneylenders, rather than going to his friends and neighbours for the finance he needed. Perhaps he did but was refused - we shall never know, but it was a highly detrimental move on his part which could have had disastrous consequences.

Near neighbours of the Hetons were the family of Anderton with whom there had been several instances of intermarriage, although the Andertons were Catholics. William's own wife Mary was the daughter of Peter Anderton and sister-in-law of Christopher Anderton, a lawyer, and a prominent member of the Anderton family at that time. William's uncle Bryan had married Katherine, daughter of Thurstan Anderton, and aunt to Christopher. Christopher Anderton was a wealthy man whom one would have thought would have been a most appropriate person to help William with his financial problems. Perhaps he was asked and declined, and subsequent events show that he may well have had an ulterior motive for this. Whatever the reason, it appears that William was obliged to fall back on London moneylenders to raise money, and to mortgage his life interest in the property to them to do so. In consequence Roger Wetherheld was not only entitled to a proportion of the rents during the lifetime of Elizabeth Bolde but also became a mortgagee of the estate, very possibly as a front man for Christopher Anderton.

The Rogues Gallery

Notwithstanding the sentiments expressed in the opening quotation to this chapter one might have hoped that William Heton could have looked to more honourable men to help him in his period of financial difficulty but in fact it seems he fell in with a group of individuals whose main purpose in life was to profit excessively at others' expense, and who seemed ready to adopt almost any methods to achieve their aims. These characters, who from time to time acted together for their own advantage, were:-

Christopher Anderton, William's brother-in-law, a lawyer practising at Lincoln's Inn, London and also engaged in moneylending.

Roger Wetherheld [or Wetherall], a moneylender, also of Lincoln's Inn.

Thomas Thurland, Master of the Savoy Hospital in London, 1557-70.

Edward Cosyn, an accomplice of Thurland.

- Perwich, a partner of Cosyn in certain highly dubious transactions.

Edward Elmar, a wealthy grocer and moneylender, of London, possibly more gullible than guilty.

In 1558 Anderton was appointed "Attorney" and Wetherheld was appointed "Counsellor" to the Charity of the Savoy Hospital and with Thurland, the Master, they conspired to defraud the Charity of a substantial part of its assets. Thurland had somehow obtained possession of the seal of the Charity and by using this without the knowledge of the Chaplains of the Hospital the trio contrived to grant excessively long leases or to sell to themselves and Perwich & Cosyn and others, contrary to the rules of the Charity, land belonging to the Charity in the counties of Middlesex, Lancashire, Yorkshire, and Westmorland.

In 1570 a Commission investigated[15] and found proven, allegations that

Thurland had abused his position and fraudulently sold goods and disposed of lands by lease or sale to his own advantage. Unprofitable leases had been granted for 30,40,50,60 and more years. The Commission found there was a lease to one Fanshaw of the manor of Dengey for 600 years, another to one Anderton of lands in Yorkshire and Lancashire for 1000 years, subsequently found to be a sale and not a lease. Thurland was dismissed from his office.

In 1583 the then Master and Chaplains of the Hospital brought an action against Edward Cosyn in respect of a lease granted to Cosyn and Perwich (now deceased) of land in Middlesex, Lancashire, Yorkshire, and Westmorland, alleging that this lease was fraudulently granted by Thurland, using the common seal contrary to the rules and regulations of the Charity.[16] Although the outcome of this action is unclear it seems that Christopher Anderton was able to avoid condemnation by producing evidence for the plaintiffs establishing the lease document as a forgery.[17] By an Indenture of 5th May 1591 Christopher Anderton and James his son undertook to pay the Master and Chaplains of the Savoy Hospital an annual rentcharge of £6.13s.4d. (£6.66) issuing out of the manor of Rumworth, Lancs.[18] Was this, perhaps, some measure of compensation to the Charity which the Andertons thought it advisable to give, to avoid further repercussions?

Although at this time the law applicable to mortgages was administered by the common law Courts of Kings Bench and Common Pleas who applied strict rules relating to the time and method of repayment of the loan by the mortgagor to the mortgagee, the Court of Chancery had begun to develop the concept of "equity of redemption" and provided a petitioner came before the Court with "clean hands" he might reasonably expect relief to be granted, subject of course to his being able to show an ability to repay, so that time was no longer of the essence.

Whilst, in 1558, the majority of Englishmen and women celebrated the accession of Queen Elizabeth I to the throne, Anderton and Wetherheld were hatching their plots and setting out to exploit this legal situation where they could. They lent money on the security of mortgages, not primarily to earn interest on the loans but more in anticipation that the borrowers would be unable to repay the loans and they would, therefore, be able to foreclose and obtain possession of the property mortgaged. Local tradition held that they were prepared to go to virtually any lengths to bring this about. In relation to the outcome of two projects upon which they were engaged, they entered into a mutual agreement,[19] on 7th December 1558, setting out the manner in which the money advanced and the expected proceeds were to be divided between them, with penalties if either failed to perform his obligations to the other.

The first of these schemes was a loan to Geoffrey Brereton Esq. or his mother Dame Jane Brereton involving an attempt to obtain "grants, bargains, sales or advantages" over their lands in Lancashire, Cheshire and Shropshire. This scheme failed, however, as the properties came under the control of Sir Thomas Egerton, the Lord Chancellor, and the conspirators were thwarted.

The second scheme was of a similar nature in relation to William Heton and his manor of Heton, where a loan of £400 was due to be repaid by 29 September 1559 to Edward Elmar. The agreement states that if William Heton does not repay this loan then Wetherheld will release Anderton from a bond for £50 which Anderton entered into to procure the "bargayne and saile of the manor of Birchley ". At the same time Wetherheld was to indemnify Anderton against any liability to Elmar for a bond which they had jointly entered into for £300, presumably to obtain the conveyance to them of any property on which Elmar foreclosed, as a result of William's inability to repay the debt.. Obviously it was very much in Anderton's interest to ensure, one way or another, that William Heton was unable to pay back the loan and redeem the mortgage. In this instance, however, his intentions were frustrated.

A Merchant to the Rescue

William Heton would have had considerable difficulty in repaying the loan by the due date, 29 September 1559, but fortunately there was a solution at hand for his predicament. He had two sons by his wife Mary; Ralph and Richard, and the eldest, Ralph, was apprenticed to a cousin of his father, another William Heton, a member of the Company of Merchant Taylors and a Citizen of London. He had married Rose Copwood and had two daughters, Adrey (sic), born 1556, and Anne, born 1557.[20]

William the merchant was a man of rather greater means than his cousin and was apparently prepared to come to the rescue when it appeared to the family that the Heton estates were at grave risk of loss through foreclosure. The loan from Wetherheld and Elmar was repaid, the merchant took over the mortgage and an agreement was reached between the two cousins whereby the life interest of William Heton of Birchley was acquired by Wiliam the merchant in the following terms:-

> "William Heton of Birchley in the Co. of Lancaster, esquire, being seised in his demesne as of fee, of the manor or lordship of Heton and Byrchley with the appurtenances, in the said County and of divers messuages, lands, tenements and hereditaments in Heton, Birchley, Rumworth, Horwich, Ulverston and Rosset in the said County, by fine and recovery with other good conveyance granted the same to William Heton of London, Merchant, and his heirs for ever"[21]

At the same time it was agreed that Ralph, the eldest son of William of Birchley should eventually marry Adrey, daughter of William the Merchant, although the girl was then only 4 years old and the marriage would not be able to take place until several years had elapsed. In this way it was proposed that the family estates would descend in accordance with the intentions of the family settlements.

Improved Estate Management

William the Merchant was a businessman and as soon as he had completed his purchase he set about maximising the return from his investment in any way he could. The Heton lands were still burdened with some heavy outgoings and the rental income was by no means generous. Leases had been granted by Richard to his sons for long terms at rents fixed some time ago and increases were not possible. Various people seemed to be occupying parts of the estate, who were reluctant to recognise the Merchant's title, and refused to pay rent and tithes to him. The jointure due to Mrs Bolde, the former wife of William of Birchley was still payable if she was still alive, the exact date of her death being uncertain. Two authorities give alternative dates[22], 1590 when she would have been 68 years of age, or 1558, when she was only 36. Obviously, if the earlier date applies, her entitlement, assigned to Wetherheld, was no longer a consideration, but if the later date, then the jointure due to her was a further drain on the estate income.

In 1565 William sued Roger Heton and his mother Alice for possession of Heton Hall and the demesne lands attached thereto.[23] Roger was the son of Richard, himself the third son of old Richard by his second wife. The younger Richard had been granted Heton Hall and its demesne lands by his father for life, but when he died in 1558 his wife and son had continued in occupation without good title. There was scope to divide Heton Hall into a number of separate dwellings and in this way and by letting or farming the demesne land William was able to increase his income by a worthwhile amount.

Having succeeded in his action against Roger and his mother, William then brought proceedings to claim possession of various other "messuages, lands and tenements and in particular the woods called Ravenhurst in Heton and Houghwood in Billinge". In this he was asserting his rights as lord of the manor to the wastes and woods of the manors of Heton and Birchley and preventing others, including one William Cheydock, establishing title by default.

The Merchant Outmanoeuvred

For nearly ten years William divided his time between the administration of his estate in Lancashire and his business in the City of London. Also living in London, and working for part of the time as his apprentice, was Ralph Heton, his daughter's intended husband and the man entitled, as remainderman, to inherit the Heton estates under the terms of the agreement made in 1552 between his father, William, and Mrs Elizabeth Bolde and her husband. As a minor he had not been a party to his father's conveyance of the estate to William the merchant in 1559, and therefore his rights as remainderman were still enforceable.

In practice as a lawyer, not far away in Lincoln's Inn, was Christopher Anderton, and it eventually became clear to William that Anderton and Ralph were colluding together to undermine his title to the Lancashire estate and bring about a situation in which Anderton would be able to purchase it for himself with Ralph's agreement. Presumably promises had been made by Anderton to Ralph which had persuaded him that such an outcome would be more advantageous to himself than the agreement reached between the merchant and his father.

When William discovered the machinations of Ralph and Anderton against him he initiated an action in 1568 before the Chancellor of the Duchy of Lancaster, seeking an injunction against Ralph Heton and Christopher Anderton, maintaining that he had held the estates in Heton, Birchley, Rumworth, Horwich, Ulverston and Rosset in fee for about nine years, having acquired them from William Heton of Birchley, but that :-

> "....certain evidences,deeds,indentures,writings and muniments concerning the premises, of right belonging to the Plaintiff,are,by sinister means, come into the possession of Ralph Heton, son of the said William Heton of Birchley, who in right is the apprentice and servant of plaintiff,and also into the possession of Christopher Anderton, esquire,being both Prothonotary, Chirographer, and "Filager" within the said Co. Palatine of Lanc. which said Ralph and Christopher Anderton by colour of the said evidence and writings have contrived to the said Ralph Heton divers untrue estates in the said premises,and have endeavoured to discredit plaintiff's title thereto and to expel him therefrom......" [24]

William goes on to claim that Anderton had persuaded Ralph to leave William's service, and that together they had entered on William's land to kill his pigeons and rabbits with guns. Furthermore he maintains that Ralph was also persuaded by Anderton to pursue an action against William for possession of land at Rumworth and elsewhere.

It would seem that for some time past Anderton had been working on Ralph Heton, probably helped by his sister-in-law, Mary, Ralph's mother, and had succeeded in persuading him that his interests would be best served by throwing in his lot with Anderton, repudiating the former agreement that he would marry William's daughter, and using his rights as remainderman to devalue William's title to the estate. Evidently loyalty to his father and the Heton family was insufficient to withstand the pressures placed on Ralph and the prospects of a substantial cash payment for his interest as soon as Anderton succeeded in his endeavours. It seems that various members of the Heton family also transferred their allegiances from one side to the other as pressure was applied. In particular Ralph's father, William, was either threatened by his wife or cajoled by Anderton with financial payments, to dissuade him from questioning the position taken up by his son. In a deposition he made on 16th March 1572/3 he stated:-

> "That he has been sundry times threatened as well by the said Rawffe, his son,as also by Marye Heton, mother of the said Rawffe,

that if he uttered anything which should be prejudicial to the title of the said Rawffe for the lands in controversy, then he should lose his living and be cast in prison where he should not see his own feet."[25]

The inference from this is that he was receiving an annuity from Anderton and if he caused trouble that would cease and without it he would be a poor man.

William the merchant had been placed in a very difficult position. He had laid out at least £1200[26] and possibly substantially more in the purchase of the Heton estates originally and without Ralph's cooperation he would not be in a position to pass the estate to his daughter or any other member of the family on his death. He was, therefore, forced to compromise and salvage what he could from the situation by joining with Ralph in the sale of their combined interests to Anderton for the maximum sum obtainable in the circumstances.

The manner in which this transaction was finally concluded is not completely clear. One would have expected it to be by way of conveyances of William's interest and Ralph's interest to Anderton in consideration of agreed sums paid to them. This would have been the most straightforward and logical way to proceed. However there is some evidence that it may not have been done that way. In a deposition made by William, Ralph's father, in 1573, he states that :-

> "William Heton, merchant taylor, and deponent's son, Rauffe Heton, mortgaged the manor of Heton, and other lands in Heton, Horwich, Rumworth, Lostock and Ulverston to the use of Christopher Anderton and his heirs."[27]

This is a very puzzling statement. It cannot refer to the mortgage of 1559 when the mortgagee was Edward Elmar and we do not know of another occasion when William the merchant and Ralph combined to grant a mortgage to Christopher Anderton. If it were true then it appears the mortgage was secured on the combined interests of the life tenant and the remainderman, effectively the entire freehold interest. We do not know when this mortgage was granted, why, and what was the eventual outcome.

There seems little doubt that Anderton's business practices were frowned upon by a substantial proportion of his contemporaries in the county who saw him as an upstart lawyer who had not behaved as a gentleman should and who had deprived the ancient family of Heton of their heritage by dubious means. He was not a popular man.

The Heton family firmly believed for generations that they had been cheated out of their hereditary estates by Christopher Anderton and various stories survived as to the ways in which this was done. In the more extreme versions it is said that the Heton messenger carrying the money to Anderton to redeem the mortgage was set upon and murdered; in another account the contention was that he was robbed of the money when travelling to repay the loan, both crimes believed to be at Anderton's instigation. A third version, which found its way into print,[28] maintained that on the last day for payment of the loan the messenger arrived at Lostock Hall, Anderton's residence, after sunset, to find the gates locked and admission refused. When he was allowed in the next day he was told that he was too late and the loan had not been repaid by the due date. Yet another account related by Rev. Gibson[29] tells that the messenger was actually let into the house but the money would not be accepted, as it was after sunset.

These stories very probably relate to the situation in 1559 and were put about to vilify Anderton although, in fact, the mortgage was repaid by William the merchant. Anderton may have first rejected the money in the manner described, but equity would have protected William, and in the end Anderton had to accept repayment.

This resentment must have rumbled on for nearly 250 years, for Partington quotes memoranda dated 13 January 1814 setting out agreements reached between various members of the Heaton family at that time, namely Lambert senior and junior, Edmund of Haigh, Jeremy, John of Bolton, Lambert of Halliwell, Thomas and one John Morris, whereby they agreed to contribute £5 each to meet the cost of employing a lawyer to investigate how the family was deprived of their property and whether it was possible to recover it. If anything could be recovered then they agreed to accept one-tenth share each, irrespective of who might be found to be heirs at law. They appointed T R Weeton, Attorney of Leigh to act for them but by 1823 he had achieved virtually nothing and in memos of that year he is describing various aspects of Heaton family history, coats-of-arms, descent etc. but without any prospect of a valid claim in respect of the lost estates. Nothing more was heard in this connection.

The Finale

Whatever the method employed, the year 1570 saw effectively the end of the Heton's long history as a landowning family in Lancashire, although disputes as to the Andertons' entitlement to the estates continued for many years. In 1573 Humphrey Winstanley and his wife Jane, formerly Mrs Gerard, and the daughter of William Heton of Birchley, son of Richard, brought an action against Anderton to try and establish their claim to the Heton estates, based on the settlement made by Richard in 1529. This attempt failed and the final record in the transfer of the Heton estates to Anderton consisted of a document dated 18th June 1576 in which Ralph relinquishes all further claims of any kind on Christopher Anderton.[30] The inference of this document is that Anderton has made payments to Ralph and also, perhaps, undertook to settle debts incurred by the young man; all, one would think, in consideration for the transfer to him of Ralph's interest in the Heton estates, although this is not specifically stated.

In a document dated 31st March 1589, Ralph and his brother Richard, describing themselves as "of Birchley", gave a bond of £100 to James and Thurstan Anderton, first and third sons of Christopher.[31] This bond would be forfeit if

A Family Divided

their mother, Mary, or father, William, make any claim on the Heton estates by way of title or jointure or if they do not acknowledge the title of the Andertons to the former Heton lands or if they do not comply with the terms of an agreement entered into between Mary and James Anderton on the 22nd June 1588. William the merchant is described in the 1589 document as then deceased.

Presumably the 1588 agreement provided for the Hetons' continued occupation of Birchley Hall for their lives, although it seems probable that William, Mary's husband, did not live there. We know that Ralph's mother lived at Birchley Hall until she died and was buried at Wigan Parish Church on 15th January 1594/5, surviving both her son Ralph and Christopher Anderton by two years. The final negotiations for the handover of Birchley Hall and lands were probably undertaken between James Anderton and Richard Heaton, Ralph's younger brother, in 1595 when Richard was living in A(th)lone, Co.Westmeath, Ireland. Despite his machinations therefore, Christopher Anderton never lived to obtain possession of Birchley Hall for which he had given his bond to Roger Wetherheld 33 years previously.

Reasons! Reasons!

What were the motives which prompted Ralph in particular to ally himself with Christopher Anderton and act in a manner which was undoubtedly contrary to the longterm interests of the Heton family, and which apparently ignored centuries of landowning tradition. Partington wrote scathingly of Ralph and William, his father, describing them as weak, improvident, deficient in family loyalty, and betrayers of William the merchant who was trying his best to keep the Heton lands within the family. This may all be true but it is worth delving more deeply into the possible motives of those involved and considering their actions in the light of circumstances prevailing in the mid-16th century. In William the father's case it was probably sheer fear of poverty which prompted his behaviour, but in Ralph's case his motivation could have been rather more complex.

The Heton estates in Lancashire had never been sufficiently extensive for the head of the family to have given freehold land to junior family members without reducing his income below the level required for the maintenance of the lifestyle which his contemporaries would expect of him. In order to preserve his income, therefore, but at the same time to provide his sons with security of tenure, Richard had chosen to grant long leases of land on the estate to his three sons, Bryan, Richard and Lambert, with the remaining demesne land farmed to produce further income for himself. Other male members of the family were required to earn their living either as lawyers or merchants, and two became clerks in holy orders . None of them had ever managed to make a particularly good marriage to an heiress which would have assured them of a substantial inheritance.

There is evidence that a typical lease, granted by Richard or William of Birchley, would be for a period of two lives plus 21 years, or for one life plus

60 years, if the extended leases granted by William of Birchley to his half-brothers were held to be valid[32]; so it could run for 40-80 years or longer. Bryan, Richard and Lambert were required to pay fixed rents for their holdings, and at the time these leases were granted, in the first quarter of the 16th century, prices had been stable for over 100 years and rents had been negotiated accordingly.[33] However, from about 1520 onwards prices for foodstuffs and other commodities began to increase at an unprecedented rate. By 1560 foodstuffs had trebled in price and other commodities had doubled[34].

Bryan, Richard and Lambert, as producers of food on the land they leased, could take advantage of these price increases, particularly as their rents were fixed at a low figure. William the merchant could also gain from the general inflation insofar as he was farming the demesne land and producing food but his income from rents was frozen on a large part of the land he owned and the jointure paid to the young widow of William of Birchley was a constant drain on the estate funds. As his general living expenses rose in accordance with the rise in prices so his position worsened.

Ralph, occupying a position in the office of the merchant, could hardly miss observing this situation and it must have become obvious to him that even when he came into his inheritance, provided he eventually married William's daughter, he could hardly expect a particularly affluent future. If Elizabeth, the widow of William of Birchley, was still alive at the time of William the merchant's acquisition of the Heton lands in 1560 she was only 38 years of age with the possibility that she might live for another 30 years, as Baines maintains she did. Furthermore, although some landowners in Lancashire were beginning to benefit from the existence of coal and other minerals on their land there was no real prospect of the exploitation of natural resources at Heton or Birchley. The real potential of the township of Heaton lay 300 years in the future with the building development which the expansion of Bolton would eventually bring but this was a prospect far beyond the imaginings of Ralph and his contemporaries.

All these adverse factors, no doubt emphasised to Ralph by Christopher Anderton, must have weighed with him when he considered his future, coupled perhaps with some resentment against his relatives whom he saw as continuing to benefit at his expense if he were to inherit the estate. As an apprentice to a London merchant he perhaps came to the conclusion that he could put a large sum of ready cash to better use, and earn with it a much greater return than he was likely to obtain from ownership of the Heton lands, burdened as they were by long leases at rents which had not kept pace with inflation, and the possible obligation to pay Elizabeth a portion of the rents for many years.

From here it was but a short step to Ralph concluding that it would be in his best interests to throw in his lot with Christopher Anderton, who, we may be sure, had promised him a rosy future. It seems his feelings of family loyalty and regard for tradition were insufficient at his young age to stand up against the pressures he was under from Anderton and his mother. Perhaps Anderton also allowed him to think that his relations, in occupation as tenants with long leases, would not be greatly harmed by a change of ownership, although the lawyer may have had a shrewd idea that he could eventually defeat any claims to the extensions of the leases granted by William of Birchley on the grounds that William had only a life interest and could not make a grant effective after his death. From then on matters took their inevitable course, as we have seen, but it is unlikely that Ralph ever benefitted from his actions to anything like the extent he anticipated. He died and was buried at the parish church of Wigan on 25th November 1592.

Notes and References.

[1] "The Tudor Age", James A. Williamson. pub.Longmans, Green & Co. 1953. Preface.

[2] The author has been greatly assisted in this chapter by having access to the articles written by Mr Tom Arkwright, a retired solicitor, in the parish magazine of St. Mary's R C church, Horwich.

[3] "The Gentry in England & Wales, 1500 - 1700" F.Heal & C. Holmes. Pub. Macmillan, 1994. p.43.
"The Crisis of Parliaments-English History 1509-1660" Conrad Russell. OUP. 1971, p.111.

[4] Partington Papers. Bolton Central Library,Archives & Local Studies. Ref.B920B.HEA.Pt. II.

[5] Partington Papers. op cit. Pleadings in the case of Myles Gerard and Jane his wife v. Elizabeth, 2nd wife of William Heton of Birchley, 32nd Henry VIII (1541).
The details of the Settlement were:-
"Richard Heton being seised in his demesne as of fee,of and in the manors of Heton and Billinge,three score messuages,three water mills,with all the lands and tenements belonging to the same in Heton, Birchley, Rumworth, Lostock, Horwich, and Ulverston-in-Furness. And also of the reversion of certain leasehold estates in the aforesaid manors held by his sons Richard, Bryan, and Lambert, he the said Richard, of such estate being seised of all and every the premises and William Heyton , his son and heir apparent, in consideration of a marriage then to be had and following,between Miles Gerard, son and heir of Thomas Gerard of Ince, Esqre.and Jane, one of the daughters and heirs apparent of the sd.William Heyton; and also in consideration that the said Thomas Gerard should assign and make over lands and tents: of his inheritance of the yearl;y value of ten marks unto the said Jane for the term of her life, and in consideration that all the lands and tents: of the inheritance of the said Thomas Gerard should descend and come to his said son Miles Gerard and his heirs male of the said Jane lawfully begotten; by Indenture dated the Xth day of the XXIst year of the reign of Henry VIII (2nd May 1529) made between Richard Heyton and William his son and heir apparent, on the one part,and the said Thomas Gerard of the other part, it was agreed that if it should fortune the sd.William Heyton to decease without issue male of his body lawfully begotten, then the one-half of all the manors, messuages, lands, tents: &c of the sd. Richard and William should wholly descend and remain to the use of the sd. Jane and to the heirs male of her body lawfully begotten, &c, &c ."

[6] Partington Papers. op. cit. Pleadings of William Heton,son of Raffe Heton in a case heard 3rd Edward VI. (1550). The actual wording of the 1530 document is as follows:-
"That Richard Heyton of Heyton,esqre., Peter Bradshaw, clerk; Adam Hulton and John

Bradshaw, esquires; Richard Tyldesley , Gilbert Hedok, and John Lever, gentlemen,were lawfully seised in fee of the manor of Heyton, with the appurtenances, and 20 messuages, 1200 acres of land, 40 acres of meadow, 100 acres of pasture, 30 acres of wood, 300 acres of moss and heath, and 3s. 1d. rent, and did at the request of the said Richard Heyton, by their deed, bearing date the 30th April, 22nd .Henry VIII. give and grant all the several premises to Jeffrey Shakerley esqre. John Langtree, esqre. Raphe Asheton,gent. John Lee, gent. Thomas Heyton, clerk, Thurston Caistor, Richard Ewen, and John Corbuall, and their heirs, to the use of the said Richard Heyton, for the term of his natural life,without impeachment of waste; and after his death to the use of William Heyton, son and heir apparent of the sd Richard, for the term of his life, without impeachment of waste; and after his death to the use of Raffe Heyton, and the heirs male of his body lawfully begotten; and for lack of such issue to divers other purposes."

7 "History of the Chantries", pub.Chetham Society, vol. 30, p. 75. [JHP]
8 Elizabeth and Anna named as sisters of John Aghton at Inquest after the death of John, 1550. Eliz . then aged 28, and Anna aged 25. Dodsworth's MSS vol.8, p.361 [JHP].
9 Depositions of Evan Heton of Birchley, taken at Wigan in a case brought in 1573 by Christopher Anderton. The deed of settlement was said to be dated 1st April 1540. [JHP states that this information was extracted by his agents Hardy & Page, genealogical researchers]
10 Lancs, & Ches. Record Society ,vol 35, p. 174. [JHP]
11 Ducatus Lancastriae, vol.2, p.255. Reported in detail by J H Partington (op.cit.),pt. II, pp. 54/55 .[There is some discrepancy with dates but the import is clear.]
12 Reported at length by J H Partington (op.cit.),pt II,p.55. The details were extracted by Hardy & Page from the pleadings of Christopher Anderton in a case in 1573 against Humphrey Winstanley and his wife Jane [former wife of Myles Gerard and elder daughter of William Heton of Birchley] .
13 Ducatus Lancastriae, vol.2, p.133 [JHP]
14 Inquest post mortem. Note 11 above.
"Lancashire Pleadings" pub. Chetham Society. P.177. [JHP]
15 "History of Life and Acts of Edmund Grindal - Archbishop of Canterbury." pub by John Hartley,London. 1710, pp. 158-160.
16 Lancs. & Ches. Record Soc.,vol 11,p.4.
17 Catalogue of the Lansdown MSS, pp 38/40. [JHP]
18 Lancs.& Ches. Record Society, vol. 24, p.36.
19 Partington (op.cit.) pt. 2, pp. 58-60 and notes 22-25. Partington sets out the Agreement in full, stating that it is " Copied from the original in the possession of T. Weld-Blundell Esq. and printed by Rev.Thomas Ellison Gibson,1876, in his work,intituled (sic) 'Lydiate Hall and its Associations', p.50."
20 Herald's Visitation of London 1568. Harleian Society, pub.1963, p.46
21 Pleading of William Heton of London,Merchant v. Ralph Heton and Christopher Anderton ,extracted by Partington's agents,Hardy & Page. [JHP]
22 E.Baines " History Directory & Gazetteer of the Co. of Lancs." 1893 ed. gives 1590. VCH of Lancs. gives 1558. A point made by Mr Tom Arkwright.
23 Ducatus Lancastriae, vol.3, p.311.
24 Partington (op.cit.) part II,pp. 62/63. Partington quotes William Heton's pleadings in full and states that these were extracted for him by his agents,Hardy & Page.
25 Partington (op.cit.) part II,note 32.
26 Partington (op.cit.) part II,note 33.
27 Partington (op.cit.) part II,note 35. Stated to have been extracted by Hardy & Page from depositions relating to an action by Humphrey Winstanley and Jane his wife, formerly

Mrs Gerard, and daughter of William of Birchley, son of Richard, against Christopher Anderton.

28 "Lancashire Legends" J.Harland & T.T. Wilkinson, pub.G.Routledge & Sons,London,1873, pp.44/45.

29 "Lydiate Hall and its Associations" Rev. T E Gibson, 1876, pp56/7.

30 Partington (op.cit.)p.66, quotes this document in Latin in full. Note 38 states that the document was copied from Ince-Blundell Deeds by J.E.Batley ,whose manuscripts are in the Chetham Library, Manchester.A translation from the Latin was carried out by Mr Ronald Smith of Bolton, 1997 as follows:-

"To all the faithful of Christ to whom this present writing shall come, I Ralph Heton, son and heir apparent of William Heton esq. late of Bircheley in the county of Lancaster, eternal greeting in the Lord. Know that I, the aforesaid Ralph in and above, fully and wholly,have determined and finalised the agreement between me the aforesaid Ralph on the one part and Christopher Anderton esq. of Lostocke in the aforesaid county of Lancaster, on the other part, of and for all Compositions, all sums of silver, money and coin and other things whatsoever, which he has, continually carried on between me, the aforesaid Ralph and the aforesaid Christopher from the beginning of the world up to the day of these present writings. And that, for other diverse good causes and considerations I have given up, relaxed and forever quitclaimed and by these presnts on behalf of myself and my heirs do give up, relax and forever quitclaim to the aforesaid Christopher Anderton and his heirs and assigns all and every sort of increases, debts, covenants, promises, accounts, suits, fines, errors and demands whatsoever which I have ever had, have, or will be able to have in the fiture or which my heirs executors or assigns will be able to have in the future against the aforesaid Christopher, his heirs or executors by any reason or pretext or matter or cause before the present date.In witness etc. this 18th day of June in the 18th year of the reign of the Lady Elizabeth , by the grace of God, Queen of England, etc. [1576]

31 Partington (op.cit.) pp.67-69 quotes this document in full, the bond in Latin, the remainder in English. Note 41 states that the document was copied from Deeds in the possession of T.Weld-Blundell by J.E.Bailey,FSA,whose manuscripts are in Chetham Library,Manchester. A translation of the Bond by Mr Ronald Smith of Bolton,1997,reads:-

"Know all men by these presents, that we Ralph Heton of Birchley in the county of Lancashire, Gentleman, and Richard Heton of the same place in the same county , Gentleman,are held and firmly bound to James Anderton,son and heir apparent of Christopher Anderton of Lostocke in the said county of Lancashire,Esquire,and Thurstan Anderton,Gentleman,second son of the same Christopher,in One Hundred Pounds of good and lawful money of England to be paid to the same James and Thurstan or their certain attorneys,executors,administrators or their assigns; to making which payment indeed well and faithfully we bind ourselves and each of us by himself for the whole and for the whole our heirs,executors, administrators, firmly by these presents,sealed with our seals. Given in the last day of March in the 31st year of the Reign of our lady Elizabeth,by the grace of God,Queen of England,France and Ireland,Defender of the Faith,etc."

32 Ducatus Lancastriae,vol. 2, p. 86 . Pleadings of Bryan Heton in the case of Bryan Heton v. Richard Heton., 1546.

33 " Inflation in Tudor and Stuart England" R.B.Outhwaite, 1969.p.10. Tabulated by A.G.R.Smith in " The Emergence of a Nation State 1529-1660" pub.Longmans 1997,appendix K, p.439.

34 Ibid.

Chapter Six

New Landlords

The Heatons were by no means unique in Lancashire in the late 16th century in losing their lands, and this happened to many families through some unfortunate circumstance, genetic mischance, personal incompetence or irresponsibility. The Heatons' management of their estates was probably no worse than that of their contemporaries but they had the misfortune to be close neighbours of an unscrupulous lawyer with expansionist ambitions which he was able to realise by playing one party off against another. In Yorkshire 9% of the gentry families lost their status between 1558 and 1642 when their estates were sold and the figure in Lancashire can hardly have been less.[1] The fate of those displaced, say Heal & Holmes[2], was normally to leave the county to seek opportunities elsewhere, to stay on as tenants to those who bought them out, to depend on the charity of their kith and kin or, in a few sad cases, to seek parish relief as paupers.

In many instances the newcomers were those who had made money as merchants, lawyers, or speculators in the land market, following the release of large acreages on the Dissolution of the Monasteries by Henry VIII. Such a one was Christopher, the founder of the family of Andertons of Lostock.

The Anderton Family[3]

The Anderton family originated in the township of Anderton, Chorley, and had been neighbours of the Heatons for several generations. From Chorley they spread to Euxton and Clayton. Christopher was the son of Lawrence Anderton of Chorley and his wife Sybil, daughter of Christopher Parker of Combe. He was born in 1533 and studied as a lawyer at Lincoln's Inn. In 1556 he married his cousin Dorothy, daughter of Peter Anderton of Anderton, and they had four sons and five daughters. The sons were James, Christopher, Thurstan and Roger and they all eventually were involved in the administration of the Heaton and Birchley estates which their father acquired from the Heatons.

In 1561/62 Christopher Anderton senior purchased the manor of Lostock from Sir John Atherton and proceeded to erect for himself a mansion which consisted of a stone built gatehouse and tower with a substantial halftimbered house at the rear, the whole property probably surrounded by a moat, the details being shown in 18th century sketches by Captain Roger Dewhurst, now in Bolton Central Library. The halftimbered Hall was demolished between 1816 and 1824, but the stone gatehouse, minus the tower, still remains and is occupied as a private house.

There were a number of instances of marriages between Heatons and

New Landlords

Andertons, both before and after the Anderton takeover of the manors of Heaton and Birchley. Bryan, sixth son of Richard Heton married Katherine, daughter of Thurstan Anderton of Anderton and aunt to Christopher, circa 1520. Mary, daughter of Peter Anderton of Anderton and sister to Christopher's wife Dorothy, married William Heton. A later marriage, according to Giblin, was between Thomas, grandson of old Richard Heton, and Dorothy Anderton of Horwich which resulted in four sons, Richard, John, Henry, and William. The later history of these four is not known although Giblin states that John Heaton (1601-1684) became a Jesuit and adopted the alias of Parker. Richard is said to have married and had a daughter Mary who became a nun at Bruges in 1657, dying in 1713.

The Succession to the Manor of Birchley

On the death of Christopher Anderton in 1592 his eldest son James inherited the manors of Heaton and Birchley. It seems he quickly leased Birchley to his brother Roger and on the death of Mary Heton in 1594, which gave the Andertons vacant possession of Birchley Hall, they put in hand the rebuilding of the Hall and its replacement by the present house. Whether any part of the older timberframed Hall was retained in the new building it is not possible to say, and a 1984 report on the building to the then Historic Buildings Council[4] gives no information on this. There is a datestone of 1594 on the front elevation of the house, accompanied by the initials "TA", being those of Thurstan Anderton, the brother of James and Roger, who apparently occupied the Hall briefly, prior to his death in 1598.

James died in 1613, leaving no sons, and the manor of Birchley was inherited by his brother Christopher, resident at Lostock Hall, who then sold the freehold of Birchley to his brother Roger, who was the tenant of the property at the time. Roger Anderton died in 1640 and was succeeded by his eldest son James, who continued to live at Birchley Hall during his lifetime. James and his wife, Ann, nee Blount, had no sons and on James' death in 1673 the Birchley estate was inherited by their daughter Elizabeth, who married John Cansfield. They had two daughters. One, Anne, married Richard Sherburne but died without children and the other, Elizabeth, married Sir William Gerard, who died in 1721. Thereafter the property descended through the Gerard family until 1888 when the Hall and the residue of the land were sold.[5] After passing through a succession of owners the Hall is now in the possession of the Sue Ryder Foundation and is used as an old persons home.

The Succession to the Manor & Township of Heaton

On the death of his brother, James, in 1613, Christopher Anderton had inherited the manor and township of Heaton and other lands accumulated by their father. Christopher, born 1559, died in 1619 and was succeeded by his son, another Christopher, born 1607 and died 1650. On his death the property passed to his son Francis, who, in 1677 became Sir Francis Anderton, 1st

*Birchley Hall as rebuilt by the Andertons c. 1594.
Crown Copyright. Reproduced by permission of the RCHME.*

Baronet, on the creation of the baronetcy of Lostock in that year, following the Restoration of Charles II in 1660. Sir Francis, 1628-1678, was succeeded by his son Sir Charles, 2nd Bart.,1655-1691 and then the estate passed to his eldest son, again Sir Charles, 3rd Bart.,1677-1705. Thereafter the estate and title passed through a succession of brothers, the 3rd, 4th, and 5th baronets, all sons of the 2nd Baronet, in very strange circumstances which will be recounted later.

On the death of the childless 5th Baronet in 1760, at which time the property was under administration by a Receiver for the Crown, the estate passed to Robert Blundell.[6] His mother, Mary, daughter of the 2nd baronet, Sir Charles Anderton, had married Henry Blundell of Ince Blundell and her son became heir when the last of her brothers died, without leaving male heirs. Robert Blundell married twice; first to Catherine Stanley by whom he had a son Henry, born 1724, who succeeded him on his death in 1773, and second to Margaret Anderton of Euxton. Henry Blundell married Elizabeth Mostyn and had a son, Charles Robert, who remained unmarried and his father took steps to bar the entail and prevent his inheriting the Heaton and Lostock estates, which he willed to his two daughters, Elizabeth and Catherine, jointly. Her father died in 1810 and Elizabeth Blundell inherited the manor of Heaton through a settlement dividing the family estates between herself and her sister.

Elizabeth Blundell had married Stephen Tempest (1756-1824) of Broughton Hall, Skipton, Yorkshire[7] and the lands of Heaton therefore passed to the Tempest family. When Stephen died, his son, Henry Tempest (1795-1860) inherited Heaton, married Jemima Trafford in 1829, and was succeeded by their son (Sir) Charles Henry Tempest of Heaton, who was created a baronet in 1866. He married Cecilia Hibbert in 1862 and their daughter, Mary Ethel, inherited the manor of Heaton. She married Miles Stapleton, 10th Baron Beaumont, in 1893. He died in 1895, when he shot himself accidently, and when Lady Beaumont died in 1937 the Heaton lands passed to their only child, Mona Josephine, 11th Baroness Beaumont in her own right. She had married Lord Howard of Glossop in 1914, and they were the parents of Miles Francis Fitzalan Howard, who inherited Heaton when his mother died in 1971 and he became Baron Beaumont, and then in 1975 he became the 17th Duke of Norfolk on the death of the 16th Duke, his second cousin once removed. It is noticeable that the families who followed the original Heaton owners and successively became landlords of Heaton were predominantly Catholic.

Thus the old manor and township of Heaton, now a district of Bolton, has, in more recent times, become a prime asset of the Howard family, increasing in value enormously as land was gradually released for building development.

Catholics in Secret

In the late 16th century Lancashire was notorious amongst English counties for the number of wellplaced individuals who continued to adhere to the proscribed Roman Catholic religion in defiance of the laws passed by Parliament in 1559. On a famous map of the county prepared by Lord Burghley, Queen Elizabeth's Secretary of State, crosses denote the houses of notorious Catholic recusants, who neglected to attend the established church, and who were believed to shelter Roman Catholic priests and secretly hear Mass in their private chapels and baptise and marry their children in their old faith. Amongst these is the Anderton residence at Euxton, but their other houses at Lostock and Birchley are not indicated in this way. This is probably because Christopher senior and his eldest son James were somewhat circumspect in their behaviour towards the established church. It was their practice to occasionally attend church and appear to conform and observe the law, whilst in secret continuing to hold to their Catholic beliefs.

When James died in 1613 and his brother Christopher inherited Lostock and Heaton he continued in the same mode of behaviour as his father and elder brother and was not greatly troubled by the authorities. However his brother Roger, who by that time was the owner of the manor of Birchley and was living at Birchley Hall, was cast in a very different mould. He was a fervent believer in the Catholic faith and did everything he could to promote his faith in the vicinity of Birchley. It was during his occupation of Birchley that the famous illegal printing press, the first such Catholic press to be operated in this country was established there, probably by Roger's cousin, Fr Lawrence Anderton, a Jesuit who adopted the alias of John Brerely or Breverly[8] and who worked secretly in England until his death in 1643. The press probably operated between 1615 and 1621 when it was raided by the authorities and closed down. During its period of operation it appears to have produced at least sixteen pro-Catholic publications.[9] Roger Anderton does not appear to have suffered any penalty for allowing his house to be used for illegal purposes, other than a probable fine, and continued to live at Birchley Hall until his death in 1640.

Roger Anderton and his wife Ann produced seven sons and four daughters. Four of their sons, John (aka Christopher), Roger, Edward and Robert became priests and three of their daughters became Poor Clare nuns at Gravelines in the Netherlands. Another son, Thurstan, is believed to have been killed at Oxford in 1643 whilst fighting in the Royalist army.[10]

The Civil War

The first engagement in the Civil War in Lancashire took place in the streets of Manchester on 15th July 1642. This was a skirmish between a small troop of cavalry under the command of Lord Strange, soon to inherit the Earldom of Derby, and the armed inhabitants of the strongly Puritan town. The Royalists retreated leaving some of their own men wounded and one of the townspeople dead.

James Stanley, Earl of Derby, the leading supporter of the King in Lancashire, was the most powerful landowner in the county and a close neighbour of the Andertons, and the Heatons living on their estates. He pressed into service many of his tenants and their sons off his estates and in the early stages of the war his illdisciplined forces ranged through the county, sacking and burning towns such as Lancaster, Preston, and Blackburn. He carried on the war brutally against his opponents, holding firmly to the maxim that those who were not with him were against him, an attitude which did not meet with the approval of the more thoughtful Royalists who could see what harm his behaviour was doing to the King's cause.

In 1643 the indiscriminate compulsory enrolment of unwilling young men into Lord Derby's forces resulted in a flow of recruits into the garrisons of the Puritan towns where their treatment was rather better. With these reinforcements the Parliamentarians were able to retake Lancaster and Preston, and hold Bolton, less than three miles from Heaton, against the attacking Royalists.[11] Finally, at Whalley Abbey on the River Calder, Lord Derby was heavily defeated, escaping with only a remnant of his cannon and troops.

The following year it was Prince Rupert, the King's nephew, who came to Lancashire with a fresh Royalist army. He was joined by Lord Derby from his base on the Isle of Man, and on May 28th 1644 attacked the austerely Puritan town of Bolton. The Parliamentarians in the town had been reinforced by fifteen hundred men from the countryside around and defended stoutly.[12] However, it was stormed and plundered by the Royalists and many of the defenders massacred. This was an atrocity which was long remembered and for which the inhabitants took their revenge against Lord Derby some years later, when he was shown no clemency and was beheaded at Bolton in 1651. This followed his capture at Wigan where he fled after Charles II's defeat at the battle of Worcester.

On June 5th 1644 Rupert entered Wigan, a largely Royalist town, where he was welcomed, and a few days later he marched on to Liverpool which he quickly captured. He then paused whilst he prepared to leave Lancashire and march to the relief of the city of York, beseiged by strong Parliamentary forces. On the departure of Rupert's army and its defeat at the battle of Marston Moor on July 2nd 1644, the Earl of Derby withdrew again to the Isle of Man to prevent this important base falling to the Parliamentarians. The result of this was that Lancashire again became largely controlled by Parliamentary forces raised by the local Puritan gentry, and so it remained for the rest of the war.

Anderton and Heaton Neutrality

Throughout the hostilities the Andertons of Lostock had tried to remain neutral and this policy appears to have been followed by their Heaton tenants, there being no record of their playing any part in the civil war or suffering any casualities. At the Parliamentary Sequestration Committee hearings held in 1649 evidence[13] was called on behalf of Christopher Anderton to substantiate his claim that at no time had he borne arms against Parliament.

Adam Monks of Westhoughton, a Parliamentary soldier, swore that after the battle of Westhoughton Common in 1642 he was taken prisoner and sent to Wigan where he saw Mr Anderton at the entrance to the town having no arms about him. The witness was a prisoner at Wigan for twelve weeks and said that Mr Anderton gave him relief and maintenance on several occasions.

Roger Nicholson of Over Hulton said that when the prisoners taken at Westhoughton were brought to Wigan he also saw Mr Anderton at the entrance and he had no weapons. He also saw Mr Anderton at Middlewich after the battle there but he was not armed.

William Morris of Lostock said that Mr Anderton, being pressed by the Earl of Derby to supply him with men and arms, to avoid doing so left Wigan and went to Prescot where he remained a certain time.

Richard Woods of Halliwell, gentleman, said that when Mr Anderton was in Wigan he sent for the witness and told him that he had two little children whom he desired the witness to take care of and provide for, because he (Mr A.) was being heavily pressed to make available men and arms for the Earl of Derby. Witness said, that very day Mr Anderton left Wigan for Prescot and thence into Wales.

Finally, Margaret Anderton of Lostock, Christopher Anderton's daughter, said that after the battle of York (Marston Moor, 1644), when Prince Rupert returned to Chester her father was detained as a prisoner at Liverpool and Chester because he would not act for the King's party against the Parliament. After the Prince left Chester her father fled and at the first opportunity went over to France, fearing that if he stayed in England he would have been forced to act against the Parliament.

The Heavy Burden of the War

Notwithstanding this attitude of neutrality by the Andertons and their tenants, they all suffered severely from the requisitions for supplies and money made upon them by both sides in the conflict, as the war moved first in favour of one side and then the other. In Heaton the proximity of the Parliamentary garrison at Bolton, during most of the war, meant that the bulk of the demands for support came from the commanders of these forces. The Constable's accounts for the neighbouring township of Halliwell, a very similar community to Heaton, have been preserved[14] and make a very revealing comparison between years of war and peace. In normal times the charges imposed by the Constable on the township never exceeded £9 per annum and were commonly much less. During the war the figures were:-

1642
"Horses etc. raised in Halliwell for the publick service" i.e requisitioned by the Parliamentary forces £14.12.4d
"Moneys pay'd to souldiers listed under Major Willoughby for service,dress and oats" £45.8.0d
"Free quarters taken by souldiers in Halliwell " £10.0.8d

1644
"Freequarters taken by souldiers in Halliwell" £14.14.0d
"Arms and horse employed and lost in the service of his Majestie and Parliament" i.e. when Bolton was attacked by Prince Rupert. It seems that both sides demanded a contribution . £54.3.0d
The Constable's charges for other matters,chiefly military, in that same year were £16.19.5d

Such burdens bore down on the whole community but the landowners had particular concerns of their own. In order to meet the onerous demands on them of the opposing armies they needed the rents payable by their tenants and therefore had to try and ensure that these were able to continue their farming activities with as little disturbance as possible by either side. A good instance of the lengths to which they had to go to accomplish this was described in evidence given before the Sequestration Committee[15] on 11th December 1649 by one George Monk.

The witness testified that in 1642 he had acted as a messenger between Christopher Anderton and Colonels Assheton and Bradshaw, Parliamentary Deputy Lieutenants for the County. It seems that Anderton was endeavouring to arrange for both sides to issue warrants in exchange for money, undertaking not to harass the farmers in the locality by taking men or cattle during the time of seeding. In a letter[16] from the colonels to Mr Anderton, which the witness procured, the two colonels accepted a payment of £10 a month and undertook to issue their warrant when they had the warrant of the Royalist commanders, Lord Derby and Col. Blair, to the same effect and written to benefit the Parliamentary supporters also. The colonels, in their letter, went on to make further demands:-

> "It is likewise required that Mr Georg's wages,which will be ten pounds at St. Mark's Day,shall be paid, as alsoe such moneys as are behind for ye poore . . . presuminge you have not contained by your letter or otherwise ye hard usage of your tenant John Fford, now prisoner at Wigan, as we are informed."

And in a postscript:-
"we likewise require the release of John Fford by your meanes."

It would seem that Anderton had to successfully complete some rather difficult and probably expensive negotiations with the Royalists if he was to obtain the warrants he required from both sides. The witness George Monk went on to say that for the second month of the agreement with the two colonels, in lieu of the money payment, the garrison at Bolton required and were sent corn and hay to the same value, thereby depriving the local farmers of much-needed fodder intended for their own animals.

The same witness also stated that on several occasions troops from the garrison at fortified Lathom House, which was Lord Derby's home and headquarters, had carried out raids and plundered goods from several places in Lostock and the adjacent area[17] which, no doubt, included the township of Heaton.

In these and various other ways the local communities suffered at the hands of the opposing armies throughout the years of the war and it can be imagined with what thankfulness they greeted the onset of peace when it finally came.

Jesuits and Jacobites

Because of their adherence to the Catholic faith, the Andertons suffered often severe legal and financial penalties but their misfortunes during the next hundred years were also brought about by unlucky chance and their own behaviour.

Christopher Anderton died in 1650 at the age of 43 and the estate was then passed down through the family, with a succession of owners dying at an early age. The Restoration of King Charles II in 1660 improved the fortunes of the Andertons of Lostock and during his reign the baronetcy of Lostock was created in 1677. Sir Francis, 1st Bart. died at 50. On inheriting and immediately after his marriage Sir Charles, 2nd Bart. settled all his estates on his son and male heirs, after making provision for his wife and future children. He died aged 36 in 1691, when his eldest son, also Charles, was only 14 years of age. Sir Charles, 3rd Bart. died aged 28 in 1705. At the time of his death he was a theology student at St. Omer College, France. He had no children to succeed him, and the lands and title passed to his brother, Sir James, born 1678.

Sir James had become a member of the Society of Jesus (Jesuits) in 1703, presumably never anticipating that the title and lands would ever pass to him. He certainly never intended to marry and have children and so, with the agreement of his mother, Dame Margaret, and the trustees of his father's settlement, he entered into a new settlement, vesting all the lands in trustees for the use of his youngest brother Francis and thereafter entailed to the male heirs. His true heir, his father's third son, Lawrence, who had become a Benedictine monk in 1704, apparently acquiesced in this arrangement and continued to live abroad, as did Sir James himself, the estate being managed largely by his mother, Dame Margaret, and the trustees.[18]

Sir James survived only five years after he inherited and died in 1710 aged 32, the title and lands then passing to Francis as 5th baronet in accordance with the terms of James' settlement. Sir Francis resided at Lostock Hall and endeavoured to make himself and his Catholic affiliations as inconspicuous as possible. However when James Stuart, "The Old Pretender", laid claim to the throne in 1715 he foolishly gave him his support when his forces entered Lancashire. He was arrested by King George's troops after the Jacobites surrendered at Preston, and was taken to London to stand trial for treason. He tried to use in his defence the fact that he was charged as Sir Francis Anderton, Bart. of Lostock, which legally he was not, but this point was not accepted by his judges. He was convicted and sentenced to hang but was subsequently reprieved in response to a general wave of public sympathy for the rebels[19], although his estates were confiscated by the Crown.

In desperation, and in an attempt to avoid ruin from the confiscation of their estates, the family then decided to reveal the whole nature of the settlement which had deprived Lawrence of his rightful inheritance. He was brought home from the continent and on 17th June 1717 he entered his claim to the estate as the eldest surviving son of Sir Charles Anderton, 2nd Bart.[20] In 1719 his claim was rejected by the Commissioners not only against himself but also against his heirs, on the grounds of his foreign education and their ineligibility as papists. He appealed against this decision and in 1722 the decision against himself was upheld but was reversed in respect of his family. Only one course now remained to Lawrence - to be confirmed in his inheritance he had to renounce his lifelong belief in Catholicism and conform to the established church. After presumably wrestling with his conscience he took this final step on 21st May 1724, when the Crown released all his estates to him and confirmed their ownership to him and his heirs.[21]

However, Sir Lawrence lived only a very short time after coming into his

New Landlords

inheritance and died the same year. By his will[22] he forgave his brother Francis the £20,000 he maintained he had deprived him of and left his estates to his brother's lawful children if any, remainder to his nephew Robert Blundell and his male heirs, or remainder to his great-nephew Henry Blundell and his heirs. Francis never married and lived another 35 years until 1760, but was never allowed to inherit. He is alleged to have said subsequently, "I wore my boots for three days against the King, and lost £3,000 a year". During his lifetime the estates were administered by a Receiver for the Crown, and on his death passed to his nephew Robert Blundell.

Receivership

This prolonged period of uncertainty and receivership was decidedly detrimental to the estates' and the tenants' interests, resulting in a lack of efficient management and an inability on the part of the tenants to get any improvements and repairs carried out by the landlord, although there also seems to have been considerable laxity in ensuring that the full rental value was obtained for the various holdings. The situation attracted speculators as is shown by the contents of a letter[23] written on 18th Sept. 1741 by Henry Escrick of Halliwell, a wealthy chapman or merchant, to a Mr Harrop of London.

> " I have made some enquiry into the affair we were talking of and I find that whilst I was in London the Stewards came over and stayed two days and received two years rent of the tenants- they are a year in arrears. It is worth £1600 or £1700 per annum. They say the Government does not get above £400 per anum. A great many of the tenants get it very cheap and they bring in very extravagant Bills for Repairs and the Stewards they take some livres (££s) as well as if it was their own land. Some is in lease and some leases are dropped. There are three Stewards,viz. Mr Chorley, Mr Hawkshead, and Mr Oliver Morris. There are two large Parks, but no deer in them. And they are given in as Parks and pay no taxes and the Steward's sons have them for nothing and lay horses and cattle into them. Mr Culceth (*an Anderton trustee*) who got the estate from Mills and Huggens is dead at London so it will be easy come at. I think it be worth while to look after it."

If all this is true then obviously the estates were being very badly managed and the Crown deprived of substantial sums and this may have been going on for many years during the period of the receivership. It appears the Stewards made only infrequent brief visits and may well have found it convenient to transfer the landlord's normal liability for repairs and improvements to the tenants in return for reductions in rent, but it would seem that this arrangement was being exploited. Undoubtedly Escrick and Harrop were looking to buy the estate cheaply but they were obviously unsuccessful and on the death of Sir Francis, when Robert Blundell inherited, it may be assumed that a more efficient system of management was introduced. Robert's succesor, Henry Blundell, was a noted art collector who, between 1771-1800, formed an exceptional collection of Greek and Roman sculpture at Ince Blundell Hall, which the Heatons' rents and fines helped to purchase, and which is now on public display at the National Museums and Galleries on Merseyside.[24]

Notes & References

[1] "The Gentry in England & Wales 1500-1700". F.Heal & C.Holmes, pub. MacMillan 1994, pp 26/27.
[2] Ibid.
[3] Information for this chapter comes from:-
(a) "Lostock Hall and the Andertons" by H Jones. Article in Halliwell Local History Society Journal, no.76, April 1998.
(b) A series of articles on "A History of Local Catholic Gentry" by Tom Arkwright, magazine of St. Mary's R C Parish, Horwich, 1996/97.
(c) "The Anderton Family of Birchley" by J F Giblin,author and publisher, 1993.
(d) Papers of John Heaton Partington,1903, op. cit.. Bolton Central Library.
(e) "Lancashire" J J Bagley.
(f) " Lydiate Hall and its Associations", Rev. Thomas Ellison Gibson, 1876.
[4] Report by Mr Peter Leach,February 1984 - Royal Commision on Historic Monuments.
[5] Giblin -op.cit.
[6] Burke's Landed Gentry, 1937 ed.
[7] Burke's Landed Gentry, 1937 ed.
[8] Giblin - op.cit.
[9] Giblin - op.cit.
[10] Giblin - op.cit.
[11] " The King's War, 1641-1647" C.V.Wedgwood 1958, Collins. P.171
[12] Ibid.
[13] "Royalist Composition Papers" - Lancs. & Cheshire Record Society,vol 24, pp 49 & 50.
[14] Halliwell Town's Book. Bolton Central Library Hampson's "History of Horwich". [JHP]
[15] " Royalist Composition Papers" op.cit.
[16] "Royalist Composition Papers" op. cit.
[17] Transactions of Lancs. & Ches.Hist. Soc.,vol.4, p.31 [JHP]
[18] "Lydiate Hall and its Associations" Fr T.E. Gibson. 1876, p.65.
[19] "Riots, Risings and Revolutions", Ian Gilmour, pub. Hutchinson, 1992, p.69.
[20] Rev. Piccope's MSS, vol. 3, p.174.
[21] Fr Gibson. op.cit., p.69.
[22] Ibid.,p. 70.
[23] Correspondence printed in the Bolton Journal of 22 January 1881
[24] "Country Life" Magazine, Aug. 6th 1998, p.70.

Chapter Seven

Gentlemen, Yeomen, and Husbandmen

Following the disposal of the Heaton freeholds in 1570 by William Heton the merchant and Ralph Heton, however this finally came about, the position of the rest of the family must have continued much as before, their change in status from a landowning family taking one or two generations to be fully felt. Those who did not depend on the occupation of land for their livelihood continued to follow their former professions of churchman, merchant, lawyer or clerk. Those who held leases or tenancies of land on the former Heaton estates would enjoy the same security of tenure as they had before, and those members of the family who benefitted from the leases originally granted by Richard Heton could continue to look forward to a further period of occupation at the concessionary rents they were paying.

When William of Birchley inherited from his father in 1535 he agreed to extend the leases of his half-brothers by a further sixty years from his death, very possibly in return for a revision of the rents paid to a figure more in line with current rental values, which would still have been low compared with inflated 1570 values. If these extensions were valid this meant that these principal leases were not due to expire until about 1605 or even later, although it is very likely there would have been other leases and tenancies for shorter periods. The change of landlord from a Heaton, the form of spelling of the name which came into common usage around this time, to an Anderton, undoubtedly gave rise to considerable resentment, but the senior members of the Heaton family might have gained some consolation from their belief that they were secure in their holdings, at low rents, for their lifetimes and possibly for up to 35 years.

There were, it is true, some members of the family whose position was not so secure; who were on short leases or tenancies at will, and they could, perhaps, not expect to receive as much consideration from a businesslike Anderton as from a more sympathetic member of their own family. They, no doubt, had cause to worry. The first to suffer was Roger Heton, son of Richard, who had already been evicted from Heaton Old Hall by William Heton in 1565, and apparently allowed to return. He was finally dispossessed by Christopher Anderton in 1570.

Amongst those who were also to experience a problem were Catherine Heton, widow of Lambert, Richard's youngest son, and their son Ferdinando. On the 12 Aug 1583 Christopher Anderton executed a power of attorney[1] in favour of Bernard Anderton, authorising him to obtain possession of a tenement or holding in Heton formerly in the occupation of Lambert Heton, deceased, and now in that of Catherine and Ferdinando. An endorsement to the document certifies that, within seven days, Bernard had entered on the land, lying next to the "Towne Crosses" and claimed possession for Christopher. It is worth noting that this event took place 12 years after Christopher Anderton acquired the Heton lands and probably about 10 years after Lambert died, so this was not a case of animosity showing itself immediately.

Whether there were a number of other Heatons put in the same situation we cannot tell, although it is a fact that some Heaton families, who may well have been tenants of Richard senior or subtenants of his sons, Richard, Bryan and Lambert, moved away from Heaton township and established themselves elsewhere after the Anderton takeover. We shall look in more detail at this exodus later and the reasons which may have brought it about.

However, there were several members of the family who were not dependent on the land for their livelihood and for them there continued to be a number of opportunities in the professions, the church and the law, or as merchants.

The Bishop

Amongst those members of the family who wholeheartedly adopted Protestantism and one of the very few who attained high office in the Church, was Martin Heton, born 1552 and Bishop of Ely from 1600 to his death in 1609.[2] Martin was the son of George, a Chamberlain of the City of London from 1563-1577 and himself a son of William, a merchant taylor and a citizen of London.. Martin's mother was Johanna, daughter of Sir Martin Bowes, Lord Mayor of London 1545. William, who died in 1523, was a first cousin to Richard of Heton and Birchley.

Martin Heton was a scholar at Westminster School; from 1571 he attended Oxford University; in 1582 he was made Canon of Christ Church; he was appointed Vice-Chancellor of Oxford in 1588. In 1589 he was made Dean of Winchester Cathedral and ten years later was nominated by Queen Elizabeth to the vacant bishopric of Ely to which he was duly elected by the Dean and Chapter and consecrated as Bishop on 3rd February 1600.

Martin is notable for his record of alienating numerous parcels of land forming part of the estate of Ely Cathedral and was much criticised for these actions. However, Bentham asserts that, in fact, these alienations were compulsory conveyances of Ely estates to the Queen, under powers granted to her by Parliament, and for which she provided in exchange other estates, by no means the equivalent in real value, but which process the Bishop was powerless to prevent[3].

The Bishop managed to fall foul of Queen Elizabeth who, in an angry letter to him threatened to defrock him for failing to carry out some instructions she had given him, or behaving in a manner of which she disapproved. He survived her wrath, however, and died on 14 July 1609, to be buried with honour in the chancel of Ely Cathedral, where his tomb, erected in his memory by his two daughters and illustrated on the front cover of this book, may be seen to this day by the thousands of visitors and worshippers who enter this magnificent building.

Descent of Martin Heton, Bishop of Ely, 1600 - 1609.

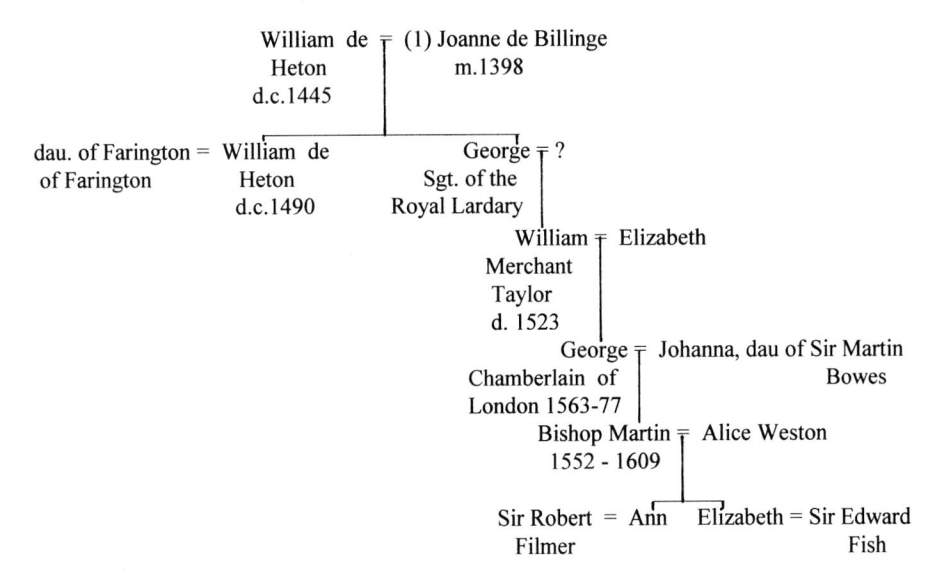

```
                    William de  ₸ (1) Joanne de Billinge
                      Heton         m.1398
                     d.c.1445
                        │
   ┌────────────────────┤
dau. of Farington = William de          George ₸ ?
of Farington         Heton           Sgt. of the
                    d.c.1490         Royal Lardary
                                          │
                                    William ₸ Elizabeth
                                    Merchant
                                     Taylor
                                     d. 1523
                                          │
                                      George ₸ Johanna, dau of Sir Martin
                                   Chamberlain of            Bowes
                                   London 1563-77
                                          │
                                   Bishop Martin ₸ Alice Weston
                                     1552 - 1609
                                          │
                              ┌───────────┴──────────┐
                         Sir Robert = Ann      Elizabeth = Sir Edward
                           Filmer                             Fish
```

Wife to an Arch-Chauvinist

Bishop Martin married Alice Weston and had two daughters, Ann, the elder, and Elizabeth. In 1618 Ann Heaton married Robert Filmer, son of Sir Edward Filmer from Kent, and bore him seven children.[4] Robert Filmer had been born in 1588, attended Trinity College, Cambridge, matriculated in 1604, and went on to train as a lawyer at Lincoln's Inn. He was knighted in 1618. He was to become wellknown for his political theorising on the Divine Right and supreme authority of Kings and his book "Patriarcha", written in 1638-40, became a standard text for Charles I and his supporters in promoting the king's cause. However, his views which we would find most extreme[5] were his contentions that, in cases of adultery, substituting a child not his own, for habitual drunkenness, and for having duplicate keys, husbands should have rights of life or death over their wives, and over their children on all occasions, although their natural affection for their children would ensure that these powers were not used "unnecessarily".

Sir Robert was imprisoned for a time by Parliament in Leeds Castle, Kent, despite Lady Filmer's strenuous pleadings on his behalf. He died in 1653 aged 65. Members of the family subsequently emigrated to North America and became associated with a number of revolutionary families including the Washingtons, Jeffersons, Byrds, Berklys and Randolphs.[6]

Citizens of London

There was a Herald's Visitation of London in 1568[7] which recorded the pedigree of William Heton, son of Brian, son of Richard of Heton and Birchley. We have met William in a previous chapter as the London merchant who purchased the manors of Birchley and Heton from his cousin William, son of Ralph, and his career has been covered there. He is thought to have died c.1589. He had two daughters, Adrey (sic) and Anne. In 1561 Adrey was betrothed to Ralph Heton, her cousin, when she was five years of age but, as we know, they were never married. We do not know what happened eventually to the two girls, whether they married or to whom.

Other London merchants were Thomas, uncle to Bishop Martin, who died 1598, aged 84, and George the father of Martin and also of Thomas Heaton who became Member of Parliament for Southampton. Thomas the M.P. had several male children but it is not possible to follow their subsequent progress here.

John Heaton, a citizen of London and a Mercer, married Jane Barnes at St. Swithins, London on 12 April 1595. Unfortunately he died only three years later and his Will was proved at the Prerogative Court of Canterbury in 1598. In it he mentions the hamlet of Billinge, parish of Wigan, "where I was born".

However the majority of the Heaton family continued to earn their living from the land and it is to Lancashire that we must look for further records of their activities.

Social Classes

Recognition of a man as a gentlemen depended on a number of factors. Lineage was important but he needed to be able to pursue an appropriate lifestyle in addition to ensure that he was accepted by the established gentlemen in the neighbourhood as their equal in social status. A man needed to live in a certain style but considerable wealth was not essential, although a successful merchant or lawyer buying himself an estate could quickly establish himself as a gentleman, provided his standard of behaviour and way of life was acceptable. A prosperous yeoman might be wealthier than the poorer gentlemen but there was a social distinction between them which both sides recognised, although gentlemen and yeomen often fraternised freely.[8] There were undoubtedly instances of the younger sons and brothers of gentlemen being regarded as yeomen and it was possible for yeomen to marry the daughters and sisters of gentlemen and, on occasions, to acquire gentry status. A yeoman and a husbandman both followed similar lifestyles and even work patterns but there was a general acceptance that a distinction existed between them socially.

Bryan, Richard and Lambert, sons of Richard of Heton and Birchley, held leasehold estates of sufficient size to enable them to sublet land to tenants, at the same time as they farmed part of their holdings themselves or under the management of bailiffs. Lambert is known to have leased four farms from his father and to have owned one himself. Bryan is on record as having an estate of approximately 220 acres. Theirs was an ancient lineage coupled with an affluent lifestyle, enabling them to describe themselves as "gentlemen", which they did for the whole of their lives.

Landlord and Tenant

As the years passed and the leases eventually expired, the descendants of old Richard's three sons, and other members of the family who had leased smaller areas of land direct from Richard or William of Birchley, found it necessary to negotiate with their Anderton landlord for a renewal of the lease, involving not only the payment of a higher rent but also a fine or premium payable to the landlord in consideration of the grant of the new lease.

In many respects the fine was more important to the landlord than the annual rent; it was a rather larger immediate payment, it was not subject to any deductions by way of landlord's expenses and it was often welcomed by the landlord as coming at a very convenient time to help with the cost of capital expenditure on the estate or elsewhere.

Partington maintains that on the expiry of their leases many of the Heaton tenants were driven from their farms by the Andertons and forced to settle elsewhere because of the bitterness generated between the Heatons and Christopher Anderton in the 1570s but this cannot really be substantiated. Whilst certain Heaton families did move outside the township to take farms, it is difficult to determine whether this was the result of a normal business failure to agree fresh terms of a lease, or a better opportunity arising for the tenant elsewhere, or, indeed, a refusal on the part of Christopher Anderton, in particular, to renew leases to Heatons as such. This does not appear to have been the attitude of his successor, James Anderton, and any later reluctance on the part of the landlord to renew a lease could have been prompted by different motives than pure malice.

Agricultural prices continued to rise during the period 1570-1640 and landlords could see the advantages of farming their land themselves in order to take advantage of higher prices for their produce. It seems very likely therefore, that when deciding whether to renew a lease the landlord would take into consideration the extent to which the land in question could conveniently be absorbed into the demesne land, the land which he farmed himself directly or under the management of his steward. Almost certainly the larger acreages which had been originally leased to Brian, Richard, and Lambert would be reduced in size, and let directly to other tenants, or taken in hand, when the leases expired and renewals were being negotiated. Naturally this would affect any subtenants also, who might have been junior members of the Heaton family. An acreage which had been sufficient to enable a man to live as a gentleman might very well be reduced to a size which obliged his descendants to accept that their social position in future would be that of a yeoman farmer and that of their subtenants as husbandmen, if they did not lose their holding altogether. This may have been one of the processes which caused movement of families to other locations in order to re-establish themselves.

An Attempt at Reconciliation

A landlord is normally reluctant to lose a good tenant and James Anderton showed himself in a conciliatory mood in 1593, when, following the death of his father, Christopher, in the previous year he apparently experienced difficulty in getting his title recognised by his Heaton tenants. Father T.E.Gibson[9] tells how he brought an action against his tenants for recovery of rent but in a document dated 17 March 1593 in his own hand he confirms:-

> "My offer at Lancaster Lent Assizes 1593,to my tenants at Heton openly in Courte wherein I shew the occasion of my suyte against them with offer to relinquishe the same if so they would but pay me ther rentes."

This attempt to avoid a lawsuit, coupled with the following remarks in the document:-

> "satisfying the country"......"the matter concerns a multitude"......"my own credit"

appear to be prompted by his wish to appear in a good light amongst his peers in the county. The ancient family of the Heatons, long resident and well-known in Lancashire, may still have been held in some esteem and a stigma may have attached to the Andertons for the dubious methods by which Christopher had brought about his acquisition of their lands. Any tenant wishing to arrange an extension of his lease might have found this a good time to open negotiations, with his landlord willing to grant his request on reasonable terms.

Those Who Moved Away

Wills, parish registers,and other records show Heaton families establishing themselves in various locations normally close to, but outside the boundaries of Heaton township and these places include Unsworth, Ainsworth, Adlington, Harwood, Middleton, and Abram. These moves appear to have taken place subsequent to the Anderton takeover of the Heaton lands and do not appear to have been harmful to the Heaton families involved since later events indicate that in most cases they prospered, sometimes quite considerably.

William Heaton died at Adlington in 1619 and in his Will settled his estate on his son, Thomas, aged only 18yrs 6mths at the time. Thomas eventually married Ellen Green, an heiress in Abram, by whom he had two sons, William and James, and he died in 1646, when his wife remarried.

His younger son, James, married Elizabeth Longworth, an heiress of Halliwell at Deane Parish Church on 20th Jan 1664. Their eldest son, Thomas, entered Brasenose College, Oxford in 1691, obtained his BA in 1694, was appointed Rector of Holwell, Beds., 1701, took an MA degree from Christ's College, Cambridge, 1704, and became Rector of Widdial, Herts. in 1718.

James Heaton is one of five men named in a document of 1694 as encroaching on the common lands of Harwood township.[10] Another of those named was James Longworth, probably a relation of his wife. Consideration was to be given "whether these five may be distrained upon or in a warrant for ejection because they have other considerable lands in ye Township having inclosed part of ye Common" Whether any further action was taken, we do not know.

This same James Heaton apparently bought the lands at Adlington which had been left to his elder brother William by their father, since in his Will dated 24 July 1721, wherein he is described as "yeoman of Harwood" he bequeathed "all those messuages, lands, etc. in Adlington which I formerly purchased from my late brother William, deceased, together with all my right title, etc. to that messuage called Height Barn in Haslam Hey: all my estate in Abram, commonly called Heaton House, and all my messuage etc. in Harwood, together with all my household goods, etc. to my son James Heaton, whom I make my sole executor." James had obviously prospered through his marriage to an heiress and his own subsequent business activities. His Will was proved at Chester in 1721.

When James Heaton II made his Will on 4 February 1741, after making money bequests to various people, £10 to one, £20 to others and providing for his wife, he left the residue of his estate to be divided equally amongst his seven younger children. J.J.Francis records that Meadowcroft Heaton, the eldest son, named after his mother's family, although not the executor, arranged the sale of a 16-acre farm for £290 to John Kirkman and distributed the proceeds amongst his brothers and sisters, Peter, Rebecka, Elizabeth, Mary, David, Ann and James.

It seems that the Harwood township mill, known as Hardy Mill, came into the ownership of David Heaton, and he spent money on it, since a datestone of 1757 bore his initials and that of his wife Margaret[11], and their daughter Betty married John Walch who became the miller subsequently.

James Heaton son of James II was overseer of the poor in Harwood for the year 1741. His son Alexander Heaton was buried at Bolton on 28 Nov 1790 aged 74.

In the formal Award for the enclosure of Harwood Common,[12] made on 29 June 1801, allocations of former common land were made to two Heatons who owned land which qualified for awards. John Heaton was allocated 1acre 3roods 2perches in respect of his ownership of Greenhalgh Fold, and Edmund Heaton was allocated 9acres 3roods 31perches in respect of holdings named as Longworths; Bottoms; and Hardy Mill. All these properties appear to have been occupied by tenants. A farm called Heatons, owned by the Governors of Brazenose College, was also a qualifying property. It was tenanted by John Scholes, but may previously have been occupied by a Heaton.

Ralph Heaton, who settled in Unsworth made his Will on 2 June 1604. He had sons James and John and at that time two unmarried daughters, Isabell and Margaret, amongst whom he divided one-third of his worldly goods, another third to his wife, and he bequeathed 20 shillings each to Elyne and Elizabeth, his married daughters, to Isaac and Ralph, his grandsons, and to Richard Heaton. Sisley, his wife, and James Sanderson were his executors. The Will was proved in 1604. His elder son James Heaton married Dorothy Kaye on 14 October 1600 and had a son Rauffe (Ralph) baptised on 15 May 1603, another son John on 16 Dec 1604 and a third son Richard on 3 Feb 1610/11. Ralph and Anne Holte were married at Bury on 1 Nov 1637. The Will of Ralph Heaton of Unsworth was proved at Chester in 1679, and the Will of Anne Heaton, his widow, in 1692. Bury parish registers contain numerous references to this branch of the Heaton family, generation after generation.

Another branch of the Heatons settled in Middleton where John Heaton made his Will on 24 July 1597, leaving all his goods, etc. to his wife Elizabeth; " but if she should misbehave (as a widow) or marry again then the one-half of my Tenement shall go to my brother Edward. Ralph Heaton to have all my wearing apparel". His wife Elizabeth and Edward Heaton, his brother, were to be his executors. Presumably John and Elizabeth had no children but many descendants of Edward and Ralph Heaton appear on the occasions of baptism, marriage, and death in the Middleton parish registers.

The Will of Henry Heaton of Middleton, husbandman, was made on 19 April 1624, naming his "now" wife Marie, and his children, Richard, Susan, Anne and Elizabeth. On 25 March 1616 a marriage licence was granted for Richard Heaton of Middleton and Sarah Hynde of Prestwich to marry at Manchester,

Thus the Heatons began to spread from their original home in the township of Heaton in Deane parish, into other parts of south Lancashire, where their prolificacy, enterprise, and the process of ramification (see Appendix I) ensured that numbers of them would continue to make their mark in the life of the district.

Working the Land

In the settlement document of 1530 the manor of Heaton is described as "appurtenances, 20 messuages, 1200 acres of land, 40 acres meadow, 100 acres pasture, 30 acres wood, 300 acres moss and heath and 3s-1d rent." The land ranges from 110 to 300 metres above sea level (360 - 985 feet). Heaton Old Hall, the ancestral home of the family, is at an altitude of approximately 165m. (540 ft). Depending on its altitude and location the land, like the majority of the Lancashire plain, would be either sand, gravel, loam, clay, or peat.[13] There is no detailed description of Birchley manor but it is likely to have been somewhat smaller and more fertile, being at a lower altitude and with a more favourable soil structure.

The principal farming activity of Heaton must have been rearing livestock with some cereals grown for the farmers' own use, and as animal feed. These would be mainly oats with some barley, and a little wheat on suitable land. Bread was made from oats, only rarely from wheat.[14] Until the late 16th century grassland was permanent pasture based on the indigenous grasses. A 3-course system was adopted; grass, corn, fallow, and for centuries agricultural productivity had remained largely static. Not many sheep were kept, except in small flocks on the higher ground which was suitable for little else, and the cattle, bought in as calves from other parts and reared as stores in Lancashire to be fattened in the Midlands, were black, multipurpose, longhorn beasts intended to produce beef, milk, tallow, hides, horn and to be used also as draught animals. Their manure was the only real fertiliser although the spreading of marl to improve the lighter soils was common practice. Dairying was also carried on, particularly in the east of the county and the production of cheese was widespread. From the beginning of the 17th century some improvements, initiated firstly by the wealthier, more experimental landowners began to spread very slowly through the farming community, although it took at least 100 years for them to become at all common, through innate conservatism, and lack of conviction as to their benefits relative to the extra cost.

The value of short-term, temporary pasture leys as a means of improving grassland began to be appreciated and ryegrass was introduced to provide more lush growth for summer grazing and better hay for winter fodder, enabling more stock to be carried on a farm of given size. The value of a crop of legumes such as beans or peas to improve the following cereal crop, or clover to sow in grassland began to be appreciated, although the reason why - the fact that legumes fix nitrogen in the soil - was not understood. Whereas turnips began to be grown in some parts of the country as winter fodder for animals, the soils of Lancashire were rarely suitable and it was little grown there. Around 1650 the potato was introduced from Ireland, and Lancashire was in the forefront of its spread, but the growing areas were mainly nearer the coast.

The increasing general population, improved economic conditions and rising prices which encouraged the landowners to take more land in hand, created better market conditions for all farmers and they prospered, whilst much of the population suffered as their wages fell in relation to the increased price of most commodities. These are probably the conditions which brought about the Great Rebuilding boom in the first four decades of the 17th century, identified by many writers, and visible to this day; with numerous buildings of that period in our present countryside.

On the security of a building lease for 99 years, or even a lease for a typical term of three lives (usually a man, his wife, and his son) plus 21 years, (reckoned as having a probable length of 42 years), a tenant farmer could feel able to provide himself with a new barn or other buildings, or even a new house, and could do so at a very reasonable price, as labour costs of craftsmen and agricultural workers had not kept pace with the increased prices he was receiving for his produce, and even the cost of building materials had not risen at the same rate as foodstuffs.[15] Similarly, a landowner, receiving higher rents and a better price for his own produce, would be prepared to invest capital in the improvement of the buildings and fixed equipment on farms which he owned, knowing that his tenants would be in a position to pay rents which would give him a good return on his outlay.

Those Who Stayed at Birchley

At this stage the histories of the manors of Birchley and Heaton began to diverge as they came into the ownership of different members of the Anderton family, as described in the previous chapter.

We cannot trace the Heatons of Birchley and Billinge much further in detail although we know that they occupied several farms on that manor and they no doubt continued to multiply and spread, and in most cases prosper on their farms, as did their cousins at Heaton and elsewhere.

The forenames Lawrence and Evan (sometimes spelt as Owen or even Hewyne) occur frequently amongst those Heatons concerned with Birchley and can cause some confusion. Evan, Owen and Hewyne are seemingly Welsh-derived names which are somewhat difficult to associate with 16th century Lancashire, although there was a Heaton family which had been established in Denbighshire, North Wales for centuries. Lawrence, employed as bailiff to William Heton of Birchley, had a son Lawrence and also another son, Evan who was himself bailiff to Richard, half-brother to William of Birchley. This Evan is named in a complaint of trespass made by Mr and Mrs Bolde in 1544 during their dispute with the sons of old Richard, when presumably he was acting for his employer Richard II in asserting rights which they believed did not truly belong to the Boldes.

Evan Heaton, yeoman of Billinge, who made his Will on 29 July 1591, was probably the former bailiff who had leased a farm and was farming himself, hardly indicating any degree of animosity between him and his landlord, who may at the time have been Mrs Mary Heaton. His brother Edward, another son of Lawrence, was a witness and he named as beneficiaries his wife Ellen and his sons Lawrence, Roger, William, Edward and his daughter Margaret. Another son, John, is mentioned in the inventory. Lawrence and Ellen are named as executors.

Another Evan Heaton, yeoman of Billinge, made his Will on 17 April 1633. The Inventory is badly damaged so we cannot tell when the Will was proved, and the total value of his property, but he named his wife, Elizabeth, and his eight children Richard, Thomas, John, William, Claire, Jane, Rachell, and Elizabeth. He made his wife his executor. His animals, consisting of 3 horses, 2 oxen, 5 cows, 2 heifers, 6 young beasts, 25 sheep would seem to indicate a farm which contained a proportion of arable land as well as pasture for livestock. It is also possible he earned additional income as a carrier, as the possession of 3 horses by a small farmer was unusual at that time.

Evan Heaton of Billinge, gent., was one of the lives named in a lease of the Tithes of Childwell in 1664.[16]

Those Who Stayed at Heaton

When William of Birchley died in 1541 the leases which his father had granted to his halfbrothers, Richard, Bryan and Lambert would have been extended by 60 years from his death, i.e. until 1601, if he had had the power to extend the leases in this way. Bryan died in 1552, Richard in 1558, and Lambert c.1573. Bryan's land appears to have been largely in Horwich and Richard's and Lambert's in Heaton. There was another son of old Richard's named Ivan but little is known about him, other than that he occupied land in Heton in 1542/3.

It seems that Christopher Anderton was able to show, in a number of cases, that the 60-year extensions to his father's leases which William of Birchley had attempted to grant to his half-brothers were invalid, as William was a tenant for life only. However, it did not necessarily follow that Anderton wished to evict the former tenants from the land but only to have an opportunity to charge a fine or premium and to increase the rents when new leases were granted to the same tenants. There is evidence that in several cases the same families continued in occupation of their farms on the basis of new leases granted by Christopher Anderton or his sons.[17]

Richard's Descendants

We have seen earlier in this chapter that Richard junior's wife Alice and their son Roger had continued in occupation of part of Heaton Old Hall after Richard's death and that William the merchant had obtained possession against them in 1565. However, it would appear that Roger subsequently reached an agreement with William whereby he continued to live at the Hall and rent land in Heaton, which he farmed. He remained unmarried and in 1570 Christopher Anderton obtained an order for possession of the land which he occupied.

Roger made a Will on 27 July 1597 which was proved at Chester on 25 April 1598. At the date of his death it seems he was still maintaining that he had an enforceable lease for 79 years from 1541 relating to Heaton Hall and adjoining land since he purported to bequeath this to his nephew Oliver Greenaugh, although he qualified this by the comment "if this lease be recovered", implying that he had already been deprived of it. He describes his holding as "all the houses, edifices and buildings belonging to the said Manor House of Heaton, with all orchards, gardines, and turbaries, pastures, closes, meadows and parcels of land and wood as at large it doth appear on the said lease". Obviously an attractive estate which he was loath to surrender since he includes in his Will a tirade against his treatment at the hands of James Anderton who at the time of Roger's death had succeeded his father as owner of the manor of Heaton.[18] Not the usual comments which one would expect to read in a Will but presumably Roger saw this as his last opportunity to show the true nature of his feelings regarding his landlord.[19]

Bryan's Descendants

In 1553 Richard, a younger son of Bryan, deposed in a statement that his father held 13 messuages and 220 acres of land in Horwich and Heton[20]. Part at least of the land leased to Bryan appears to have passed to his son Augustine and then to his grandson, Rauffe, whose Will was made on 17 March 1626 and proved in 1628. In it he names his second wife Mary, his children Richard, John, Thomas, and Elizabeth, and his father, Augustine, who apparently outlived his son. Rauffe provided £6 a year maintenance for life to his father out of his holding known as Holyn Hey, apparently let and producing rent. He confirms his own occupation of another farm, leased from Christopher Anderton II for his own life and those of his wife and son Richard. This appears to have been a fairly new lease for which he had undertaken to pay a fine or premium of £100 in instalments, some of which were already paid and the balance of which he instructed his executors to now pay. Mary and Richard were named as his executors.

A Brother/Sister Dispute

Rauffe (Ralphe) had provided in his Will of 1626 for a legacy to his daughter Elizabeth, and her brother Richard, as executor, was responsible for giving effect to this. However it seems he failed to do this and Elizabeth was obliged to petition Thomas, Lord Coventry, Keeper of the Great Seal of England, for redress.

Her petition document[21], although damaged and illegible in part, makes fascinating reading. She recites the fact that her father made his Will on 17 March 1626 wherein he provided that each of his children should receive one-fourth part of one-third of his estate and out of a further one-third part the sum of £20 should be divided equally between his four children and that also she should receive her mother's best gown, "witch was worth the some of tenn poundes att the least". The residue of this one-third part was to go to Richard if he married his father's "then wife's daughter" (i.e. his stepsister), otherwise it was to be distributed amongst the other three children. She says that, within one month, her "mother in care" (stepmother), Mary, renounced her executorship, leaving Richard as sole executor.

Elizabeth, in her petition, states that the total value of her father's personal estate consisting of " goodes, Chattells, Leases, Jewells, plate, Cattell, beastes, oxen, hay or corne graine and other utensells of husbandrie and household stuffe" was £128.18s. plus debts of at least £100 more owing to her father, and a fourth part of one-third. part of this belongs to her. She goes on to say that her brother did not marry his stepsister and consequently the sum of £6.13s.4d. is due to her together with other sums which she cannot "certainely tell and declare", her brother having apparently kept her in the dark over the value of the various assets and what had come into the executor's hands. Although she "hath often in a friendlie and lovinge manner demanded all her said severall legacies and hath desired the said Richard Heaton (to pay her that which) belonges to her by virtue of the said Will, yett the said Richard Heaton without any just cause or reason, doth altogether refuse to part with same or to lett your Oratrix (Petitioner) knowe what is due to her". She goes on to say that the only way she can obtain redress is to sue in a Court of Equity, and petitions his Lordship to issue a Writ of Subpoena, directing Richard Heaton to appear before the Court of Chancery to answer to all her complaints on oath and abide by any orders and directions which the Court may issue to protect her.

We do not know the outcome of this case but it is to be hoped that Elizabeth was eventually able to obtain satisfaction and receive everything to which she was entitled. How modern it all sounds and how typical of questions now raised regularly in the legal advice sections of weekly magazines.

An Early Death and its Consequences

Richard Heaton succeeded his father, Rauffe, in occupation of the farm, which seems to have been a prosperous holding. Richard, as we know, did not marry his stepsister but married Anna and their children were Ralph, baptised at Deane, 15 July 1638, another son Frances, and a daughter Anna, baptised 20 December 1646. Unfortunately Richard died young and unexpectedly and was buried at Deane on 25 May 1647. He did not make a Will, and Administration was granted to his wife and Thomas Lightbowne of Halliwell, possibly a relative of hers, at the Bishop's Court in Chester on 18 November 1647. The Inventory of his goods shows a total value of £280.1s.10d with cattle at £84.11s.4d, a quite considerable amount. His eldest son was only aged 8 at the time and with Richard's death the lease of the farm expired. If his widow had wished to renew the lease then a further substantial fine would have been payable to their landlord, her father-in-law having paid £100 perhaps only 25 years earlier. Alternatively, as a young widow in comfortable circumstances she may well have had the opportunity to remarry.

Thomas Heaton, brother to Richard, married Dorothy and occupied a farm at Halliwell. He held the offices of Churchwarden at St. Mary's, the parish church of Deane in the year 1654, and Parish Constable in 1661. His wife died and was buried at Deane on 6 December 1647.[22]

We know very little more about this family. There were a Ralph and Frances Heaton, both living in Heaton, appointed Trustees of Deane School estate on 29 June 1659,[23] but they are highly unlikely to have been the sons of Richard and Anna as those two would both have been under 21 at the time. On 8 August 1665 a marriage licence was granted to Ralph Heaton of Heaton, gent, and Deborah Bridocke, spinster, of Cheetwood, Lancs. to marry at either Manchester or Eccles, but we know nothing further of Ralph after that. When Frances died in 1686 he was living in Haigh, a few miles to the west of

Heaton. In 1697, an allegation that no impediment to a marriage existed was sworn by Frances Heaton of Haigh, gent, very possibly a son of the first Frances. The fact that two further generations of this family were able to describe themselves as gentlemen, would seem to indicate that they had prospered wherever they had moved to.

Lambert's Descendants

Lambert Heaton was the youngest son of Richard of Heton and Birchley. Lambert lived at Heaton Hall and held four farms in Heaton, leased from his father, and one further farm which he may have owned himself. It seems he was not disturbed by Christopher Anderton during his lifetime and that he lived rather longer than his two brothers, Richard and Bryan. Lambert probably died circa 1573 and some years afterwards Christopher Anderton commenced proceedings against his widow Catherine and their son Ferdinando to gain possession of certain land in Heaton, as described earlier in this chapter. Anderton was successful in this and on 12 August 1583 authorised Bernard Anderton to enter on the land and take posession.

Notwithstanding this loss of some of his father's land it seems that Ferdinando continued to farm elsewhere in Heaton. In 1583 and later years he entered into an arrangement with Sir Richard Shuttleworth of Smithills, through Sir Richard's steward, to provide storage space for the tithe corn of Heaton which was due to Sir Richard. On other occasions Ferdinando provided board and lodging for Sir Richard's workman whilst the corn was cut and threshed in his barn.

The payments[24] made to Ferdinando were:-

> 1583, " for houseroome of the tythe corn of Heaton - 10s." ; " for the tablyinge of Robert Aspden whilst the saide tythe corne was in thresshinge - 22d".
> 1584, "for house rowme of the tiethe corn of Heaton, 7s.: and 13d for the tableing of Roberte Aspden when the same was throshen."
> 1586, " 4s for seven and twyntie melles (meals) for thosse which lade the tythe corne of Hetone, after towe pence a melle." : " 10s for his barne to laye the tythe corne of Heitone in"

Partington suggests that the fact that Ferdinando Heaton's barn was so often empty indicates that his own farm was not particularly productive or he was a poor farmer. If such was the case one would not have expected him to survive very long either as a tenant or an owner/occupier. An alternative explanation is that Ferdinando was occupying a house and farm buildings which were too large for the acreage of land which he had, they having been intended to serve the larger acreage which Lambert leased. They may have been Heaton Hall itself and its barns. Houseroom for threshed corn meant literally that - the grain was placed in the great arks or chests which appear in most farmers' inventories at the time and these were located in chambers in the house to keep it dry and prevent it sprouting and being spoilt. Unthreshed corn was kept in the barn.

Ferdinando, son of Lambert was executor to his father's Will, made in 1573, but we do not know who he married and when he died and who precisely his children and grandchildren were.

As the 17th century opens, some confusion arises from the fact that there were two contemporary Ferdinando or Ffardinando (the spelling varies) Heatons occupying farms in Heaton. We are obliged to fall back on circumstantial evidence to decide relationships between various Heatons as the parish registers for Deane, where many of them were born and lived, have not survived earlier than 1637 nor apparently have any relevant Wills or other documents of this period been preserved.

However, there is a substantial body of evidence relating to Ralph Heaton of Heaton, gent, which places him in the right place, at the right time, names his wife and some of his children, but not his father, nor confirms his relationship with Lambert Heaton, born circa 1619, died 1676, from whom a number of presentday Heatons can trace their descent, he being the author's 7xgreatgrandfather . On the balance of probabilities it would be reasonable to say that Ralph was the son of Ferdinando and the father of Lambert.

A Rather Puzzling Transaction

In 1652, in a legal action between Sir Edward Mosley and Ralph Heaton, complainants, and Sir William Gerard, defendant, Ralph Heaton of Heaton, gent, made depositions[25] or witness statements, in which he stated that he was 63 years of age or thereabouts, putting the year of his birth as about 1589. The action referred to the manors of Etwall and Hardwick in Derbyshire, purchased by Sir Edward Mosley from Sir William Gerard in 1641, for a total of £9,000 and in his deposition Ralph Heaton stated that he was a joint purchaser with Sir Edward, his contribution to the purchase price being £2,500, which fact was later endorsed and witnessed on the deed of 5 August 1641. One of the witnesses to the endorsement was Atherton Heaton, very probably Ralph's eldest son, born 1617, and presumed brother to Lambert, and the signatures of Mosley, Gerard and Heaton were confirmed by other witnesses .

This action related to Sir Edward Mosley's claim to be relieved of an obligation to pay rentcharges of £60 and £20 per annum secured on Etwall lands but the original transaction of 1641 is unusual, not least in the fact that Ralph Heaton was able to lay his hands on £2,500, a very considerable sum for a minor provincial gentleman to raise. It is possible that he was acting as agent for one of the principal parties who actually put up the money. Mosley may not have wanted it to be known that he was laying out the full purchase price at a time of stringency or perhaps Gerard, who was a Catholic and connected to the Heatons by marriage in the previous century, wanted to dispose of the property, to avoid its possible confiscation, but at the same time wished to retain a concealed interest. We do not know the eventual outcome of the case or anything more of Ralph's involvement with Etwall and Hardwick but further research amongst any available Mosley or Gerard papers could perhaps throw more light on this rather puzzling transaction.

Ralph Heaton married Philadelphia Atherton at Leigh parish church on 5 January 1613. Their eldest son was Atherton, named after his mother's family, and baptised at Leigh on 1 May 1617. It seems very likely that their second son was Lambert, born circa 1619, and named after his greatgrandfather. There may well have been other sons, Richard and Frances. The Frances Heaton, living in Heaton, who was appointed a Trustee of Deane School estate on 29 June 1659 could have been Ralph's son, aged about 35 at the time.

Ralph died and was buried at Deane on 12 October 1652. He obviously had made something of a mark in the locality and had a wide circle of contacts. We do not know whether he farmed on any sort of scale or was something of an entrepreneur, but it is to be hoped that one day further research will be able to throw more light on a somewhat mysterious individual whose activities we know too little about.

Lambert Heaton, yeoman, the author's 7xgreatgrandfather, farmed in Heaton and lived through the Civil War, when he endeavoured to remain neutral, and his experiences during that very difficult period would be as described in the previous chapter. He married Ann Pilkington at Bolton Parish Church on 11 August 1640. They were living at Heaton Old Hall soon after 1650 but it is likely that more than one family were occupying different parts of the building at the time. We do not know the exact extent of his farm but the value of his goods and chattels and personal effects when valued in January 1675/6 was £123.15s.7d., showing him to be in a fair way of business. The inclusion of "loomes" in the long and interesting Inventory shows that, like so many farming families in the locality they supplemented their income by the production of woven woollen and linen goods.

His Will was proved at Chester on 20 May 1676 and he was buried at Deane Parish Church on 23 January 1675/6, the very same day on which his wife was buried in the same place. Their children were Ferdinando, Alexander, Lambert, all baptised at Deane on 26 October 1645, Anna, baptised 10 October 1647, died 1648, Anna baptised 25 March 1649, Isabella, Gabriel, baptised 16 November 1652, Esther, baptised 25 March 1655, died 1656, Esther, baptised 6 October 1656, Noah, baptised 9 January 1658/9, John, baptised 17 February 1660/1, and Richard, baptised 5 May 1663.

Lambert and Ann married by licence granted at Chester on 8 August 1640 and their bondsman, who guaranteed thier appearance at the marriage, was Oliver Morris of Heaton. The Morris family also lived in part of the Old Hall and obviously the two families knew one another very well. When Alexander, Lambert's second son, was seeking a wife he needed to look no further than their close neighbours and he married Alice Morris at Deane Church on 29

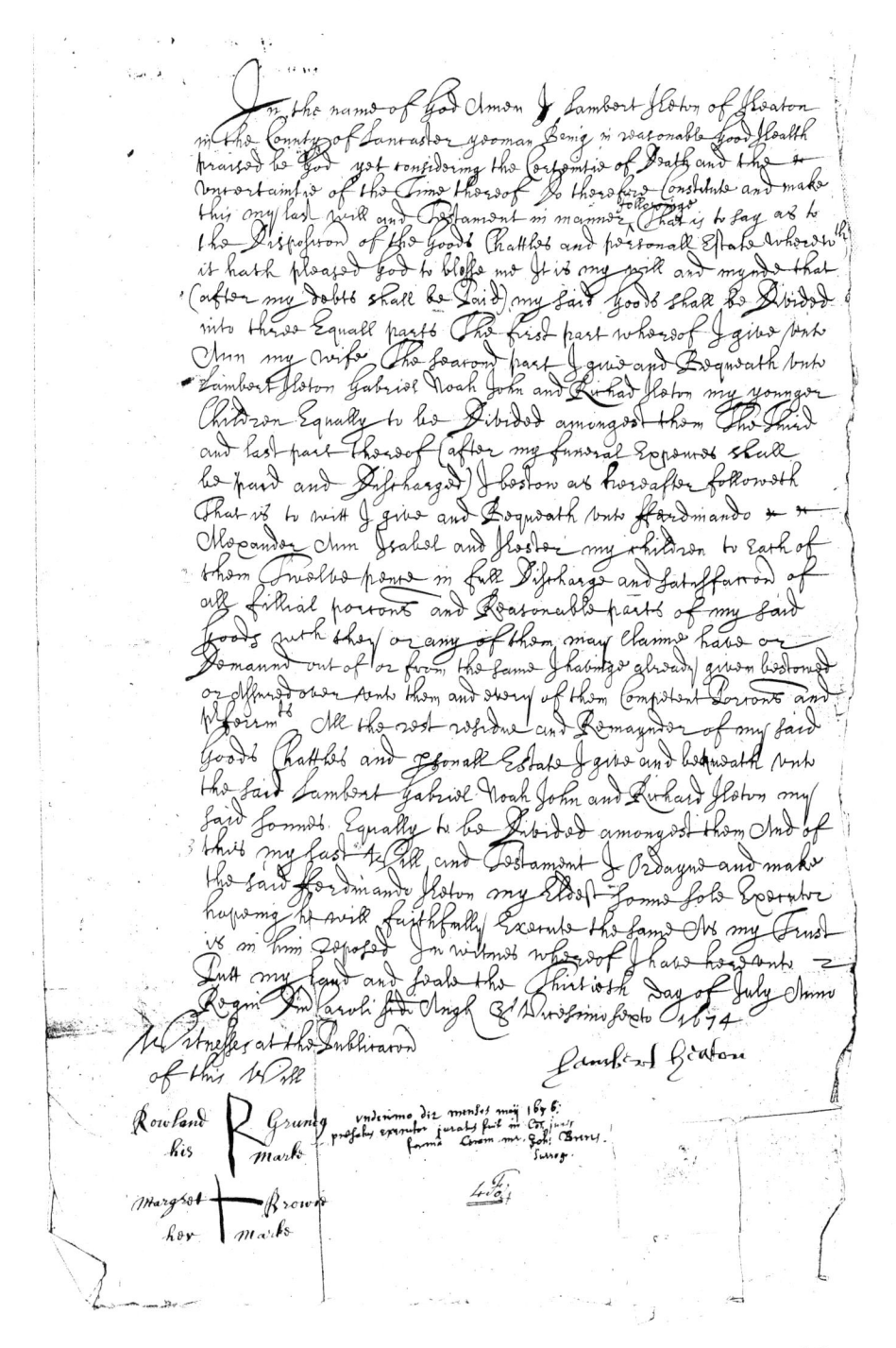

Will of Lambert Heaton, yeoman, 1619-1676. Reproduced by courtesy of County Archivist, Lancashire Record Office, ref. WCW.

June 1663, their marriage licence having been granted at Chester only two days before on 27 June, with James Pilkington of Sharples standing as bondsman.

Alexander, Lambert and Ann's second son, died in 1702 without making a Will and on 10 August of that year Administration was granted in the Bishop's Court at Chester to Martha Heaton of Heaton, spinster, and James Heaton of Heaton, his son. His goods and chattels, valued at 1 July 1702, totalled only £19.13s.2d., a surprisingly small amount in view of his father's opinion, expressed in his Will, that he had given "competent portions" to Alexander and his elder brother Ffardinando. It seems he was not able to amass a more substantial sum from his own farming activities, and may well have lost money.

The children of Alexander and Alice were Anna, born 1664; Martha, 666; Beatrix,1669; James,1672; Margaret,1674; Lambert,1676; and Alexander, 1682. James Heaton married Elizabeth, daughter of James Bradshaw at Bolton Parish Church on 21 March 1701. After they were married they took over Ravenhurst Farm, Heaton on lease, and succeeding generations of Heatons remained tenants of this farm for over 150 years. The story of the Ravenhurst branch of the family, from whom the author is descended, will be told in a later chapter.

The remaining younger children of Lambert appear to have progressed satisfactorily. All married and had several children, male and female. Noah, the fifth son, receives a special mention as occupying a farm known as "Leigh's Land" in Halliwell, in consequence of which he served as Churchwarden for the township at Deane parish church during 1694.[26]

A Successful 17th Century Farmer

Lambert's eldest son Ffardinando, apparently named after his great-grandfather, would seem to have been the most successful member of the family farming in Heaton during the 17th century, notwithstanding that from about 1650 prices had ceased to rise steeply and farmers no longer had the advantage of inflation being in their favour. He had a lease for life of two farms from Sir Charles Anderton. One, known at the time as "Higher House", was later known as Clough Farm, and a later farmhouse of that name still exists near Chorley New Road, Bolton. The other farm, named "Lower House", Partington states, was located where it would now be on the south side of Chorley New Road and to the west of Lostock Junction, Bolton.

The value of Ffardinando's goods and chattels when appraised on 6 December 1704 was a total of £290.0.0d, and it is noticeable that of this amount £172.0.0d was represented by "Bills, Bonds and ready money" so he may also have carried on business as a moneylender. The number of animals and the farm equipment mentioned on the Inventory, including a malt mill, would seem to indicate that these were livestock and arable farms and the inclusion of "two spinnings" tends to show that the family income was supplemented by the production of yarn, although there is no mention of looms for weaving.

Ffardinando bequeathed his interest in the two farms to his eldest son Lambert, and he divided his possessions into the usual three equal parts, giving two parts to be divided equally between his son John and his daughter, Elizabeth. From the third part he gave 5s.0d to his married daughter Ann Ward, 1s.0d to her husband, Ralph, and 1s.0d to their son, Robert. He also gave Lambert "one great garner ark standing in the chamber, one livery table standing in the Parlour, and one great brass pot". All his wearing apparel was divided equally between his sons Lambert and John, and the residue of the third part went to his wife. He appointed Margery, his wife, and Oliver Stones, probably her nephew, to be his executors. The Will was proved at Chester on 16 June 1705.

A Century Closes

By the end of the 17th century the Heaton families in Lancashire had consolidated their positions as farmers and businessmen and, over a period of 100 years, had moved from a state of uncertainty as to the likely nature of their relationship with their new landlords to a situation in which numbers of them had established themselves securely and acquired the trust of their landlords and the respect of their community. They now showed increased confidence in their own ability to continue to provide for their families and conduct their business activities on an increasingly sound and prosperous basis in a competitive situation, without reliance on the monetary inflation and nepotism which had tended to shelter their 16th century ancestors.

Notes and References

1. "Lydiate Hall and its Associations", Rev. T E Gibson, 1876, p.55.
2. " History of Ely" James Bentham, 2nd ed., 1812, pp195/197.
3. Ibid.
4. "Filmer-Seven centuries of a Kent family" John L. Filmer 1975. Research Publishing Co. Ltd.
5. "Crisis of Parliaments" Conrad Russell 1971. OUP. P.199
6. J.L.Filmer op.cit.
7. Harleian Society 1963.
8. "English Yeoman of Tudor & Early Stuart Age", M. Campbell,1960,pub. Merlin Press,London, pp. 55/56.
9. " Lydiate Hall and its Associations" Father T.E. Gibson,1876, p.55.
10. "The Enclosure of Harwood Commons 1797-1801", J.J.Francis, pub.Turton Local History Society 1990, p.8.
11. Papers of J.H.Partington,1903. Bolton Central Library,ref. B920B. HEA. JHP apparently saw this stone at the end of the 19th cent.
12. J.J.Francis,op. cit., pp. 17/18.

13. "Agrarian History of England & Wales", vol V 1640-1750 D. Hey, ed. J.Thirsk 1984, pp.60/61.
14. Ibid., pp. 62-65.
15. " Inflation in Tudor and Stuart England" R.B.Outhwaite, 1969.p.10. Tabulated by A.G.R.Smith in " The Emergence of a Nation State 1529-1660" pub.Longmans 1997,appendix K, p.439.
16. Partington,op.cit. Note 11 to part 2, page 52 refers to all the above.
17. Ibid. part 2,p.72.
18. Ibid.part 2,p.43.
19. In his Will ,Roger further complicated the matter of the Anderton's title to Heaton lands by stating that James Anderton pretended to have obtained title from a Richard Heton living in Ireland and claiming to be Richard, son of Ffernando Heton, whereas that Richard was known to have died of the plague in London 20 years earlier. The Richard in Ireland was probably the second son of William Heton and brother to Ralph the remainderman. The transaction referred to was, in all likelihood, the arrangement whereby the Andertons obtained vacant possession of Birchley Hall on Mary Heton's death in 1594. Roger appears to be obsessed and totally confused.
20. Ibid.part 2,p.45.
21. PRO ref. C3/404/148.
22. Partington, op.cit..Pt.2,note 2a to p.72.
23. Ibid. pt.2,p.73.
24. Shuttleworth Accoounts, pub. by The Chetham Society,pp.13, 21, 33, 34. [JHP]
25. PRO Refs. C21/M17/14 ; C14/m14/14.
26. Hampson's History of Horwich, 1883. [JHP]

Chapter Eight

Towards the Industrial Revolution

Many economists hold to the view that an efficient system of agriculture is a definite prerequisite for the industrialisation of a nation[1]. The slow improvement in agricultural efficiency which took place during the later 17th century was the foundation for the improvement in farming techniques and management which began to gather pace during the following hundred years. Enclosure of former common lands also contributed to a more efficient system of agriculture but the township of Heaton was not subject to any formal Parliamentary enclosure procedures during the 18th or 19th centuries, the land having been divided into smaller, hedged fields, and these amalgamated into individual farms many years earlier, under the system of estate management operated by the Heaton landlords.

Improved Farming Techniques

The initial simple improvements referred to in the previous chapter were only very slowly adopted by the majority of farmers and it was after 1700 before there was any general recognition of the benefits resulting from the use of these methods. Lancashire farmers were amongst the last to introduce clover into their pastures and it was not until about 1720 that this became general[2]. Jethro Tull's invention of the seed drill in 1700 revolutionised the growing of cereals, improving both cultivation and yield as seeds were sown in rows and no longer broadcast, enabling weed control by horse-hoeing to be carried out. Potatoes were being grown in east Lancashire by the early 18th century and proved to be a very profitable crop, much in demand.[3]

The growing of leguminous plants such as peas and beans to fix nitrogen into the soil largely eliminated the need for a period of fallow in the rotation. Although complete drainage of heavy land had to await the introduction of clay drain pipes in the 19th century, nevertheless land was often improved in the 18th century by the use of drainage trenches filled with stone or brushwood. All these methods, coupled with improved seed varieties, served to increase the yields of cereals and other crops.

There were also changes in the nature of livestock production. At the start of the 18th century the tendency was to increase the number of sheep flocks, rearing sheep breeds which were noted for the quality of their wool, with their value for meat and manure being secondary. Later in the century, sheep-farmers preferred to cross ewes from the hill sheep breeds with the Border Leicester rams, bred by Robert Bakewell and his followers, to produce the more prolific half-bred animal which was then crossed again with a Downland ram to give a larger, meatier sheep carrying a good fleece.[4]

Towards the end of the 18th century sheep feeding techniques improved with a greater understanding of the need to ensure that ewes were well-fed before mating to obtain maximum prolificacy, and after lambing to maintain a good supply of milk.[5] Lambs were allowed to grow on to mature sheep, more than 12 months old, and the meat was sold as mutton.

Cattle were reared on the temporary leys and better permanent pasture but even so the grasslands of Lancashire were not sufficiently lush, nor was the winter feed of hay, oats and chopped straw adequate to fully fatten large numbers of animals. Most of the livestock farmers reared calves, which they bought in, up to store quality only and then sold the cattle on to the Midland graziers to finish. Only a small proportion of the Lancashire herds were able to be fattened in the county. It was not until the 19th century that the increase in the urban population justified the cost of finishing numbers of cattle in the county. The later years of the 18th century saw the improvements in profitability which followed the gradual replacement of the original black, longhorn breed of cattle with the Shorthorn and its crosses, a good dual-purpose animal that efficiently converted grass and fodder into meat and milk.[6]

Textiles

All this time the production of textiles by spinners and weavers on the farms continued and agriculture and industry were inseparable in the county. The adoption of the flying shuttle and then the introduction of Hargreaves spinning jenny in the 1760s revolutionised textile manufacture in the home and what had previously been part-time jobs for spinners and weavers became full-time occupations for men, women and children. The incomes and wealth of the yeoman farmers of Heaton and similar districts of Lancashire improved, and they gradually moved into the position where numbers of them found themselves able to use their capital resources and practical knowledge of the textile trade to embark on more ambitious projects involving the construction and equipping of factory buildings, the organisation and training of a larger, specialised workforce, and the marketing of a much larger volume of finished products. Thus the world's first Industrial Revolution was launched on the backs of such men and their contemporaries,[7] who bore the risks and only sometimes reaped the rewards. How some of them fared in these new enterprises we shall see in a later chapter.

New Leases

Shortly after the death of Ffardinando Heaton, Margery his widow, renewed the lease[8] of Lower House farm. The date of the lease was 1 March 1705 and the terms were broadly to the effect that Sir James Anderton of Lostock, Baronet, let to Margery Heaton the messuage and land known as Lower House, being approximately 12 acres "of ye measure there used". There were various measurements of an acre in use in Lancashire and Cheshire and not all corresponded to the present statutory acre of 4840 square yards. Some were up to twice that area, (e.g. a Lancashire acre was the equivalent of 1.86 statute acres). Sir James reserved to himself all the mineral rights, all the timber and all the hunting and fishing rights with all necessary access over the land to enable him to enjoy these. The lessee had the right to dig marl, clay and stone to use on the premises. Margery and her heirs or assignees, to whom she might transfer the lease, were to hold the property on lease for the lives of John and Lambert, her sons, and Robert Ward, her grandson. The rent was to be 14 shillings per annum, payable half-yearly at Christmas and Midsummer at Lostock Hall, plus "four fat hens or 2 shillings in lieu, two fat capons or 2 shillings in lieu" as Sir James might choose. All corn and grain grown was to be ground at the landlord's mills at Heaton or Lostock and not elsewhere. The miller, employed by Sir James, would take a percentage of the grain as a fee. A memorandum on the lease states that Margery took formal possession on 16 May 1707 but in practice she had probably occupied the farm since her husband's death. There was, no doubt, a fine or premium payable for the lease but the amount of this is not stated.

In many respects this would be a standard form of lease in use generally at the time. It is noticeable that the lease does not stipulate the type of farming which is to be carried on or what is to be grown or who is responsible for repairs. The only remedy the landlord seems to have is a right of re-entry or re-possession for nonpayment of rent or for "waste" generally, which probably covers bad husbandry and poor farming practices, resulting in neglect of the land and buildings.

Ann, daughter of Ffardinando and Margery, had married Ralph Ward, yeoman, of Halliwell and Robert was their son. Ralph was parish constable of Halliwell in 1721 and Robert held the same office in 1725 and 1738. Elizabeth, a younger daughter of Ffardinando and Margery, married Robert Marsden, a weaver.

Also on 1 March 1705 Sir James Anderton granted to Lambert Heaton, eldest son of Ffardinando, a lease of Higher House farm, comprising the house, buildings, and 40 acres of land for the lives of Lambert, Martha his wife, and their nephew Robert Ward. The rent is not known but in other respects the terms of the lease would seem to be similar to the one granted to Margery. The fact that the terms are not particularly stringent may well indicate the degree of trust that had arisen between Sir James; his agent, probably Robert Kellett of Lostock who witnessed the leases; and the family of Ffardinando Heaton.

Very Long Leases

Lambert and Martha had seven children of which one died in infancy. The survivors were all baptised at St. Mary's, the Parish Church of Deane: Ferdinando on 6 Feb.1707; Mary, 6 Feb. 1709; Ann, 26 Sep.1712; Lambert, 4 Apr 1714; Elizabeth, 25 Dec 1717; and Martha, 21 Aug 1720. Mary married William Horrocks of Rumworth and Ann married John Eatock of Heaton.

Descendants of Lambert Heton, youngest son of Richard Heton of Heton and Birchley (d.1534).

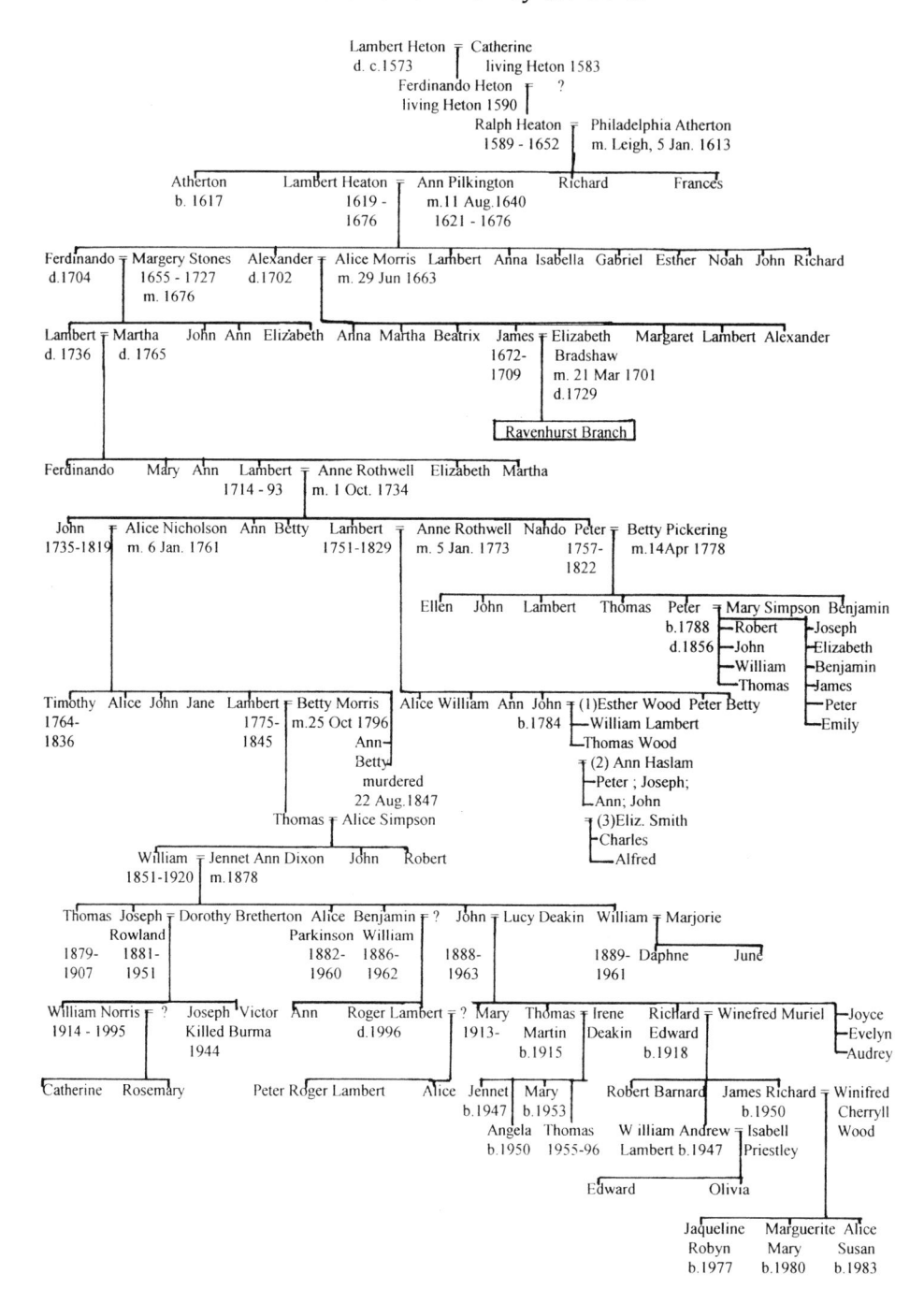

Lambert Heton = Catherine
d. c.1573 | living Heton 1583
Ferdinando Heton = ?
living Heton 1590
Ralph Heaton = Philadelphia Atherton
1589 - 1652 | m. Leigh, 5 Jan. 1613

Atherton | Lambert Heaton = Ann Pilkington | Richard | Frances
b. 1617 | 1619 - 1676 | m.11 Aug.1640
 | | 1621 - 1676

Ferdinando = Margery Stones Alexander = Alice Morris Lambert Anna Isabella Gabriel Esther Noah John Richard
d.1704 | 1655 - 1727   d.1702 | m. 29 Jun 1663
 | m. 1676

Lambert = Martha   John Ann Elizabeth   Anna Martha Beatrix   James = Elizabeth   Margaret Lambert Alexander
d. 1736 | d. 1765   1672- Bradshaw
                                               1709   m. 21 Mar 1701
                                                      d.1729

[Ravenhurst Branch]

Ferdinando   Mary Ann   Lambert = Anne Rothwell   Elizabeth Martha
                    1714 - 93 | m. 1 Oct. 1734

John   = Alice Nicholson Ann Betty   Lambert = Anne Rothwell   Nahdo Peter = Betty Pickering
1735-1819 | m. 6 Jan. 1761   1751-1829 | m. 5 Jan. 1773   1757-   m.14Apr 1778
                                                                     1822

                                  Ellen John Lambert Thomas Peter = Mary Simpson Benjamin
                                                        b.1788 ├─Robert   ├─Joseph
                                                        d.1856 ├─John   ├─Elizabeth
                                                                ├─William   ├─Benjamin
                                                                └─Thomas   ├─James

Timothy Alice John Jane Lambert = Betty Morris   Alice William Ann John = (1)Esther Wood Peter Betty   ├─Peter
1764-   1775- | m.25 Oct 1796   b.1784 ├─William Lambert   └─Emily
1836   1845   Ann   └─Thomas Wood
                                    Betty   = (2) Ann Haslam
                                    murdered   ├─Peter ; Joseph;
                                    22 Aug.1847   └─Ann; John
                           Thomas = Alice Simpson   = (3)Eliz. Smith
                                                                       ├─Charles
                                                                       └─Alfred

          William   = Jennet Ann Dixon   John   Robert
          1851-1920 | m.1878

Thomas Joseph = Dorothy Bretherton Alice Benjamin = ?   John = Lucy Deakin   William = Marjorie
        Rowland   Parkinson William
1879-   1881- 1882-   1886-   1888-   1889- Daphne   June
1907   1951   1960   1962   1963   1961

William Norris = ?   Joseph Victor Ann   Roger Lambert = ? Mary   Thomas = Irene   Richard = Winefred Muriel ├─Joyce
1914 - 1995   Killed Burma   d.1996   1913- Martin   Deakin Edward   ├─Evelyn
                    1944   b.1915   b.1918   └─Audrey

Catherine Rosemary   Peter Roger Lambert   Alice Jennet Mary   Robert Barnard   James Richard = Winifred
                                                            b.1947 b.1953   b.1950 Cherryll
                                                            Angela Thomas   William Andrew = Isabell   Wood
                                                            b.1950 1955-96   Lambert b.1947 Priestley
                                                                        Edward   Olivia

                                                                              Jaqueline Marguerite Alice
                                                                              Robyn   Mary   Susan
                                                                              b.1977   b.1980   b.1983

Lambert Heaton, yeoman, farmed Higher House farm for thirty years at the beginning of the 18th century. Agriculture was in a strong position during this period with mostly good harvests, stable prices, and with gradually improving techniques of husbandry being slowly introduced. On the 27 September 1735 Lambert assigned[9] a moiety or half part of his lease of Higher House farm to his eldest son Ferdinando in consideration of "his natural love and affection" and a payment of £80 by Ferdinando to Lambert. Lambert was to pay "one-half of the rent, boons,etc. and the one half of all lays, taxes, etc. wherewith the whole messuage shall be charged". Apparently in order to pay for this assignment; on 17 November 1735, Ferdinando borrowed £60 from his aunt Elizabeth Marsden, Thomas Stones of Heaton being his guarantor. Lambert Heaton died early in 1736 and on 6 September 1736 Martha, his widow, and Ferdinando, her son, jointly borrowed £20 from Oliver Morris of Heaton.[10]

Lambert made his Will on 8 September 1735, stating that he had already settled the moiety of the property he owned in Heaton (i.e. Higher House farm) on his wife for her life and after her death it was to go jointly to his four daughters. He left small sums of money to his four daughters, all his clothing equally between his sons, Ferdinando and Lambert, and the residue of his personal belongings to his wife. Martha and Ferdinando were appointed executors. The Will was proved at Chester on 24th May 1736 and the inventory attached was valued at £92.15s.1d. by Daniel Foster and Richard Mason on 16 April 1736.

Martha Heaton was buried at Deane on 28 March 1765, probably aged over 80. As she was so extremely long-lived it meant that the leases of Higher House farm ran, in practice, for at least 60 years from 1705.

The Landlord's Problems

It was during Lambert's occupation of Higher House farm that the Anderton family began to experience their worst problems, as related in a previous chapter. From 1715 a period of great uncertainty began and from 1725 the management of their estates was in the hands of a Receiver appointed by the Crown, with the consequences already described. The tenants may have found that the lax management gave them certain advantages but undoubtedly they suffered in other ways by not having a landlord available to spend money in carrying out improvements to the buildings and farmsteads generally.

Ferdinando, eldest son of Lambert, to whom had been assigned half of Higher House or Clough farm, died childless, and it was left to his younger brother, another Lambert Heaton, born 1714, to carry on the line and make a success of the family business. On the 1st October 1734 he married Anne, daughter of Peter Rothwell of Halliwell. Their children were John, baptised at Deane, 20 Jun.1735; Lambert, 10 Apr.1737, (died young); Ann, 23 Mar.1739; Betty, 4 Jul.1744; Lambert, 24 Nov.1751; Nando, 11 Aug 1754; Peter,20 May 1757.

Cattle Disease hits Farmers

It seems that for some years after his marriage Lambert II farmed his mother's half of the Clough by arrangement and possibly his brother's half also. One serious setback which he had to contend with in 1746-8 was a cattle disease which decimated herds throughout the country and which the farmers and commentators of the time termed a "murrain". Throughout England boards were set up to ensure that infected herds were isolated, movement of cattle was restricted, cattle were slaughtered which showed any sign of infection, and carcases were burned or buried immediately. The disease was stamped out after three disastrous years for livestock farmers.

Less Paternalism, More Commercialism

The paternalism which was displayed by Sir James Anderton in his dealings with the family of Ffardinando Heaton at the beginning of the century was less pronounced as the century advanced and a new management took over. However, it must be said that Lambert Heaton II appears to have been fully capable of holding his own in the more commercial atmosphere which began to prevail. He overcame his various problems and became one of the most successful Heaton farmers of the 18th century.

On 4 April 1754, Lambert took an assignment of a lease of Longshaw Ford farm from James Pendlebury of Upholland. The Indenture of Assignment[11] states that James Pendlebury, chapman, held a lease granted by Francis Anderton of Lostock on 21 June 1675 for "a term of lives" which he agrees to assign to Lambert Heaton, yeoman, in consideration of a payment of £70. We do not know how long the lease was likely to run as it had already been in existence for 79 years but it was obviously of some length to justify a payment of such an amount. The rent payable by Lambert Heaton was £10 p.annum as is evidenced by an interesting receipt,[12] worded as follows:-

> " Received the 20th day of June 1754, by order of Robert Blundell Esq., and for his use, or as shall otherwise be ordered by the High Court of Chancery, from Lambert Heaton, Ten pounds, being one year's rent in full for an estate late Pendlebury's and due for the year 1754 - by Richd. Brettargh."

Richard Brettargh was the Blundell family's attorney and land agent. It is noticeable that no entitlement or even the existence of Sir Francis Anderton, found guilty of treason in 1715, is acknowledged, and Robert Blundell is recognised as the heir to the estate, which he was to inherit fully in 1760 when Sir Francis died unmarried.

On the 6 October 1755 Lambert sublet the Longshaw Ford farm of 18 acres to Robert Taylor of Heaton for a term of 3 years at £22 per annum,[13] providing himself with a useful profit of £12 a year, although it is possible he had to carry out some improvements to obtain this higher rent. Short leases at rack rents but with no premium on ingoing, as in this instance, were becoming more common.

On 2 February 1762 a memorandum[14] was entered into between Richard Clayton, Jonathan Case, and Robert Blundell of the one part and Lambert Heaton of the other part to the effect that Lambert was to take the Longshaw Ford farm, estimated at 28 acres, for the term of three years at a yearly rent of £14, clear of all rates and taxes. The memorandum describes the farm in interesting detail as containing a 3-bay house, a 2-bay cottage, a 1-bay stable and a 5-bay barn, a bay being on average about 16ft (4.875m) depth x 12ft (3.65m) width. On this basis a two storey, 3-bay house would be approximately 1150 sq.ft. (107sq.m). The names of the fields are all given and provide some indication of their nature, the use to which they were put, and the form of cultivation they had received, e.g. the Higher Limed, the Lower Limed, the Marled Earth, the Calf Croft, the Rye Croft, the Rough Moor hey, the Kiln Lime hey, the Lower Meadow and others.

This lease was renewed on 2 February 1769 for a further three years at the same rent, and on 12 October 1774 Henry Blundell granted a lease of Longshaw Ford farm to Lambert Heaton for seven years at a rent of £20 per annum, Robert Blundell having died in 1773. A farm with this name still exists to the east of Walker Fold Road, Bolton. Approximately one kilometre to the north-east lies Pendlebury's Farm, very possibly also associated with the James Pendlebury from whom Lambert took the assignment of Longshaw Ford farm.

A Valued Tenant

Two further important transactions are recorded between Lambert Heaton and the Blundell family of Ince Blundell.

On 2 February 1770 he entered into an agreement[15] with Robert Blundell to renew the lease of the whole of the Clough farm. The new lease was for eleven years at a rent of £32 per annum, clear of "all Parliamentary leys and taxes", for 38 acres, "of the large measure there used", implying that it could have been rather more than 38 modern statutory acres. The consideration for the grant of the lease was Lambert's undertaking to erect a new barn on the holding by the following summer, entirely at his own expense except for timber, which presumably was to be cut from the land. Included in the lease was a four-bay dwellinghouse (about 1500sq.ft./143 sq.m.) and ten bays of farm buildings. The fields were all named in the lease and several of the names indicate the nature of the cultivation carried out and have been perpetuated in the names of properties which exist at the present time, e.g. The Garden Orchard, the Barn field, the nearer Water Meadow, the Marled Earth, the Barley croft with the Clough, the Ravenhurst Clough, etc.. Robert Blundell reserved to himself all the rights in minerals, timber and game. Lambert was to get immediate possession of the land, and possession of the house and buildings from 1 May 1770.

The second important agreement[16] which Lambert entered into was in 1780 and was apparently designed to secure the future of his son Lambert junior.

It was an Indenture of Lease made 13 November 1780 between Henry Blundell as landlord and Lambert Heaton senior and Lambert Heaton junior as tenants. It refers to a farm "commonly called by the name of Lambert Heaton's Farm" but it is obvious from the field names quoted that it is, in fact, the Clough farm which is referred to, plus some additional land, since the acreage is now stated to be "50 acres and 14 perches of the measure there used". The Lease was for 7 years from 2 February 1781 for the land and from 1 May 1781 for the house and buildings. In other words it was a 7-year extension of the lease granted in 1770, but including Lambert junior as a tenant so that he could continue in occupation should his father die during the term of the lease. The rent was to be £40 per annum and in addition the tenants were "to maintain and keep in good order and condition one Hound or other Dog and one Gamecock for the use and pleasure of of the said Henry Blundell without receiving any gratuity for the same". Robert Blundell had not bothered to have such a clause as the latter in his leases so it would appear that Henry Blundell took his sporting activities more seriously than his father.

The Game Laws[17]

Clauses such as the above in leases are evidence of the increasing interest in game preservation being taken by the larger landowners. Although there is no indication of any specific disputes, during the 18th and 19th centuries, between the Heaton tenant farmers and their landlords in relation to the enforcement of the Game Laws and the strict preservation of game nevertheless, in common with 90% of country dwellers they no doubt felt resentment and frustration at the sight of a countryside amply stocked with game which they were prevented from legally taking by strict laws, with severe penalties imposed on those who broke them.

In the farmers' case they were doubly offended. Not only were they prevented from taking the occasional pheasant or rabbit for the pot, except with the landowner's specific permission, but they were also forced to watch the depredations by protected birds, deer and rabbits on their crops, and vermin such as foxes on their lambs, chickens, and piglets, without the ability to respond. Large shooting parties, or battues were held to which the sporting landowner would invite a number of guests and these could cause extensive damage to crops and disturbance to livestock.

Game laws had existed since the 14th century, and although initially fairly loosely applied for most species, by the end of the 17th century game preservation had become a much more organised business. Landowners were intent on keeping the taking of game as a monopoly for themselves and their guests and as the majority in Parliament they had the power to do this. An Act passed in 1671 made it illegal for anyone to take game other than an owner of freehold land worth not less than £100 a year or a 99-year leasehold on land worth £150 a year or more. A person thus qualified could take game not only on his own land but elsewhere, irrespective of whether he owned the land or not. The 1671 Act also empowered the lord of the manor to appoint gamekeepers to search for and confiscate guns, nets, and other poaching equipment and to kill dogs in the ownership of unqualified persons. The law operated very harshly and sometimes perfectly harmless pet dogs and those belonging to other gentry were killed on the orders of qualified gentry.

Only hares, partridges, pheasants and grouse were rated as "game"; deer and rabbits were property, owned by the person on whose land they were enclosed. The penalties for stealing "property" were, if anything, more severe than those for poaching game. An Act of 1723 made stealing deer punishable by death and Acts of 1770, 1773, and 1800 increased all the penalties for poaching until armed poaching at night was punishable by 7 years transportation, and for armed resistance to capture the penalty was death. Stealing was also punishable by death or transportation. The penalties for these offences in England and Wales were the severest in Europe. So severe were the penalties that judges and juries were disinclined to find accused persons guilty and many cases were dealt with by magistrates, often qualified landowners, sitting alone without a jury.

An Act of 1755 banned the sale of all game by anyone, even qualified landowners and the only legal way of obtaining it was as a gift from a qualified person. In these circumstances, despite the severe penalties, poaching was rife, either from bravado, poverty, envy or commercial greed. Poaching in gangs was common and fights between poachers and gamekeepers resulted in men being killed on both sides. Poachers had the general sympathy of country dwellers and found a ready market for the game they poached amongst the more affluent members of the community.

Landowners resorted to the use of mantraps and spring guns as deterrents to poachers but these were quite indiscriminate implements and it was not uncommon for quite innocent people to be harmed by them, whilst they do not seem to have been a particularly effective deterrent to poachers. They were not made illegal by Act of Parliament until 1827 after several attempts to do so.

In 1831 the sale of game was permitted on licence and it gradually became more readily available legally, although it was not until late in the 19th century that the severest penalties for poaching were finally repealed.

A Prosperous Yeoman

Lambert Heaton senior survived ten years after he joined with his son, Lambert junior, as tenants of Clough farm with a new lease commencing in 1781. He made his Will on 6 October 1791 and although no Inventory of his goods and chattels survives it is obvious that he was a man of some substance since he owned a number of properties which he passed to his family at his death. Several houses which he owned in Spring Gardens, Bolton were bequeathed to his sons John, Lambert, and Nando and his daughter Betty, and another house in Halliwell which he held on a 999 year lease and which was occupied by his son Peter, he left to him. All the properties were charged with the payment of a 40/- annuity to his wife Anne who was thereby assured of an income of at least £10 per annum, plus her share of the residue of his estate which was to be divided equally amongst his wife and children. Anne, John and Lambert were appointed executors and the Will was proved at Chester on 22 April 1793.

Lambert senior died, aged 79, a highly respected person in the locality, a churchwarden at the Parish Church of Deane for the township of Heaton in 1742, 1745, 1758 and 1760 and a prosperous yeoman farmer.

An Early Industrialist

John Heaton, the eldest son of Lambert and Anne appears to have done very well for himself by obtaining a long lease of Old Hall Farm which probably involved him living with his family in part of the Heaton Old Hall. His lease, which was for a farm of 70 acres "Cheshire measure", ran for many years, and was at a rent of £94 per annum. In addition to his farming activities he conducted a small cotton goods manufacturing business and was also a chapman or merchant. He was churchwarden for Heaton at Deane Parish Church for the years 1777 and 1779. Undoubtedly he was an astute man of business and one of those robust Lancashire yeoman farmers who, by combining their farming and manufacturing skills, paved the way for the start of the Industrial Revolution, which their capital and practical expertise were to launch a few years later as one of the first steps in making Britain the manufacturing centre of the world. His enterprise in building his first cotton mill at Picton Street, Doffcocker and the involvement of his son Lambert in this business is described in a later chapter.

Portrait of John Heaton, 1735-1819. Farmer and early industrialist. Builder of Picton Street Mill, Doffcocker. (Reproduced by courtesy of Bolton Local Studies Dept.)

On 6 January 1761 he had married Alice Nicholson at Deane Parish Church. Their children were Lambert who was baptised on 22

Nov.1761 but who died 8 years later; Timothy, baptised 5 Feb.1764; John, 27 Jul.1766 but who died in 1767; Alice; John, 10 Jun 1769; Jane, 12 Sep.1772; Lambert, 23 Sep.1775; Ann, 22 Dec.1776; Betty, 22 Jun.1783.

John died on 17 February 1819 and his Will, made on 25 August 1818 shows him to have been a quite considerable property-owner. He owned a factory and adjoining land in Halliwell, one-half of which he bequeathed to his son Timothy and the other half to his youngest daughter, Betty Pilkington, together with a house in Spring Gardens, Bolton. His other children and grandchildren also received various houses in Heaton and in Spring Gardens. A house in Spring Gardens went to Timothy; to the children of his late daughter Jane Baker he gave a house in Spring Gardens plus the house in Heaton in which he lived himself; to John a house in Heaton and one in Spring Gardens plus a "building formerly used as a stable"; to Lambert a house in Heaton and one in Spring Gardens, subject to Lambert repaying to Timothy the £25 he owed him, otherwise the executors could sell part of his legacy to repay the debt. To his daughter Alice Hodgkinson he gave two houses in Heaton with a house in Spring Gardens and the house at the back of the stable building above. However as Alice's houses were better than the others she was made responsible for paying the chief rent of 19s. p.a. due to Henry Blundell Esq. in perpetuity. Finally he bequeathed to his daughter Ann Pendlebury two houses in Heaton and a house in Spring Gardens. His son Timothy and John Longworth, farmer of Heaton, were appointed executors.

Timothy, son of John and Alice, a weaver by occupation, remained unmarried and lived in his own house at Delph Hill in Halliwell. He died on 26 April 1836 and in his Will he directed that his properties in Halliwell and Great Bolton and his personal effects should be sold and the net proceeds divided equally amongst his brothers and sisters.

John, second surviving son of John and Alice, was a weaver and shopkeeper, living in Heaton. He married twice, firstly to Ann Lee on 30 November 1790, by whom he had Alice and Richard. His second wife was Esther Morris, whom he married on 9 September 1795 and their children were John, Timothy, Betty, and Esther. In 1803, John junior and his father were assessed for Poor Rate in Heaton at £19.12s.6d in respect of "a factory and other premises" and "a cottage and spinning room". It would seem, then, that John and his father were in partnership together in a cotton spinning business, but not at the Picton Street mill, which by that time was being worked by John's younger brother Lambert.

Lambert was the youngest son of John and Alice and he married Betty Morris at Deane Church on 25 October 1796. Their children were Alice, Maria, John, Mary Ann, William, Jane, Thomas, Sarah and Ann. His business ventures were many and varied and not always successful. The enterprises with which he became involved are described later.

Lambert and Betty's son Thomas succeeded his mother in the occupation of Hodgkinson's farm in Heaton where he stayed until 1858 when he moved to

126 Towards the Industrial Revolution

Late Eighteenth Century Haymaking. Courtesy of National Library of Wales.

Townley's farm in Farnworth where he built up a successful dairy business and was able to buy the freehold. He married Alice, daughter of William Simpson of Halliwell by whom he had three sons, William, John and Robert. On his retirement he relinquished occupation of the farm to his son John.

William and John, sons of Lambert and Betty, married two sisters, Janet (Jennet) Ann and Rose, daughters of John Dixon of Old Hall Farm, Heaton. William had a great future before him after he joined his cousins Thomas and Joseph Rowland Heaton, sons of Peter Heaton of Delph Hill Mill, in a cotton manufacturing enterprise. The story of their success is related in a later chapter.

An Important New Road

We have seen how Lambert senior tried to ensure that his second son Lambert junior would have some security after his death by joining him in the tenancy of the Clough farm, jointly with himself. In this he was successful and Lambert junior occupied Clough farm for 35 years after his father died. He married Ann, daughter of Thomas Rothwell of Halliwell on 5 January 1773 at Deane church and their children were John, baptised 25 Dec.1773 but who died young; Alice, baptised 21 Sep.1776; William, 3 Jan.1779; Ann, 19 Jun.1781; John, 23 Jan. 1784; Peter, 1 Apr. 1787; Betty, 14 Nov. 1790.

Lambert was churchwarden for Heaton at Deane Parish Church in 1825 and 1826 and appears to have been a successful farmer. He quit his farm in 1828 and towards the end of his tenancy the first of the developments took place which were, during the 19th century, to transform the township of Heaton from a purely rural location into a largely builtup area. Mr Henry Tempest, who had just inherited the estate from his father, decided to speculate on the construction of a new turnpike road, in collaboration with other landowners, who presumably all anticipated that the opening up of an area of their land for development by this new road would result, in due course, in a considerable increase in its value plus the tolls from the turnpike road.

The following advertisement appeared in a local newspaper on 4 September 1824:-

> "To Road Makers. To be let by ticket at the house of Reubon Gorton, the Whitster's Arms, Little Bolton, on Thursday , the 23rd September, the fencing off, forming, paving, stoning, and sanding a new length of road leading from Bolton to Chorley, beginning at the Whitster's Arms afsd. and ending at Anderton Ford Bridge, Horwich, in length about 5 1/2 miles, of new road to be formed, in breadth about 20 yards.Mr Pickering of Halliwell, surveyor of the said road, will show the plans.
> - John Albinson, Clerk to the said Road."

The new road, to be known as Chorley New Road, passed virtually through the middle of Clough farm and whereas nowadays a farmer in this situation would receive compensation for disturbance and severance, the unfortunate

Lambert probably received nothing more than a proportionate reduction in the amount of his rent for the land which had been taken from him.

Around 1828 Lambert Heaton retired and went to live at "The Hill", Halliwell where he died on 2 June 1829, aged 77, and his widow Ann died on 7 September in the same year, aged 82 years. Lambert left no Will and Administration was granted to Richard Smith in 1829.

William, eldest surviving son of Lambert and Ann, farmed at Woodside farm, Heaton all his life. He married Sarah, sister of Richard Smith his father's Administrator and they had two children, Peter and Mary.

John, William's younger brother, was married three times. His first wife, Esther Wood, he married in 1806, when he was serving as a lieutenant in the militia, and they had two surviving sons, William Lambert (1808-1835) and Thomas Wood (1809-1886). By his second wife, Ann Haslam, he had Peter (1813-1832), Joseph (1815-1834), Ann (1817-1843), John (1819-1870). His third wife was Elizabeth Smith and their children who survived to adulthood were Charles (b.1829) and Alfred (1837-1874). Thomas Wood and his half-brother John went into partnership as millowners and their story is recounted in a later chapter. Charles and Alfred eventually took over a business which their father started and this too is described later.

Nando, fourth surviving son of Lambert senior and Anne married Rebecca Horrox on 24 December 1776. Their surviving children were Mary, Lambert, William, John, and Alice. This family were farmers and weavers in Heaton. Nando was buried at Deane on 28 November 1816 and his widow on 18 January 1836. Lambert, the eldest son, married firstly Mary, daughter of James Heaton of Ravenhurst. She died aged 26 and he then married his first cousin Betty, youngest daughter of Lambert and Ann Heaton, and widow of John Horrocks. They occupied Adises farm, Middle Hulton, where he died on 11 March 1864, aged 81 and she died 26 February 1875, aged 84 years. The other two sons William and John both became weavers.

Peter, youngest son of Lambert senior and Anne, married Betty Pickering, daughter of Oliver Pickering of Lostock Hall farm on 14 April 1778. Their children were Ellen, John, Lambert, Thomas, Peter, and Benjamin. Peter junior, baptised 13 March 1788, was destined for much bigger things as the founder of a business which went on to become the most successful Heaton cotton enterprise, and which claimed eventually to be the largest private cotton-spinning company in the United Kingdom. His story is related in the later chapter on "Trade & Industry".

Murder !

In a family which can be traced back over 28 generations and shown to be as numerous as the Heatons, it would, perhaps, be surprising if one or two members did not suffer a violent end. It is ironic, however, in the case about which we know most, that the victim should be an innocent, elderly, female member of the family, living in supposedly quieter times in the 19th century

Betty, youngest daughter of John and Alice Heaton was born in 1783 and married Robert Pilkington. When her uncle Peter died in 1822, she and her husband moved to live on Pool Fold farm which Peter had occupied and which his son Peter junior then took over. It was reported[18] that her husband's conduct towards her became increasingly violent culminating in a very violent assault in July 1835. She then took out a summons against him and in order to avoid a prison sentence he agreed to live apart from her and not molest her in any way. He also conveyed to trustees for her sole use the property which her father had left to her and which had come under his control. It is said that his lifestyle deteriorated to the extent that he was sleeping in barns and only working as and when absolutely necessary.

Betty lived at Pool Fold farm with her son John Pilkington until 1842 when they left and went to live at Longshaw Fold farm with her son, William Pilkington. John seems to have been of a somewhat similar temperament to his father for in March 1847 he was sentenced to 9 months imprisonment for a savage assault upon William Kershaw at the Doffcocker Inn.

According to the evidence of witnesses, whilst John was away in prison, on 22 August 1847, Robert Pilkington came to the farm about 7.00 a.m. and asked to be allowed to come in and light his pipe at the fire. William, his son, admitted him and when his pipe was alight, the farm servant, Bridget Dean, asked him to leave but he refused and sat down by the fire. William and Bridget were about to go out to make milk deliveries to their customers and rather than leave old Betty Pilkington alone with her husband they took her with them. When they returned about 9.00 a.m. a minor remark made by Betty apparently annoyed her husband who jumped up, seized a poker, and hit her twice on the head with it. She fell to the floor and he was about to hit her again when Bridget Dean caught the poker and tried to wrest it from him but he then hit her with it. Betty did not utter another word and died shortly afterwards. She was 64 years of age.

During all the commotion the murderer had fled but he was soon apprehended and was brought before the justices at Bolton the next day, 23 August, when he was committed to stand trial at the Assizes on a charge of murdering his wife. At the Assize Court on 16 December 1847 Bridget Dean and William Pilkington gave evidence of what had occurred. Counsel for the accused tried to persuade the jury that his client's violent behaviour was caused by a series of accidents which had befallen him since 1830, and that he was not responsible for his actions, but after only a ten-minute retirement the jury returned a verdict of "Guilty". The judge passed sentence of death but the Home Secretary subsequently commuted the sentence to one of imprisonment for life.

Entrepreneurial Cousins

As the Industrial Revolution is born we see the majority of the Heatons still earning their living from the land and small-scale cotton manufacturing businesses, but a number of them showing greater ambition and prepared to accept the risks of embarking on various larger-scale enterprises. We have the initiator John Heaton, builder of Picton St. Mill and his son Lambert; Peter Heaton of Delph Hill Mill and his sons, Thomas and Joseph; Thomas, brother of Peter, an engineering inventor; millowners John and Thomas Wood Heaton, halfbrothers and partners; their millowning father, John, and his other two sons Charles and Alfred who succeeded him in his business; and William Heaton, great-grandson of John of Picton St. Mill, and eventually to go into business with Thomas and Joseph in a most successful cotton spinning enterprise.

The next chapter tells the story of the Ravenhurst branch of the family and there also are to be found those who sought a future in trade and industry, some successfully but others the reverse.

Notes and References

[1] "The First Industrial Revolution", Phyllis Deane, 2nd ed.1998. Cambridge UP. P.37.
[2] "Farmers of Old England", E.Kerridge 1973, pub.Allen & Unwin, p.124.
[3] "Agrarian History of England & Wales", vol.V. I, p.64.
[4] Ibid, vol.V1, p. 42.
[5] Ibid, vol.VI, p. 332.
[6] Ibid, vol.VI, p. 342.
[7] Ibid, vol. V. I, p. 84.
[8] J H Partington. Papers at Bolton Central Library ref. B920B.HEA, ptII, pp. 82/83.
[9] Ibid.PtII, notes to page 84.
[10] Ibid.
[11] Ibid. PtII, p.92.
[12] Ibid.
[13] Ibid.
[14] Ibid. PtII, p.93.
[15] Ibid.Pt. II, p.94.
[16] Ibid. notes preceding p.95.
[17] "Riot, Risings & Revolution", Ian Gilmour, 1992, p. 193 et seq. "Agrarian History of England & Wales" vol. VI, pp 830, 924. "Gentleman & Poachers" P.B.Munsche, 1981, Camb.UP, p.134 et seq.
[18] Partington, op.cit.. Notes to Pt.2, p.99.

Chapter Nine

The Ravenhurst Branch

The solid, stonebuilt, farmhouse of Ravenhurst (now renamed Raven House) still exists, although in a much altered state, fronting on to The Lane, immediately south of Chorley New Road, Bolton, in what is now a largely built-up area. This farm, of at least 20 customary Cheshire acres initially and probably rather more modern statutory acres, was occupied by various members of the Heaton family for over 150 years from 1701 to 1859.

The first Heaton occupier of Ravenhurst was James, son of Alexander and Alice Heaton. He was born in 1672 and on 21 March 1701 he married Elizabeth Bradshaw at Bolton Parish Church. Immediately after his marriage he took over Ravenhurst farm on a lease from Sir Charles Anderton's trustees. Unfortunately he lived only 8 years after his marriage and died and was buried at Deane Parish Church on 6th February 1709, aged only 37. His children by Elizabeth were Alice, born 1702; John, 1704; Ann, 1707; and Betty, who died young. He left no Will and Administration was granted at the Bishop's Court at Chester to his widow and James Pendlebury of Heaton. The total value of his farm goods and chattels was £37.18s.10d.

His widow Elizabeth stayed on at Ravenhurst for another 20 years, managed the farm, and raised her children. On her death in 1729 Administration of her effects was granted to her son, John Heaton, and George Bradshaw, a member of her family, for the benefit of her two married daughters, Ann and Alice. Ann married Robert Kay of Aspull and Alice married James Ormrod of Harwood and became the ancestress of a notable family of Bolton cotton spinners. Elizabeth must have managed Ravenhurst farm competently, for the value of the goods at the farm had increased at her death to £82.17s.9d, substantially more than the figure 20 years earlier.

Union with the Ryleys

On 6 August 1728 John Heaton, son of James and Elizabeth, married Elizabeth Ryley, daughter of Edmund Ryley, yeoman, of Heaton and Lostock, granddaughter of Edmund Ryley, and sister to Edmund Ryley of Heaton and Rumworth. She was descended from a long line of yeoman farmers; many of them named Edmund, generation after generation. She undoubtedly introduced the christian name Edmund into the Heaton family as a change from the numerous Lamberts, James, and Johns. After her a large number of male members of the family were either given or adopted the name Edmund, as were the author, his father and grandfather.

After his marriage John took a farm at Rumworth, on a tenancy from Mr Nathaniel Nuttall of Hungerhill, but when his mother died in 1729 he moved to Ravenhurst and shortly afterwards he renewed the lease for a term of three lives plus 21 years (generally reckoned as likely to run for 42 years). On the strength of this new lease he carried out extensive building work at the farm, where he stayed until 1750. He and his wife Elizabeth had seven children; James, born 1730; Elizabeth, 1733; George, 1736; John, 1738; Edmund, 1740; Rachel; and Ann. Rachel appears to have died young. When James married in 1750 his father gave up possession of the farm to him and moved with his wife to Wigan where he was living in 1760. When he died in 1766 he was living in a house in Deansgate, Bolton. After he moved from Ravenhurst it is obvious that he kept himself busy and prospered, as is indicated by the various properties and investments which he mentions in his Will.

A Diversity of Interests

John Heaton's Will was dated 2 May 1765, and in it he made generous provision for his youngest daughter Ann, who appears to have been something of a favourite of his or perhaps he felt the other members of his family were already well provided for. He left her a tenement at Heigh, probably an area of farmland let to a tenant, and two tenanted houses, to be hers when she reached 21, and until then she was to have £20 to be raised from the tenement. A few years later Ann married John Rudge a grocer of Bradshawgate, Bolton, and a member of a prosperous family.

John Heaton's daughter Elizabeth had married John Dearden and he bequeathed to her, for life, the house in Bradshawgate in which he himself lived. After her death the house was to pass to John Dearden, her son.

George, the second son, received two tenanted houses, one newly erected, together with " the little house nearby". He was also to inherit a pew at Blackrod church "while his lease at Brincup continues" and after his lease expired the pew was to go to the children of third son John for ever. John himself was to receive two tenanted houses and fourth son Edmund received one tenanted house. Sums of money were given to various grandchildren and cousins. All John senior's children except James were required to pay their mother Betty 20/- a year each, thereby ensuring her an income of at least £5 per annum.

A final interesting reference in John Heaton's Will is to four pairs of looms which he owns and which are out to various people on hire at a charge of 4/- per pair a year. John junior was to receive two pairs and use the proceeds of one pair to buy books or pay for the schooling for some of the poor of Heaton. The other pairs were to go to Edmund and Noah, a cousin of the deceased, the latter being required to give the 4/- p.a. to "the preacher at the Methodist building in the Acres". It is very possible that not only did John hire out the looms but he also supplied the cotton yarn and bought the goods manufactured on them for resale, in much the same way as knitting machines are hired out to outworkers and their knitted garments bought back, in modern times.

The Ravenhurst Branch of the Heaton Family.

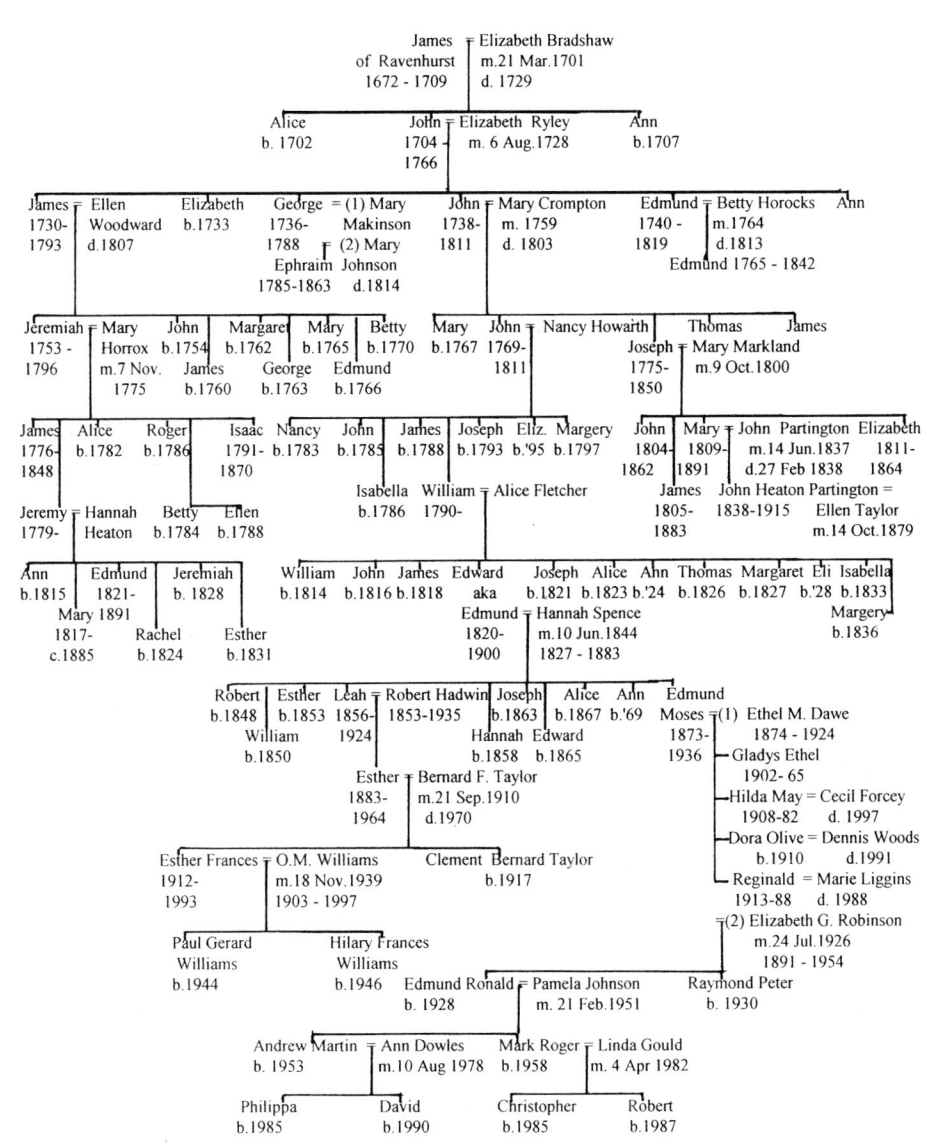

```
                              James    = Elizabeth Bradshaw
                              of Ravenhurst  m.21 Mar.1701
                              1672 - 1709    d. 1729
                    ┌──────────────┼──────────────┐
                  Alice         John = Elizabeth Ryley      Ann
                  b. 1702       1704 -  m. 6 Aug.1728       b.1707
                                1766
  ┌────────┬────────┬──────────┬──────────────┬────────────────┬──────────────┐
James = Ellen   Elizabeth  George  = (1) Mary     John = Mary Crompton   Edmund = Betty Horocks   Ann
1730-   Woodward b.1733    1736-     Makinson    1738-   m. 1759         1740 -   m.1764
1793    d.1807             1788    ┌ (2) Mary    1811    d. 1803         1819     d.1813
                                     Ephraim  Johnson                          Edmund 1765 - 1842
                                     1785-1863  d.1814
┌────────┬───────┬─────────┬─────────┬────────┬──────────┬────────────────┬─────────────┐
Jeremiah = Mary  John    Margaret  Mary   Betty   Mary   John = Nancy Howarth    Thomas         James
1753 -    Horrox b.1754  b.1762    b.1765 b.1770  b.1767 1769-               Joseph = Mary Markland
1796      m.7 Nov.  James          George  Edmund          1811              1775-    m.9 Oct.1800
          1775     b.1760         b.1763  b.1766                             1850
┌───────┬──────┬──────┬──────┬──────┬──────┬──────┬──────┬──────┐    ┌──────┬──────────────┬────────┐
James   Alice  Roger  Isaac  Nancy  John   James  Joseph Eliz. Margery   John   Mary = John Partington Elizabeth
1776-   b.1782 b.1786 1791-  b.1783 b.1785 b.1788 b.1793 b.'95 b.1797    1804-  1809-  m.14 Jun.1837   1811-
1848                   1870                                              1862   1891   d.27 Feb 1838   1864
┌──────┬──────┬──────┐         Isabella  William = Alice Fletcher            James   John Heaton Partington =
Jeremy = Hannah Betty  Ellen   b.1786    1790-                               1805-   1838-1915   Ellen Taylor
1779-    Heaton b.1784 b.1788                                                1883                m.14 Oct.1879
┌──────┬─────────┬────────┐   ┌──────┬──────┬──────┐     ┌──────┬──────┬─────┬──────┬──────────┬─────┬────────┐
Ann    Edmund    Jeremiah    William John  James  Edward  Joseph Alice  Ann  Thomas Margaret   Eli   Isabella
b.1815 1821-     b. 1828     b.1814 b.1816 b.1818  aka    b.1821 b.1823 b.'24 b.1826 b.1827    b.'28 b.1833
       Mary 1891                                  Edmund =Hannah Spence                                Margery
       1817-    Rachel   Esther                   1820-   m.10 Jun.1844                                b.1836
       c.1885   b.1824   b.1831                   1900    1827 - 1883
              ┌──────┬───────┬──────┬─────────────┬──────┬──────┬──────┬──────┐
            Robert  Esther  Leah = Robert Hadwin Joseph Alice  Ann   Edmund
            b.1848  b.1853  1856-  1853-1935     b.1863 b.1867 b.'69 Moses =(1) Ethel M. Dawe
                    William  1924  Hannah  Edward                    1873-     1874 - 1924
                    b.1850          b.1858 b.1865                    1936    ├ Gladys Ethel
                           Esther = Bernard F. Taylor                         1902- 65
                           1883-    m.21 Sep.1910                            ├ Hilda May = Cecil Forcey
                           1964     d.1970                                    1908-82    d. 1997
                                                                             ├ Dora Olive = Dennis Woods
         Esther Frances = O.M. Williams      Clement Bernard Taylor            b.1910      d.1991
         1912-            m.18 Nov.1939      b.1917                          └ Reginald = Marie Liggins
         1993             1903 - 1997                                          1913-88    d. 1988
              Paul Gerard       Hilary Frances                              =(2) Elizabeth G. Robinson
              Williams          Williams                                       m.24 Jul.1926
              b.1944            b.1946   Edmund Ronald = Pamela Johnson        1891 - 1954
                                         b. 1928        m. 21 Feb.1951      Raymond Peter
                                                                            b. 1930
                           Andrew Martin = Ann Dowles    Mark Roger = Linda Gould
                           b. 1953         m.10 Aug 1978 b.1958       m. 4 Apr 1982
                                  Philippa        David       Christopher    Robert
                                  b.1985          b.1990      b.1985         b.1987
```

During his lifetime John Heaton senior had made provision for his children in various ways and we will consider these later. For the moment we will stay with the occupiers of Ravenhurst.

Further Generations at Ravenhurst

James, the eldest son, is not mentioned in the Will but he had taken over the lease of the Ravenhurst farm in 1750. He married Ellen Woodward and by her had twelve children, although only eight survived to become adults. All were baptised at Deane parish church. Jeremiah was baptised 11 Jan.1753; John, 8 Sept.1754; Betty, 25 Jan.1756 (died young); Margery, 16 Jun.1757 (died young); James, 6 Dec.1760; Margaret, 26 Jun.1762; George,19 Dec.1763; Mary 10 Mar.1765; Edmund, 13 Feb.1766; William, 1 May 1768 (died young); and Betty and Rachel, twins baptised on 24 Mar. 1770, but only Betty survived.

James Heaton occupied Ravenhurst for 43 years, dying in 1793, aged 63. In addition to Ravenhurst he was also able to lease Dobhill farm from Henry Blundell Esq. increasing his acreage to over 40 customary acres, anything up to 80 statutory acres, so evidently his farming activities were successful and his relations with his landlord and the landlord's agent were good. He spent money on the house and buildings at Ravenhurst and there is a plaque in the gable wall of the house with the date 1759, a heart, and the initials J E H of James and Ellen Heaton indicating, presumably, a loving marriage, and the date that alterations were carried out to this part of the house.

He can be seen as a typical yeoman farmer of the period, concentrating on improving his breeding of sheep and cattle and his yields of cereal crops, attending the recently introduced agricultural fairs, agricultural society meetings and markets to learn what his neighbours were doing, what new techniques were being introduced and what the more innovative landlords and their agents in the district were recommending. Regrettably, these good years were to be followed by a period during which a number of disappointments and unfortunate occurrences for the family took place.

In 1775 James and Ellen's eldest son Jeremiah, took over the lease of Dobhill farm on his marriage to Mary Horrox at Deane Parish Church on 7th November of that year. They had 8 children of which 7 survived to adulthood, these being James, born 1776; Jeremy, 1779; Alice, 1782; Betty, 1784; Roger 1786; Ellen, 1788 and Isaac, born 1791.

James Heaton died and was buried at Deane on 3 October 1793. In his Will dated 5 September 1793 he directs that his son Jeremiah shall inherit Ravenhurst farm but that he must allow his mother to live in "the house at the east end" for which she is to pay a rent of two guineas a year. She can occupy this accommodation for the remainder of the lease if she lives that long. James also directs that all his farming stock and household goods, except any pieces which his wife wants for herself, shall be sold and the proceeds invested, the interest therefrom being paid to his wiife for life. After she dies the principal sum is to divided amongst all his children equally. Ellen herself died and was buried on 15 April 1807.

We do not know the circumstances of James and Ellen's other children but presumably he regarded them as well provided for as he made little mention of them in his Will. The provisons he made might have worked out well for everyone but unfortunately Jeremiah lived only three years after he inherited, dying on 16 June 1796. At the time his eldest two sons were 20 and 17 years old respectively. The terms of the lease of Ravenhurst are not known, but if Jeremiah's death caused it to terminate then a fine or premium would no doubt have had to be found to effect a renewal for a further term.

After Jeremiah's death his widow Mary carried on working the farm herself with the help of her sons. Her eldest son, James, was joined with her in the lease and never married. She lived another 36 years, being buried at Deane on 16 March 1832. After her death James appears to have given up occupation of the farm to his youngest brother, Isaac, who had taken possession by 1840. James died and was buried at Deane on 13 July 1848, aged 71.

A Tragic Mistake

Isaac Heaton never married and lived at Ravenhurst with his housekeeper, Elizabeth Hulme, and a farm servant and labourer, Ralph Markland. By this time the farm appears to have expanded to 44 acres. As he grew older Isaac wished to make arrangements for a comfortable old age and his solution was to come to an arrangement whereby the lease was assigned to Ralph Markland, who was to marry Elizabeth Hulme, and they were to be responsible for looking after him and providing him with food and shelter at Ravenhurst for the rest of his life. He also transferred the farm stock and household furniture to them, as apparently they had nothing of their own. His reason for doing this was apparently because he distrusted his own family and wished to ensure that none of them got their hands on his possessions after his death.[1]

This arrangement, whereby Isaac deprived himself of everything he possessed, was put into effect in 1853 when Elizabeth and Ralph were both 23 and Isaac was 62 years of age, and it turned out to be a grave mistake. Ralph Markland apparently proved incapable of running the farm himself, ran up debts, neglected the farm and failed to pay the rent. Within five years Markland was in a hopeless position and the landlord took steps to evict all the occupiers and repossess the farm. This probably happened about 1858/9 as Markland is recorded in the Poor Rate Books for Heaton as tenant in 1857 whereas in the census of 1861 the tenant was a man named Alexander Pate. Isaac seems likely to have spent his remaining years in poverty and died in 1870 aged 79 in Bolton.

Other Sons of Ravenhurst

We have seen what provision John of Ravenhurst made for his various children when he died in 1766, and that his eldest son James had taken over the farm in 1750. George, his second son, lived until 1760 on a farm in Heaton, when he moved to a farm at Brinsop, Westhoughton, where he lived the rest of his life. He married twice; firstly to Mary Makinson, but they had no children and after she died he married Mary Johnson at Deane on 23 Oct 1774. They had three children who did not reach adulthood and then a son Ephraim who survived them. George died 1 Dec 1788 and Ephraim took over the farm. Mary died 3 Feb 1814. Ephraim was buried at Horwich Church on 6 Aug.1863 aged 78, and his wife followed him on 21 Oct.1863 aged 73.

John, the third son of John and Elizabeth of Ravenhurst, was apprenticed to a Mr Plumbe of Wigan to learn the trade of weaving and manufacturing cloth. However in 1759 he was fortunate enough to marry Mary Crompton, only child of James Crompton of Bolton and heiress of her greatgrandfather, Joseph Crompton.. On his marriage his father broke the entail by a common recovery on a small estate which he owned at Blackrod, enabling him to transfer to this younger son, this property which otherwise would have had to go to his eldest son. The estate is described as four dwelling houses together with land of about four acres and a pew in the gallery of Blackrod chapel.[2] This process was completed on 23 Aug. 1759 and shortly afterwards John and his new wife moved into one of the houses at Blackrod where he carried on the business of a small manufacturer of textile products and a chapman or merchant.

Deane Moorside Farm

This continued until 1769 when John leased 12 acres of land (Cheshire measure) in Over Hulton from William Hulton Esq. for a term of three lives plus 21 years. On this land he built a farmhouse, barn, shippons for 12 cows, plus further outbuildings, and moved into this farmstead, which was given the name Deane Moorside, in 1771. John leased his estate in Blackrod on 1 March 1771 to three members of the Prescott family; William of Abram, weaver, James, weaver and John, victualler, both of Blackrod, for eleven years at a rent of £14.13.6d. per annum.[3]

John and Mary had two children born at Blackrod; Mary born 1767 and John born 1769. Children born at Deane Moorside were James, born 1771 (who died young), Elizabeth, born 1773 (who also died young), Thomas, Joseph, born 1775, and James, born 1778. John senior continued to work the farm and carry on his other businesses until his son Joseph married in 1800 when he let the farm to him and moved, with his wife Mary, to live in Bradshawgate, Bolton. Mary died there and was buried at Deane on 14 June 1803, when John moved back to Deane Moorside, where he lived until his death in 1811 when he was buried with his wife at Deane on 4 June. With the exception of Joseph, the sons of John and Mary all went into trade or industry and their exploits are described in the next chapter.

Joseph, fourth son of John and Mary, was initially apprenticed as a weaver but when he married Mary Markland of Snydle Hall, Westhoughton on 9 Oct.1800 his father let him into occupation of Deane Moorside farm. Joseph and Mary had several children who died young and only John, born 1804,

James, born 1805, Mary, born 1809, and Elizabeth, born 1811, survived to adulthood. Joseph lived all his life on the farm where he was born, as did his sons who never married. Joseph was Overseer of the Poor and Relieving Officer for Over Hulton in 1801/2 and his son James occupied the same posts from 1856-70 and was Churchwarden for Over Hulton from 1867 to 1877. His sons took over the running of the farm from him when he became ill in 1845 and he died on 19 July 1850, aged 75. John died and was buried on 5 Oct.1862 and James on 30 Apr.1883. This Heaton family had occupied Deane Moorside farm for 114 years, from when they built it in 1769 to 1883.

Joseph and Mary's daughter Elizabeth married John Stanning on 22 Apr.1835. She died on 3 May 1864. Her husband, after rising to the position of manager, in 1865 was taken into partnership at Halliwell Bleach Works by Col. R H Ainsworth. In 1871 the partnership was dissolved and Stanning senior left, with his son John, to establish his own business at Leyland Bleach Works. John junior succeeded his father at Leyland and later became Joint General Manager of the Bleachers Association on its formation in 1900.[4]

The Family Historian

The other daughter, Mary, married John Partington of Middle Hulton on 14 June 1837. Tragically, he died on 27 February the following year and their son John Heaton Partington was born posthumously later that year. Mary lived with her brothers, James and John, at Deane Moorside farm for over 40 years. She died 18 June 1891, aged 82 years.

John, her son, also lived at Deane Moorside for many years until in 1879 he took a tenancy of Yew Tree Farm, Over Hulton and on 14 October 1879, at the age of 40, he married Ellen Taylor, a 41 year-old spinster of Chiphill Farm, Rumworth. They had no children. He became the historian of the Heaton family, encouraged and backed financially by William Heaton of Lostock, and carrying out a great deal of research towards the end of the century. He deposited the bulk of his papers and notebooks at Bolton Central Library in 1903, when he was living at Bridgewater Place, Middle Hulton. He died in 1915.

A Fortunate Batchelor

Edmund Heaton, fourth and youngest son of John and Elizabeth of Ravenhurst went into the business of a tanner at Wigan. He married Elizabeth (aka Betty) Horrocks. Their children were Edmund, born 1765; Betty 1769, died young; William, born 1771, died young; Elizabeth, born 1776, died 1800. The tanning business of Edmund senior was successful and he moved to live at Curfey House in Haigh where he died on 27 July 1819, aged 79. His wife had died on 9 December 1813 aged 82.

Edmund Heaton alone survived to inherit his parents' wealth. He never married and he used some of his money to purchase an estate of small farms in one of the upland parts of Horwich. He lived on one of these farms, New

Field, and the others were let to various tenants, some of them members of his family. He died on 14 December 1842 and was buried at Horwich New Chapel. A certificate attached to his Will gives the value of his personal estate and effects at not more than £600, which cannot have included the land he owned.

Upland Farms

The estate which Edmund bought is situated little more than one mile north and north-east of Horwich town centre just outside the boundary with Heaton township, at an altitude of around 1000ft (300m) above sea level, where there lies a group of small farms, on the edge of Smithills Moor. These farms had connections with a number of Heaton families through most of the 19th century and many of them now remain largely unaltered in appearance from that date. Their names include Slack Hall, Burnt Edge, New Field, Cow Hey, Sheepcote, Higher Derbyshires, and Tar Hall. This estate of small tenanted farms had been bought by Edmund towards the beginning of the century. The farms were largely poor pasture land suitable only for sheep and a few hardy cows and it must have been difficult to obtain much of a living from them. They seem to have been occupied by families who had experienced financial problems and were not in a position to rent and stock a larger, more productive holding. Most of them were not solely reliant on farming

Slack Hall Farm, Horwich. Home of William and Alice Heaton, the author's great-grandparents, in the 1820s.

for a livelihood and pursued other occupations as well, usually weaving or working in one of the local factories.

The first Heaton family recorded as occupying one of these farms is that of William and Alice Heaton, the author's great grandparents. They were in financial straits following the collapse of William's father's business in 1797, about which more is written in the next chapter. They lived at Slack Hall farm in the 1820s, but in 1841 this farm was occupied by James and Alice Kirkman and their son Joseph, all weavers, and apparently not very dependent on farming. The son was the Joseph Kirkman, son of James, to whom Edmund Heaton left these farms in his Will in 1842, the Kirkmans being related to his mother. Edmund Heaton himself was living at adjoining New Field farm with just his housekeeper, Mary Hearst, to whom he also left an annuity.

Jeremy (aka Jeremiah), the second surviving son of Jeremiah and Mary Heaton of Ravenhurst was only 17 when his father died in 1796. He stayed on the farm with his mother for some years but then appears to have married and struck out on his own. We do not know where he was first able to rent a farm but the 1841 census shows him as occupying Sheepcote farm, next to Slack Hall, as a widower aged 60, with a number of unmarried sons and daughters and a granddaughter living with him. These were Ann, age 25, weaver; Mary, 23, weaver; Edmund, 20, weaver; Rachel, 18, weaver; Jeremy, 13, weaver; Esther, 10. The granddaughter was Amelia, age 4, but whose daughter she was we do not know.

In 1851 the family, still with all the same members, had moved to Burnt Edge farm nearby. Surprisingly, none appeared to have got married or left home and the occupations of Mary, Rachel and Esther had changed to that of a "billier" in a factory with Jeremiah (Jeremy) also working in a factory. Ann did the housework and Edmund helped his father as a farm labourer.

By 1861, old Jeremiah had died, the family had given up Burnt Edge farm and Ann, Mary, Edmund, Jeremy and Esther are recorded as living in part of Pinchmans farm where Robert Marsden is the head of the household although Ann is herself stated to be a farmer of 14 acres. Jeremy has a job as a banksman and Esther is working as a reeler. Rachel and Amelia, who by then would have been aged 38 and 24 respectively, have left home, presumably to get married, although it is possible one or both may have died.

In 1871 Jeremy and his wife Ann, were living at Little Dakins farm nearby where they were farming 12 acres, but had no children.

By 1881 Mary, Edmund and Esther had moved to New Field farm, where Mary, now aged 64, was head of the household, farming 20 acres, with her brother and sister working on the farm and in the house. At Cow Hey farm nearby were living Jeremy Heaton, age 53, Mary's brother, and his wife Ann, age 43. There were no children living with them. At this date Slack Hall was unoccupied but both it and New Field are quite habitable at the present time. A few years later Mary had died, the tenancy of New Field farm had expired and Edmund, rendered homeless, died in Farnworth workhouse on 12 April

1891. Esther's whereabouts are not known. This is the last record of any Heaton families living on these difficult upland farms, but more may be known when the 1901 census is allowed to be open for inspection on 1 January 2002. The names of Slack Hall, Sheepcote, New Field, Little Dakins and Marsden's farms still appear on current Ordnance Survey maps.

19th Century Farming.

In the closing years of the 18th century and at the beginning of the 19th Britain was at war with the French Republic and the Emperor Napoleon Bonaparte. During this period up to 1815 both arable and livestock farmers thrived without much competition from abroad, and with demands from the Government for increased supplies of food, wool, hides, flax and other materials needed to feed and equip the army, navy and the civilian population. In 1791 the Corn Law had been passed which prohibited the import of grain whilst the price in England remained below a certain figure. This too helped to keep prices of cereals at a high level and was particularly beneficial to the arable farmers of southern and eastern England.

For twenty years after the war prices assumed a level which, although lower than in wartime, still enabled livestock and arable farmers to maintain a fairly comfortable existence and this situation continued until the late 1830s with just a few minor peaks and troughs in the general level of prosperity in agriculture. During this period the farmers who experienced the worst economic conditions were those reliant on growing wheat on heavy clay soils[5] where costs were high. Those growing crops on light soils or rearing livestock were not badly affected by any fall in prices. There was considerable unrest amongst the general working population at the continued application of the Corn Laws which many maintained were keeping cereal prices artificially high and thereby increasing the price of essential foodstuffs throughout the country. Finally in 1846, in response to these protests but in the face of opposition from the landed interests who foresaw a fall in farm rents and arable farmers who anticipated a steep fall in prices, the Government repealed the Corn Laws. In the event however, the result was not a drastic fall in rents or prices and landowners and farmers weathered the change without undue difficulty.

From 1840 the railway network began to spread throughout the country and easier communications, growth in the urban population, general rise in the standard of living in the industrial towns as incomes increased, and the spread of improved agricultural techniques, led to several decades of rising prosperity amongst farmers, whose own standard of living noticeably increased, particularly amongst the wives and daughters of the larger arable farmers. Some commentators expressed the view that these women with their fancy clothes and piano playing had lost the practical qualities they needed to function competently as the wife of a farmer in their turn, and no longer had the abilities of their forebears who:-

> "Never looked further than her father's farm nor knew more
>   Than the price of corn in the market or at what rate
>   Beef went a stone? That would survey your dairy
>   And bring in mutton out of cheese and butter,
>   That could give directions at what time of the moon
>   To cut her cocks for capons against Christmas,
>   Or when to raise up goslings." [6]

Rising rents enabled landowners to spend more money on farm buildings and other permanent improvements to the land. A particularly favoured measure was the provision of improved land drainage following the introduction of clay drainpipes in about 1845 and mole drainage in 1850.[7] The whole agricultural community accepted the desirability of improved drainage, seeing it as the way to a general rise in productivity throughout the country, and the Government encouraged the work by making available cheap loans to landowners for this purpose.

Lancashire was predominantly a livestock farming county, such cereals as were grown being primarily barley and oats for animal feed and a little wheat for farmers' own use for breadmaking. Farms on the better land in Heaton and the neighbouring townships were typical mixed farms of this period, rearing sheep for mutton and wool, cattle for meat and milk, keeping hens and pigs, and growing grain and fodder crops for animal feed. They benefitted considerably by their proximity to a number of rapidly expanding towns around about which created good markets for milk, cheese, and meat. Bolton, the nearest town, had a population of around 5000 in 1750, 12,000 in the 1790s, 20,000 at about 1810 and then increased at a tremendous rate to over 60,000 by 1851 and to 180,000 by the end of the century.[8] Whereas it had previously been the custom of Lancashire livestock farmers to buy in calves and sell them on as store cattle to graziers in the Midlands to fatten, it now became worth their while to fatten animals themselves in view of the considerably increased markets for meat nearby, and the willingness of local consumers to pay higher prices. Although several members of the Heaton family were moving into industry, a substantial number still earned their living from the land and they benefitted from the general increase in agricultural prosperity.

Even the small upland farms on poorer land north of Horwich, which we have seen some members of the Heaton family occupying through most of the 19th century, gained some benefit from the improved markets expanding nearby. Their small sheep flocks produced lambs which they sold on as stores to farmers on better land to fatten and the one or two cows which they were able to keep could produce milk which they could sell to households in nearby Horwich. However, it was essential for them to have other sources of income unless they were able to enlarge their holdings, as Mary Heaton seems to have been able to do at New Field farm by 1881. It is even possible that their landlord would be willing to carry out some drainage and reseeding for them which would have undoubtedly improved the poor grassland with which they had to work.

Agricultural Depression!

About 1874 a drastic change took place in the economic position of agriculture in this country which was to last until near the end of the century. Increasing imports of cheap wheat produced from the virgin prairies of the USA and Canada, which were being ploughed up for the first time, flooded into the country in the free trade situation which had been created after the repeal of the Corn Laws. The position of the arable farmers in eastern and southern England deteriorated rapidly as prices plummeted, and a recession set in which was to affect corn growers for over twenty years. Commentators took the view that the high standard of living to which these arable farming families had become accustomed for the previous thirty years was to prove their downfall as they found it very difficult to economise to the extent necessary to cut their costs to a level commensurate with the prevailing prices.

For a large part of the 19th century the long leases which had been the norm in previous centuries had tended to fall out of favour, both with landlords and tenants. As prices fluctuated at frequent intervals both parties began to prefer the flexibility of an annual tenancy or short lease. This did not imply less security for the tenant as landlords definitely preferred to keep a good tenant whom they knew and many families farmed for generations on the basis of annual tenancies only. The advent of customary payments for tenant right, improvements, unexpired manurial values, etc. on the termination of a tenancy gave further security to a tenant whose landlord was reluctant to incur such expense if he gave notice to quit.[9] Many farmers on annual tenancies of arable farms took the opportunity to give their landlords notice to quit and salvage as much of their capital as they could, rather than stay on their farms losing money year after year. Much land in the eastern and southern counties was unlettable even at rockbottom rents and land had to be taken in hand and farmed by the owners or sold.

However what was disastrous to the arable farmer was beneficial to the livestock farmer whose bills for animal feed were reduced as cereal prices fell. In the competitive situation which frequently prevails between the arable and livestock farmer this was a period when it was a case of "horn up/corn down", contrary to the position at the end of the 20th century when it has very definitely been "corn up/horn down".

Notes & References

1. T J Arkwright "History of Ravenhurst", privately published 1994. Copy in Bolton Library. Mr Arkwright was once the owner of Ravenhurst (Raven House).
2. Partington Papers, pt2, notes to p.117. Bolton Central Library, ref. B920B.HEA.
3. Ibid.
4. "Cotton Mills of Bolton 1780-1985" J H Longworth. Pub. Bolton Museum & Art Gallery ,1986, p.104.
5. " Essays in Agrarian History", ed. W E Minchinton, vol.2, David & Charles, 1968. R J Thompson, p. 61
6. Play by Phillip Massinger," The City Madam", Act II,Sc.2.
7. "Essays in Agrarian History, R J Thompson, op.cit. p.63.
8. J H Longworth, op.cit., pp. 11-13.
9. "Essays in Agrarian History", vol.2, op.cit., G E Mingay, p.16.

Chapter Ten

Trade and Industry

For centuries the Heatons had relied on the land for their income, either as landowners receiving rents or as yeomen and husbandmen actually engaged in farming. Quite frequently the farmers also carried out small-scale spinning and weaving of wool and cotton on their farms, or by employing outworkers. However, in the late 18th century, with the national economy expanding, we first see members of the family prepared to accept the risks of becoming involved in larger-scale manufacturing, committing their capital and expertise to the establishment of businesses which were amongst the first to be launched in the new Industrial Revolution.

King Cotton

A cottage industry to process wool into cloth had been established in Bolton and district probably by the late 12th century. In the reign of Richard I a cloth measurer had been appointed whose function was to measure all cloths for sale and mark them with the King's seal.[1] This would seem to indicate the existence of a substantial trade in woollen cloth at that time and this continued for centuries as a local cottage-based industry, expanding both into the processing of locally-grown and Irish flax into linen and eventually, in the mid-17th century, into cotton, imported firstly from the Middle East and then from the southern states of the USA.[2] Combining farming with cotton spinning or weaving was a very common practice in the area, enabling a farmer owning or renting a small acreage (20-50 acres) and having a building suitable as a loom shed, to earn a very respectable income[3], several times that of a purely agricultural worker. Mostly this was a family enterprise but sometimes these men became small capitalists, owning their buildings and plant and employing others as journeyman weavers.

Others aspired to greater heights with the ambition to become part of the expanding industrial scene. The first mill in Bolton was erected by James Thweat in 1780 on the north bank of the River Croal opposite King Street, and this building, St. Helena Mill, still exists, although it ceased operations as a cotton mill in 1979, and is now used as offices. Samuel Crompton, the inventor of the spinning mule took up residence in King Street in 1791, living there until his death in 1827. It is claimed that he worked his mule for a time in St. Helena Mill, before moving across the river to another mill in 1802.[4]

Members of the Heaton family were no exception to this desire to become industrialists on a larger scale and whether they were to be successful or not we shall see.

An Enterprise that Failed

Chronologically the first, and unfortunately the worst-case scenario amongst our ambitious cotton entrepreneurs was John Heaton, the author's great-great-grandfather. John was born in 1760 and was baptised on 28 February of that year at Deane parish church, the eldest son of John and Mary Heaton, nee Crompton. John Heaton senior had inherited a small estate at Blackrod from his father and in addition he acquired land at Deane Moorside, Over Hulton from William Hulton Esq. on lease for three lives and 21 years. He built a farmhouse, barn, shippon and other outbuildings at Deane Moorside and moved there to live in 1771.

John junior was born at Blackrod and like his father was a weaver and small manufacturer. On 27 October 1782 he married Nancy (aka Ann) Howarth at St. Mary's Church,Deane. Nancy had a small Farm at Nevy Fold in Horwich in her own right and John's father conveyed to him the estate at Blackrod on his marriage. John and his wife were, therefore, fairly prosperous with two farms and a small cotton goods manfacturing business. However, John soon felt the urge to improve his fortunes further by embarking on a major investment in larger-scale cotton spinning and manufacturing. To raise the capital to enable him to achieve this ambition, by 1794 he had sold his own farm at Blackrod and that of his wife at Nevy Fold and sunk the proceeds into a factory, machinery, and business at Rylstone near Skipton in Yorkshire.

In many ways this was a logical move to make, which deserved to succeed. There was an undoubted bottleneck between the demand for yarn by weavers and the ability of hand spinners to satisfy it. It had always required the output of three or four spinners to keep a weaver supplied and the general introduction of the flying shuttle around 1760 had aggravated this, as it enabled the weavers to work much faster. However the invention of Hargreave's spinning jenny and Arkwright's water-frame revolutionised spinning which began, to an increasing extent from 1770, to be located in factories. By 1790 these developments had provoked considerable unrest amongst the hand spinners of Lancashire at the prospect of large-scale production by machinery in mills, powered by either water or steam. Several riots had broken out, premises were set on fire and machinery wrecked.

John Heaton was probably accustomed as a farmer to make trips to the Craven area around Skipton to buy calves, a common practice amongst Lancashire cattle rearers. He would have learnt that there was no such unrest in Yorkshire where the establishment of cotton spinning mills was welcomed[5] He may also have heard that a former corn mill at Rylstone nearby was to let for cotton spinning and this seemed to present an opportunity for him to set up his new business, even though the mill had a few disadvantages, principally that of difficult acess, being several hundred yards from a good road, and the neighbours objecting to the use of the track from the road by carts bringing materials to and from the mill. This dispute was only apparently resolved after arbitration by a London barrister.[6] The author observed, on a recent visit to this site, that a prominent notice is displayed where the track leaves the existing road in Rylstone, pointing out that access is for foot traffic only, so this would seem to be a dispute that has possibly been rumbling on for 200 years! Nothing now remains of the mill, it and its successor having been demolished by 1826.[7]

John decided to go ahead with this new enterprise; moved his family into a house in Rylstone and began to buy materials for the machinery which he had to instal, from Kirkstall Forge in 1794.[8] However, he obviously experienced difficulties in establishing a fully viable business in this location and although he struggled on for a few years, probably selling his yarn to local weavers or sending it to Manchester; by 1797, a bad year for the cotton trade generally, he was bankrupt and owing large sums to his creditors. Instead of facing up to the situation, accepting his responsibilities to his wife and children and trying to salvage something from the disaster, he fled the country to avoid his creditors and possible imprisonment for debt. His wife was obliged to sell what she could of the machinery and stocks at the mill to try and make some payment to the creditors. Letters were received from him for a few years from South America but finally ceased and nothing more was heard from him. It is believed he died of yellow fever in Rio de Janeiro, probably in 1812. Thus failed, somewhat ignominiously, the first Heaton attempt to establish a substantial cotton manufacturing business.

John and Nancy Heaton had eight children; Nancy born 1783; John, 1785; Isabella, 1786; James, 1788; William (the author's great grandfather),1790; Joseph, 1793; Isabella (aka Elizabeth), 1795; and Margery, 1797. The first six were born in Horwich and the last two in Yorkshire, but all of them were baptised at St.Mary's Church, Deane, the latter two, Elizabeth and Margery, 10 and 8 years after their births, respectively, on 15 April 1805.

In the space of five years Nancy had moved from a prosperous and comfortable way of life to a state of destitution as a mother of children aged from 14 years to a few months. The eventual fate of Nancy and her family will be recounted later but for the moment we will confine ourselves to consideration of another Heaton entrepreneur.

A Survivor

Contemporaneously with John Heaton's ill-fated business venture, another member of the family to attempt to realise his ambition to become a major manufacturer was Lambert Heaton, born 1775 and baptised at Deane Church on 23 September of that year, the third son of John and Alice Heaton, nee Nicholson.. John Heaton was a prosperous farmer who had himself built a small mill at Picton Street, Doffcocker in the 1790s but this business was soon taken over by his son, Lambert. It is claimed that Samuel Crompton's mules were operated there in 1798, manufactured by the firm of Dobson & Barlow.[9]

Lambert Heaton was an enterprising individual, being a farmer and manufacturer of cotton goods, a combination which was very common in this part

Picton Street Mill, Doffcocker after conversion to houses in the late 1800s. (Photograph by courtesy of Bolton Local Studies Dept.)

of Lancashire at that time. He occupied Hodgkinsons Farm of 25 acres in Heaton for nearly 50 years where he had his warehouse and "taking-in" room. He employed a considerable number of handloom weavers as outworkers at their own premises.

On 25th October 1796 he married Betty Morris at Deane Church. Their children, born between 1798 and 1818 were Alice, Maria, John, Mary Ann, William, Lambert, Jane, Thomas, Sarah and Ann. Mary Ann, Sarah and Ann died young.

In 1800 at the age of 24, with financial help from his father, Lambert embarked on the construction of Delph Hill Mill, Chorley Old Road, Doffcocker, one of the first cotton mills built in this location. However, the speculation does not appear to have been successful for on the 5th January 1802 the following advertisement appeared in Harrops Mercury.[10]

> "To be Sold by Auction at the Nag's Head in Bolton, on Thursday, the 28th January 1802, for the remainder of the term of 999 years, a few years of which are only expired...
> Lot 1. All that new erected and well built Stone Factory, five storeys high, called Heaton's Factory, situate in Halliwell, together with 35 perches of Building Land ...and
> Lot 2. The Fee-simple... in all those six messuages, cottages,or dwellinghouses with the Loom-houses...,near the said factory.
>
> The above premises are eligibly situated on the side of the Turnpike Road leading between the populous trading towns of Bolton and Chorley, and little more than 2 miles from the said town of Bolton; and are now in the possession of Mr Lambert Heaton, subject only to the yearly ground rent of £14.12s.0d during the term.
>
> For further particulars apply to Mr Richard Wylde and Mr William Appleton, both of Bolton aforesaid, Cotton Merchants; or to Mr Hopwood of Horwich, in the said County, Whitster; or at the office of Mr James Croft, of Bolton afsd. Attorney-at-Law."

Presumably the ground rent was payable for the mill premises only as the property comprising Lot 2 appears to be freehold. The equipment in the mill consisting of "19 Spinning Wheels,nearly new " were also available for purchase if so desired by the purchaser of the mill. The ground rent was payable to Thomas Nuttall Esq. of Hungerhill, Rumworth, who owned the freehold. It seems that not long afterwards Mr Nuttall sold the whole of his estate here to Henry Tempest Esq., the principal landowner in the area.

Lambert appears to have survived this setback because he is on record as continuing his activities as a farmer and manufacturer of cotton goods still employing a number of handloom weavers, and being described by Baines in 1825 as a "Muslin Manufacturer of Heaton".[11] However, financial problems were to beset him again because four years later a notice appeared in the Bolton Chronicle newspaper to the effect that-

> "The Commissioners appointed in a Commission of Bankruptcy, dated 14th August 1827, awarded against Lambert Heaton of Heaton in the Co. of Lancs: Cotton Manufacturer Dealer and Chapman, intend to meet on the 7th July 1829, to make a final dividend, &c.
> Dated 13th June 1829.   Woodhouse,Solicitor."

Once more, however, it seems Lambert overcame his problems and carried on at least his farming activities. When he made his Will on 13th July 1841 he left all his Farming Stock, Household Furniture, ready-money, and debts, together with his house in Spring Gardens, Great Bolton, to his wife Betty for her life; and after her death to be equally divided amongst his surviving sons and daughters, namely, Alice Wood, Maria Heaton, John Heaton, William Heaton, Jane Pendlebury, and Thomas Heaton.

He died on 13th July 1845 aged 69 years and his wife, Betty, died on the 26th December 1854 aged 80 years and they are buried at the Wesleyan Chapel in Bridge Street, Bolton, where also is buried Maria, their daughter, who died unmarried on 14th June 1856, aged 56 years.

The failure of John Heaton's business and Lambert Heaton's relative lack of success highlights the risks and difficulties facing the pioneers of the cotton industry in trying to establish thriving enterprises. For every successful entrepreneur there were undoubtedly a number of failures.

Rescue

In 1797 Nancy Heaton was absolutely destitute, having been deserted by her husband and needing to somehow support several young children. Fortunately, as soon as her husband's family heard of her plight they rallied round to find her and offer her help. She was soon found, impoverished, with her family in Manchester, and her three brothers-in-law, Thomas, Joseph and James Heaton, the second, third and fourth sons of John and Mary Heaton, born in 1764, 1775 and 1778, respectively, undertook to take the children into their own homes and in other ways to offer aid and relief to their mother.

Letters written in 1809 and 1816 by Thomas Heaton in Liverpool to his father and brothers in Bolton recount certain of the later activities of his nephews James, Joseph and William Heaton sons of John and Nancy Heaton, and show that whilst some members of the family were able to overcome their problems fairly successfully, others had very great difficulty in obtaining a livelihood. At the age of 21 in 1809 James set up in business at Roscoe Lane, Berry St., Liverpool, where he apparently prospered although we do not know what type of business it was. There he was joined by his brother Joseph, then aged 16[12]. In the year 1816, further correspondence from Thomas to his brothers shows the problems being experienced by Joseph and William, his nephews, in trying to earn a living. The elder, William (the author's great grandfather), was then aged 26, and Joseph was 23.[13]

William had married Alice Fletcher at Deane Parish Church on 31 December 1812. They eventually had 13 children; William born 1814; John, 1816; James,1818; Edward (the author's grandfather), 1820; Joseph, 1821; Alice, 1823; Ann, 1824; Thomas, 1826; Margaret, 1827; Eli, 1828; Sarah, 1831 (died young); Isabella, 1833; Margery, 1836. The parents appear to have had some changes of heart concerning the particular religious persuasion they wished to follow. John, James, Edward, Joseph, and Ann were all baptised at Horwich New Chapel (Independent) on 15 February 1826. Margaret was baptised there on 25 March 1828, Thomas on 8 April 1828, and Eli on 27 January 1829. William was baptised at St. Peter's, Bolton on 17 July 1814 and others at St.

Mary's, Deane, even though one might have expected them to have been baptised at Horwich New Chapel.

William was already married with one child and was in desperate straits when he turned up again in Liverpool in 1816, looking to his brother James or his uncle Thomas to help him find work and somewhere to live. Somehow it would appear that his situation gradually improved, very possibly through help afforded him by his second cousin Edmund Heaton of Horwich, a wealthy bachelor who was referred to in the previous chapter as owning an estate consisting of a number of small farms in the vicinity of Burnt Edge, north-east of Horwich. Edmund lived on his own farm at New Field, Horwich and next door was Slack Hall farm which William and his family occupied in the 1820s and where he would have had the opportunity to earn some income from the land, by keeping sheep and cattle but his prime occupation and principal source of income would have been as a handloom weaver, helped by other members of his family.

This combination of farming and weaving was still a common practice in the area, although by that time (the 1820s/30s) the handloom weavers were experiencing increasing difficulty in competing with the production of the looms in the new factories powered by steam. Whereas in 1795 a handloom weaver could earn a good income of 33/- (£1.65p) per week from his loom, by 1814 this had been reduced to 24/- (£1.20p) per week,and by 1819, the year of Peterloo, it had dropped again to the appallingly low figure of 9/- (45p) per week.[14] The handloom weavers were in a desperate situation but they valued their independence so much that many of them still refused to give in and apply for work in the mills. By 1850 however the generation that had seen their industry decimated by the growth of the factory system had died out and the trade of handloom weaving that had served so many of them so well for centuries had finally disappeared.

Gratitude

Unlike most members of the Heaton family who were members of the Anglican Church of England, Edmund Heaton of Horwich was a Presbyterian and a devout member of Horwich New Chapel (Independent), where he was buried on the 14th December 1842, aged 78. This chapel was founded in 1716 and rebuilt in 1803. The late baptisms of eight of William's and Alice's children there between 1826 and 1829, and presumably the attendance of the family there for worship, could possibly indicate action taken to express gratitude to Edmund for help given around that time, which appears to have included the grant of a tenancy of Slack Hall, the farm which William and his family were occupying at the time of the baptisms.

Another expression of gratitude might well be the fact that William's fourth son, although named Edward at his baptism, by 1841 had changed his name to Edmund, and he was known by this name throughout his life. Although the name Edmund had been common amongst the Heatons for generations,

Trade and Industry 151

by the 1830s the only surviving member of the family with that name was Edmund of Horwich, who was unmarried and without children. The fact that with his death the name would disappear in the family may well have prompted him to ask William and Edward to agree to a change of name for the latter, to which they apparently agreed. There is no documentary evidence confirming this arrangement however, and when Edmund of Horwich made his Will on 22nd September 1840, he made no provision for William and his family. Perhaps by then he thought he had helped the family sufficiently during his lifetime,or there may even have been a falling-out between Edmund and William. Anyway, in his Will, Edmund left his entire estate to Joseph Kirkman, a relative of his mother, and nothing at all to any of his Heaton relatives.

Recovery

The 1841 census shows the family living at Tar Hall, Halliwell and comprising William and Alice, his wife, their children, Edmund (formerly Edward), Joseph, Ann, Eli, Sarah, Isabella, and Margery; the two eldest boys, John and James, and two daughters, Alice and Margaret having by then left home. All the male members of the family are described as "coalminers", even Eli, aged 10! It would seem that by then William had decided that to make a living as a farmer/weaver was now impossible and the earnings from

Traditional grass bleaching process with cloths laid out on a croft, running water nearby and chimney for steam power.
(Reproduced by courtesy of Bolton Local Studies Dept.)

coalmining with four family members working were much better. However the decade was well termed the "Hungry Forties" and it is estimated that 60% of the workforce in Bolton at that time was unemployed. The author's grandfather Edmund (as we shall now call William's and Alice's fourth son) decided to move elsewhere to find work and first went to the district of Chadderton in Oldham where he presumably felt the prospects would be better. This proved to be correct, and the job he obtained was as a crofter in a bleach works, an ocupation which was to form the basis of the business he subsequently built up and which was to provide a livelihood not only for himself, but for other members of his family also.

Bolton and district had been noted for the bleaching and finishing of cloth since the 16th century and the early bleaching process included the boiling of the cloth in a mixture of lime, soured buttermilk and a weak alkali made from plant ashes. A good supply of soft water was required. After treatment the cloth was pegged out in the sun on extensive areas of land termed crofts.[15] Hence the name "crofter" for a worker in a bleach works. However by the mid-19th century most of the bleaching works had turned over to the newer chemical methods of bleaching, thereby considerably shortening the time taken in the process.

Edmund was not only to find work in Chadderton but also a wife, for it was here he met a young girl named Hannah Spence, daughter of Anthony and Esther Spence. This was probably in 1842/3 and Hannah was no more than 15 at the time. She and Edmund were married at Oldham Parish Church on 10th June 1844, when she was only 16, and he was 24. In 1843 her father had become landlord of the Horton Arms, Streetbridge, Chadderton, a position he held until 1861 when he was killed in an accident.[16] The Horton Arms still exists in Streetbridge, but much changed from the mid-19th century.

Edmund and Hannah stayed in Chadderton for a year or two but they then moved to Glossop in the neighbouring county of Derbyshire where Edmund again obtained work as a crofter at a textile print works. On the 5th April 1848 their first child, Robert, was born. Whilst they were living in Glossop their second son, William, was born blind on 7th February 1850. Shortly after the birth of William the family returned to Horwich and in April 1851, at the time of the census, they were living at White Gate Farm, close to Edmund's father, with Edmund still working as a crofter at one of the local bleach works, of which there were many. William was then a 60-yr old widower, living at Higher Derbyshires Farm, Rivington, with his two sons, Joseph and Eli, both bleacher operatives, and three daughters, Alice, Isabella and Margery, all unmarried. Alice and Margery looked after the house and helped on the farm and Isabella worked as a dressmaker.

The Bleacher

By 1853 Edmund and his family had moved to Pendleton, Manchester, where he first set up his own small business as a cotton waste bleacher. The

Trade and Industry 153

family stayed here until after 1858, during which time three more children were born, Esther in 1853, Leah in 1856, and Hannah in 1858. By 1861 they had moved again to Chadderton, where their sixth child Joseph was born in 1863, and their seventh child Edward in 1865. From Chadderton they moved to Moston, Manchester where two more children, Alice and Ann were born in 1867 and 1869 respectively. They were there until 1871 and then followed a move to Holts Farm, Lees, Ashton-under Lyne, where their last child, Edmund Moses Heaton, the author's father, was born on 10th January 1873. Hannah had been producing children for 25 years so there was a quite considerable age-gap between the first and the last, and Edmund was 53 when his youngest son was born.

Why they moved so often we do not know but every move involved Edmund finding suitable premises with a house, workshop, and good supply of running water for his bleaching business and it is noticeable how the vari-

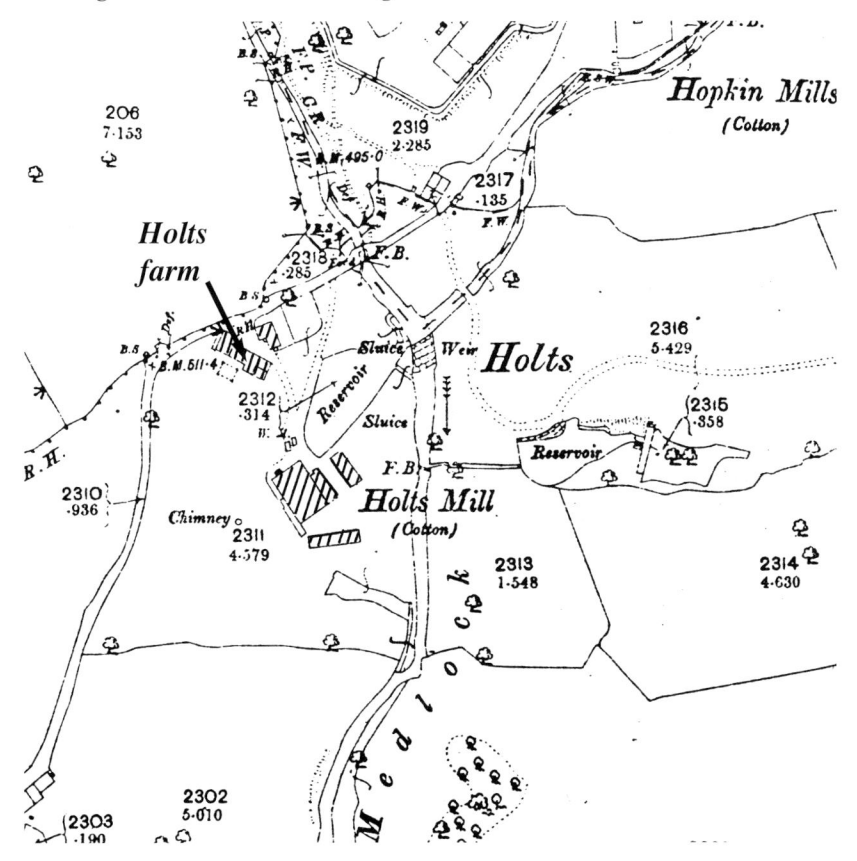

Map of Holts Farm, Lees, where the author's father was born and his grandfather carried on his business of cotton waste bleaching.
Note living accomodation in farmhouse and cottages, with mill, reservoir, stream and engine house.

ous places where they settled met these requirements. At Moston the water came from the Dean Brook, at Chadderton the River Irk, and at Lees the River Medlock. There was a final move by the family to Cherry Row, Streetbridge, Chadderton where they were living in 1881, and again the reliance was on the River Irk for the supply of water needed for the bleaching process.

Of the various locations at which the business was carried on, the site at Holts Farm, Lees is the easiest to identify. Edmund was then employing probably 10 people, some being members of his own family, including his elder brother William and eventually his nephew Eli, William's son. The buildings consisted of the farmhouse, occupied by Edmund's family, and four cottages or converted farm buildings, occupied by his workers and their families. The bleaching was carried out in a mill close to the river where there was a ford and a weir with a sluice which raised the water level and allowed the water to fill a shallow reservoir adjacent to the mill. The land is now part of a community park along the course of the River Medlock, and although all the buildings have been demolished the features of the ford, weir, sluice, reservoir configuration and sites of the buildings are clearly visible after 120 years. It seems probable that Edmund was also engaged in farming here as his predecessor at the premises is noted in the 1871 census as being a master bleacher, also farming 15 acres. Even as a young boy, Edmund Moses would have grown up with a knowledge of farming, and this was an occupation which he was to pursue for a number of years, later in life.

Hannah Heaton died on 25th January 1883 at the house in Streetbridge, Chadderton, leaving Edmund to look after the children still living at home, Edward, aged 16, Ann, 14, and Edmund Moses, 10. He continued his apparently successful business until he retired a year or two later when it seems that the business was taken over by his nephew Eli. Edmund lived on until the start of the 20th century and died at Salford on 8th April 1900, aged 79. His early life, when his father was struggling to recover from the family impoverishment resulting from the failure of John Heaton's business at Rylstone, must have been very difficult and it is greatly to his credit that, without the benefit of a proper education, he was able to establish himself in a business and build this up to the position where he could give his own children a much better start in life. At least three of them, Esther, Hannah, and Edward, decided to emigrate to the USA, but not as an act of desperation, rather as a considered decision, seen as being able to provide them with the opportunities that would be more difficult to find in the Old Country. The girls made good marriages and the men all found positions which would provide them with a reasonable lifestyle. Even William, who had the disadvantage of being born blind, became a marine store supervisor, married, and had a child. Edmund junior was apprenticed at the new premises of Ferranti in Oldham which opened in 1879, and he eventually qualified as an electrical engineer, an industry then in its infancy and a decision which displayed considerable foresight on his part or that of his father.

Some Minor Enterprises

John Heaton and his wife Mary, nee Crompton, whom he married in 1759, had farms at Blackrod and Deane Moorside and he was in a prosperous way of business as a farmer, chapman (merchant) and small manufacturer. They had four sons and one daughter who lived to adulthood, John of Rylstone, Thomas, Mary, Joseph, and James, born 1760, 1764, 1767, 1775, and 1778 respectively.

Thomas was apprenticed to the trade of printer and stationer and his father set him up in a shop at no. 195 Deansgate, Bolton. However he was unable to make a success of this business, and when it soon failed he departed to London and left the shop and his debts for his father to deal with. After a while he returned to Lancashire and opened a shop at no. 24, Ranelagh Street, Liverpool. He was very fortunate in his choice of wife, for his marriage to Ann Maria Taylor seems to have transformed his life which thereafter gave no cause for complaint by his family or his business associates.

They married in Liverpool on 27 March 1809 and letters from Thomas and Ann Maria to his father, show the extent of his penitence, although he writes, perhaps, in a somewhat patronising manner. However, no father receiving such a letter as his new daughter-in-law wrote, could have failed to feel that his son's choice of wife seemed very auspicious.

From Thomas Heaton to his father. Dated 4 March 1809.

> " Dear Father,
> From the time you left me I have continued to mourn that any bitter words should ever have passed between us. I now pray you look back on the whole of my conduct. Those instances in which I have in any way given you pain of mind I am sincerely sorry and grieved for, and beg your forgiveness and blessing. In a few weeks you will have one more Daughter-in-Law, about thirty-three years old, bearing the name of Ann Maria, daughter of Mr Taylor, a miller on the North Shore, near here. In her I observe some of the high, much of the good, and a capability for being my friend. The family I think very well of. There is diligence, economy, and real private goodness of character. You will ask what property? One hundred pounds now and several more in future...The day of the ceremony is not yet fixed...I do not presume to desire that you will be either present or absent, but I pray with sincere love and duty that you will follow the desire of your own mind...If you should choose to communicate the contents of this to my brother Joseph and my brother James my love and brotherly regard is with them and my sisters. I hope to recover their good opinion also."

From Mrs Ann Maria Heaton to her father-in-law. Dated Saturday 10 June 1809.

"Dear Father,

It gives me pleasure to hear that your health is so much better. I feel grateful to you, for what you have been pleased to do for us. With respect to your wish, that my husband would pay the whole of the debt due to his brother,[17] trust me, you cannot desire that more earnestly than I do, or than he does himself. And it is our intention by honest industry and careful economy, to enable ourselves to discharge all debts as soon as possible. - Thus,my dear Father, with the firm intention in our hearts, to act upon every occasion according to the excellent precept of our Saviour's - do unto all men as thou wouldst they should do unto thee - we hope, - we pray, that the blessing of God may always, and upon every occasion, prosper our endeavours to do what is just and right. - I remain, with every good wish for your happiness, and the happiness of all belonging to you.

Your dutiful Daughter,   Ann Maria Heaton "

It seems that Thomas and his wife lived up to their good intentions. Their business prospered, they were able to pay off all their debts and they earned the esteem of their relatives and friends. It is only with regard to their own family that they suffered misfortune. They had two pairs of twins, all of whom died in infancy,and their son John Crompton, born 27th January 1810, survived his father but died unmarried. Thomas died on 7th August 1817, but his widow was still living in 1857.[18]

Thomas was a man who seemed very conscious of his ancestry, since a paper in his handwriting, seen by Partington, gives details of the Heaton coat of arms, impaled with that of Taylor, his wife's family, together with details of the Ravenhurst branch of the Heaton family, from the late 17th century. The Taylor arms were described as "Azure a chevron between three escalop shells argent. Crest, on a wreath of colours a nags head erased argent".

When Thomas Heaton relinquished his first shop at 195 Deansgate, Bolton, his father placed his only daughter Mary in charge there to ensure the continuance of the business, which sold books and stationery, tea, coffee and groceries as well as the milk and butter produced on the farm at Dean Moorside. James, Thomas's younger brother had also been apprenticed as a printer and stationer and he was sent to help his sister as soon as he was available. Together they managed the shop until 1807,when James married Esther Heyes of Westhoughton, and Mary then ended her participation in the business.

James Heaton had a successful business career. He was, for a time, proprietor of the "Bolton Chronicle" during the early years of its existence, and he also obtained the appointment of Stamp Distributor for Bolton and District before 1825. When he retired from business his son John succeeded him and carried on until 1855, when the business was sold. James went to live in a favoured location at Lark Hill, St.Georges Road, Bolton, where he bought a

Trade and Industry

plot of land and built a house in 1825. He died there on 8 June 1854 aged 76 years. Esther, his widow, died on 6 September 1870, aged 86 years.

The Inventor

The constant drive for improved efficiency in all fields of industrial production gave considerable scope to men of an imaginative and inventive mind and one of those who took advantage of these opportunities was Thomas Heaton, third son of Peter and Betty Heaton, nee Pickering, of Pool Fold Farm, Halliwell, and brother of Peter Heaton junior who was mentioned in a previous chapter and whom we shall hear of further in connection with Delph Hill Mill. When Thomas married he lived in Chorley and worked a small coalmine in Adlington on his own account. In about 1850 he gave up the mine and moved to Blackburn where he opened an office as a Consulting Engineer. His practical mining experience stood him in good stead and he developed several improved items of equipment.

On 11th September 1855 he took out a patent for "Improvements in Pumps", no. 2055 of 1855. On the 24th March 1856 he took out another patent, no.690 of 1856, concerning " Invention for Self-Acting Doors and Gateways" Shortly after obtaining this patent Thomas Heaton moved to Bolton where, on 15th June 1857, he took out a further patent, no.1667 of 1857 entitled "Improvements in Self-Acting Doors and Gateways", describing it as "improvements upon an invention for which I obtained Letters Patent dated 24th March 1856".

The later improvement, patented in 1857, apparently proved to be a much simpler and more effective method of achieving the desired result. It is described in the patent as "... fixing horizontal levers at each side of of the passage or doorway turning on pivots; I curve the said levers so that each of them nearly meet at their extreme points, and pass through holes or appertures in the doors or gates, in which holes or appertures I fix friction pulleys, to allow the ends of the said levers to pass easily through them. The doors or gates slide on crossbars or rails,... so that when a horse, person or tub,etc. comes in contact with the aforesaid slightly curved shafts pressing laterally against them, the said lateral force pushes the doors or gates sideways into recesses prepared for them,which will remain there as long as there is anything pressing against them; but the moment they are freed from the said lateral pressure, the doors or gates will close of themselves, either by means of a simple pulley and weight to draw them back to their closed position, or by giving the horizontal cross bars or rails on which they slide a slight incline from the centre."

One of the worst features of the early Industrial Revolution was the employment of young children down coal mines as "trappers", spending all their working time alone in damp dark conditions waiting to open safety "trapdoors" between sections of mine galleries whenever a line of trucks came along.

The use of Thomas Heaton's invention by the Duke of Bridgwater's Trustees in some of their collieries, and by other colliery managers and proprietors certainly meant that the use of children for this dangerous work was reduced, but unfortunately it was never taken up on a sufficiently large scale to make the continued employment of small children as "trappers" unnecessary throughout the industry and Thomas Heaton's comparatively early death prevented him promoting his invention more widely.

A Major Success

Undoubtedly, the greatest success amongst those Heatons who became involved in the cotton industry followed on from the foundations already laid down by John Heaton and his son Lambert.

When sold in 1802 Delph Hill Mill passed first into the ownership of Messrs Darbyshire & Chorley and then subsequently was owned by Mr John Mawdsley until 1835 when it was repurchased by another member of the Heaton family, Peter, second cousin to Lambert who built the Mill originally, and brother of Thomas, the inventor.

Peter, fourth son of Peter and Betty Heaton, nee Pickering, was born in 1788 and married Mary Simpson of Halliwell. Their children were Robert, born 1808; John, 1810; William, 1812; Thomas, 1814; Joseph, 1816; Benjamin, 1818, died in infancy; Elizabeth, 1821; Benjamin Dukinfield, 1823; James, 1824; Peter Rowland, 1826; Emily, 1828; and Noah Oswald, 1831, who died in infancy.

Peter and his family lived from 1822 on his father's farm at Pool Fold in Halliwell, his wife Mary being the manager and principal worker on the farm. She was a strong, active woman of farming stock who took a keen interest in farming matters well into her old age.

At about the time he took over Delph Hill Mill in 1835, Peter and his family moved to Hollin Hey Farm. He worked the Mill in conjunction with his two sons Thomas and Joseph, trading as Peter Heaton & Sons. When he retired from business he handed over the Mill to his sons and at the same time he relinquished Hollin Hey farm to his son, William. With his wife and two daughters he then moved into York House, Rumworth, later transferring to Blue Bonnet Hall, Over Hulton, and finally into a house in Bath Street, Little Bolton. He died on 2 November 1856, aged 68, his wife having died, aged 70, on 9 March 1853.

Thomas and Joseph never married and on succeeding their father in 1848 in the management of the Mill they both moved in to a house named Lieutenants in Halliwell where they lived together for the rest of their lives. Thomas was the expert with machinery and Joseph was most knowledgeable about all the processes of cotton spinning. Both were industrious and skilful in the business and the firm prospered year after year. The Heatons initially were both spinners and weavers with mules and looms but later they abandoned weaving to concentrate on spinning. In 1851 during the Great Exhibition at the Crystal Palace, Heatons exhibited very fine yarn in the textiles section. The business continued to make progress with constant improvements being made to the buildings and machinery. The Poor Rate Assessments over a number of years indicate the efforts made to improve the premises. Pre-1835 - £174-10-6d; 1840 -£189-6-4d; 1849 - £302-16-0d.

In 1855 however, on Friday 23 March, disaster struck! At about 3 o'clock in the morning the Mill was found to be on fire and before help could arrive to deal with the blaze the whole building was well alight. The worst nightmare of any millowner had been realised and by 5 a.m. the roof had fallen in and the mill building was a ruin. The Engine House, Engine, and Warehouse were however, saved. The damage was estimated at £16,000 and the insurance cover was £12,000 for the buildings,machinery, and the stock of finished cotton goods and raw materials. The Heaton's loss, therefore, was very substantial at approximately £4,000. Neverthless the owners raised the necessary additional capital, rebuilt the mill and re-equipped it with improved machinery. The Poor Rate Assessment after the rebuilding was increased to £394-2-6d.

Following the rebuilding of Delph Hill Mill, Thomas and Joseph came to the conclusion that it would be more advantageous for their business if they had greater space closer to the Lancashire & Yorkshire Railway where they would have a direct line to Liverpool where the raw cotton from Egypt and America was landed and from which the finished products were shipped abroad. They, therefore, acquired a long lease of a site adjoining the line at Lostock Junction in Heaton, and of which their ancestors had once owned the freehold. Ironically,the person from whom they obtained their lease was Henry Tempest Esq., a member of the family who succeeded the Blundells who succeeded the Andertons who succeeded the Heatons themselves as lords of the manor and owners of the township of Heaton.

On this site Thomas and Joseph built a much larger mill housing 50,000 spindles and this mill became operational in 1860. Unlike large numbers of Lancashire cotton firms, the Heatons were able to minimise the effect of the shortage of raw cotton resulting from the American Civil War by switching to the finer cotton from Egypt and the Sudan. In 1865 William Heaton, the son of Thomas and Alice Heaton and great-grandson of John Heaton, builder of Picton Street Mill, started work at the mill, aged 13. The Heaton brothers worked the new Lostock Junction Mill with great success and an increasing volume of business for several years. At about the time they completed Lostock Junction Mill they decided to let Delph Hill Mill to Mr James Whittaker, which arrangement continued until 1872 when William Heaton, who had been appointed a manager at the age of 20, bought the premises, committing all the capital he had to the venture.

William Heaton had been born at Townleys Farm in 1852 and married Janet Ann Dixon, daughter of John Dixon of Heaton Old Hall in 1878. They were living at Bessybrook Hall, Lostock when their first son Thomas was born in 1880, to be followed by Joseph Rowland, born 1881; Alice Parkinson, 1882; Benjamin William, 1886; John, 1887; and William, 1889.

Thomas Heaton died on 7 October 1877, aged 63 years. Thereafter Joseph managed the mill at Lostock Junction with William responsible for Delph Hill Mill. This arrangement continued until Joseph's death on 26 December 1884, aged 68, when William took over ownership and management of the entire firm, and changed its name to William Heaton & Sons. Delph Hill Mill was let again from 1884 to 1900, this time to Mr Robert Whittaker who operated 18,366 spindles there. Then William Heaton again took possession. and operated the mill in conjunction with Lostock Junction. In 1900 No.2 Mill at Lostock Junction was built with a capacity of 100,000 spindles,and No.1 Mill at Lostock Junction was enlarged in 1886, 1895, and 1899. The end of the century saw the firm in a commanding position in the production of fine cotton yarns and claiming to be the largest private company in that business in the United Kingdom.

William Heaton was a wealthy man who was proud of his lineage. He adapted the family's ancient coat-of-arms as the corporate arms of his company and he encouraged and financed John Heaton Partington to pursue his research into the family history, paying for the services of agents to search out the old documents which Partington needed when he himself was not able to gain access to them. For many years Partington worked at his research and finally in 1903 he completed it and deposited the bulk of his papers and notebooks in Bolton Central Library, where ever since they have been an invaluable archive for later researchers.

A Hosiery Business

Second only to Thomas, Joseph and William Heaton in the degree of success their businesses enjoyed was the family of John Heaton, born 1784 and second surviving son of Lambert and Ann Heaton, nee Rothwell. John was first cousin to Lambert Heaton, founder of Delph Hill Mill, and was married three times, first to Esther Wood in 1806, then to Ann Haslam in 1812, and thirdly to Elizabeth Smith in 1825. These marriages produced only four children who survived beyond their twenties and several died in infancy.

In Piggott & Dean's Directory of 1821/2 John Heaton is described as a hosier and muslin manufacturer of 175 Deansgate, Bolton but some time prior to 1836 he went into partnership with Mr John Brimelow of Rumworth and they formed

William Heaton of Lostock (1852-1920). Proprietor of William Heaton & Sons Ltd. (Reproduced by courtesy of Bolton Local Studies Dept)

the firm of Heaton & Brimelow, manufacturing cotton hosiery at Derby Street Mill, Bolton. John died on 1st February 1837 and Mr Brimelow carried on the business alone until John's sons, Charles, born 1829 and Alfred John, born 1837 came of an age when they were able to take over the management jointly. After Alfred Heaton died in 1874 the Derby Street premises were sold. Charles set up a new business as Charles Heaton, Cotton Spinner, Weston St., Great Lever with a private address at Marlborough House, Hesketh Park, Southport (1888 Directory). Partington, writing in 1903, states that at that time Charles Heaton, then 74 years of age, was carrying on business on his own as proprietor of a large mill in Great Lever. In 1919 the firm became Charles Heaton & Son Ltd.

Egyptian Mills

John and Thomas Wood Heaton, halfbrothers, and sons of John Heaton by his first and second wives, built a mill and established a successful spinning business at Egyptian Mills, Slater Street, Bolton in 1837 and operated it for a number of years. John died 18 Jan. 1870 aged 50. Thomas retired to Blackpool and died 3 Dec.1886 age 77.[19] He was an Alderman and Justice of the Peace for Bolton. Both he and John made generous donations to the new Mechanics Institute in Bolton in 1868. The business subsequently passed into the hands of John Knowles & Son and their successors[20]. Part of the premises was demolished in 1985, when the cleared site was used for housing, but the remainder of the building is still in use for business purposes.

Notes and References

1. E.Baines "History,Directory & Gazetteer of the Co. of Lancs." 1825 (2 vols).
2. J.H.Longworth "The Cotton Mills of Bolton 1780-1985". Bolton Museum & Art Gallery ,1987. P. 10.
3. F.Musgrove "The North of England",pub.Basil Blackwell,Oxford,1990,pp.258 and 272. States that in 1770 an agricultural worker's average wage was 7/- per week and that in 1795 a handloom weaver could expect to earn 33/- a week from his loom.
4. J H Longworth. op cit. p.15.
5. "Yorkshire Cotton",Dr George Ingle. Carnegie Publishing 1997. P.6.
6. "Rilston & Hetton Cotton Mills", G. Ingle. An article in Yorks. History Quarterly,vol 3, issue 1,August 1997.
7. G.Ingle. Ibid
8. G.Ingle. Ibid
9. "Bolton: its Trade and Commerce". pub.1919.
10. Partington Papers. Ref. B 920 B. HEA, part 2, p.100. Bolton Central Library
11. E.Baines. Op. cit. Vol. 2, p.275.
12. Partington Papers. Op.cit., p.118, note 2. The following letter is quoted

"4th March 1809
Dear Father,

My brother's son James has taken a house at Roscoe Lane,Berry St. here at £24. His brother Joseph is come to him. I have given him the fustian suit which I reserved on breaking John's indentures - they fit Joseph well, and James, as I learn from himself, has much encouragement in his business."

13 Partington,op.cit. p.118, note 2 quotes the following letter,the original of which he states he saw:

25th October 1816

Dear Brother Joseph,
Your namesake, our nephew, came within these few months back, I understand, very much in rags, to the door of his brother James,who lives in this street (i.e. Ranelagh St.) and who clothed and employed him. Joseph's family of course came soon, and James took a habitation for them. William and his family have since joined them. James got William a warehouse -man's situation, at 11/- (55p) per week but the work was so much harder than William had been accustomed to,that he could not stand to it, and was obliged to apply to the Dispensary for the recovery of his health; and is better. James has bought a horse and cart with a view towards their livelihood by carting goods or coals for lesser housekeepers.- Chance custom was found to be so much occupied by those who supply it regularly, that a few days served to show the fallacy of this. James has applied to the owners of lesser steam engines and works, so as to obtain employment for William in bringing coals from the neighbourhood of Prescot. James finding some difficulty in dealing with Joseph, had an indenture of apprenticeship drawn up. Joseph is now the second time gone from his family your way..."

14 Musgrove,F. Op.cit. p272.
15 Longworth J.H..Op.cit.p.100
16 "A History of Chadderton Pubs" by Rob Magee.Published 1986 by Neil Richardson,375 Chorley Rd,Swinton,Manchester, pages 25/26.
    The following refers to the Horton Arms, 19 Streetbridge,Chadderton.
    "On Saturday 2nd December 1843 Anthony Spence moved into the pub. He was still Landlord in 1861,but he was killed that year when he was ejected from a gig travelling at speed at the bottom of Street Lane near the Bridge Inn.He was 54 years old."
17 Partington Op.cit., p.120, note 1, states that Thomas owed £100 to his brother James on security of a Bond,and James,somewhat harshly,insisted that his father should deduct this £100 from Thomas's share of his father's estate.Thomas agreed to this on James giving up posssession of the Bond to his father which he did on 12th June 1810.
18 "Transactions of the Historic Society of Lancs.and Cheshire",vol.9, p.265. [JHP]
    At a meeting held 6th Nov. 1856, Mrs Ann Maria Heaton, of Edge Hill,donated:-
    Copper Calendar 1782: Commemorative Medals - Roscoe,Broughton: Copper political tokens: Seven halfpenny tokens of the last century ,and various others.
    Ibid.vol.9, p.277.
    At a meeting held 1st January 1857, Mrs Heaton donated a map of Chester, dated 1643.
19 Partington, op.cit.. Notes to p. 103.
20 J H Longworth, op.cit.p.148.

Chapter Eleven

The Twentieth Century

For over four hundred years the family of the Heatons of Deane had been engaged in the process of ramification (see Appendix 1) which had greatly increased their numbers in south-east Lancashire. A glance at the family trees in this volume which show some of the descendants of the 17th-century Lambert Heaton and Anne Pilkington will give an indication of the total numbers of male Heatons born during the last three centuries from those lines alone. It is possible, therefore, to complete only a few of the lines of the various Heaton families which now exist and who are descended from those earlier Heatons whom we have named.

During the closing years of the nineteenth century the majority of the members of the Heaton family were still engaged in their traditional occupations of farming and textile manufacture and the trades associated with these two industries. Their social and economic positions were very widely separated. Edmund Heaton, farm labourer, had died a pauper in Farnworth workhouse in 1891 and a number of Heatons were earning a poor living on small upland farms above Horwich. At the other extreme, William Heaton, millowner of Lostock, had a very successful cotton spinning business and by 1900 he had just built his no. 2 mill at Lostock Junction. When he died in 1920 he was a multi-millionnaire in 1990s currency. Many members of the Heaton family were working in firms of various sizes, mainly associated with the textile industry or forms of engineering or mining or in one of the growing service industries. Farming, full- or part-time, whilst still important, comprised the main activity of fewer than it had previously as many more moved into industry and commerce.

The Township of Heaton

The first development which heralded any change in the predominantly agricultural character of Heaton was the building of Chorley New Road as a turnpike road in 1825 as described in chapter 8. This was to open up an area of land which was, later in the century, to become a fashionable high-class residential area. The 1849 first edition of the Ordnance Survey map shows the entire area as agricultural with some quarrying undertaken. The site of Lambert Heaton's Delph Hill Mill, built in 1800, is throroughly rural and is surrounded by farmland. The line of the Lancashire & Yorkshire Railway Co. from Bolton to Preston is shown but Lostock Junction did not exist. Many of the place-names which we have come across in relation to the Heaton's farming activities in earlier centuries are shown.

There may have been a few small artisans' houses built in that part of

Heaton nearest to Bolton where it abutted an already existing built-up area but the biggest potential for development in Heaton was in the provision of houses for the affluent families of Bolton manufacturers and members of the legal and medical professions. Heaton was well situated to form the site of a fashionable suburb for the wealthy. It was to the west of the town of Bolton so the prevailing wind tended to blow the smoke and fumes from the mills and factories in the opposite direction. It was well-wooded so the large houses could be on secluded sites and enjoy considerable privacy. The land sloped gently to the south and there were good views from several locations. The existence of Chorley New Road and Lostock railway station provided good access and transport links with Bolton and other towns.

The principal landowners in the latter half of the nineteenth and the early twentieth century when numerous expensive mansions were built in Heaton were the Tempest family and their successors the Beaumonts, and they were very willing to make building plots available, either on long building leases or freehold, to those who wished to provide themselves with a comfortable home on an attractive site in this fashionable suburb. Families from Bolton who acquired plots and built themselves mansions included the Knowles, Mellors, Wolfendens, Taylors and Lords, cotton magnates; and the Tillotsons, printers; Magers, brewers; and Dobsons, textile engineers.[1]

During the Late Victorian and Edwardian period, with the economy booming, development of these large houses went on apace but the radical social changes and shortage of domestic staff which followed the First World War meant that many of them were too large and expensive to maintain for single families, and other uses had to be found. Some were converted to flats, private schools or offices and many were demolished so that numbers of smaller houses at much higher densities could be built on the cleared sites.

The district of Heaton, formerly administered by a Rural District Council, had been absorbed into the borough of Bolton in 1898 and in 1974 the Borough Council, recognising the special character of the area around Chorley New Road, and acknowledging that much of the development which had taken place on the cleared sites of former mansions was not particularly attractive, designated the area as a Conservation Area and laid down a policy which was to be applied in future to proposals for development within it "so as to reflect and enhance the existing character of the area".[2]

Elsewhere in Heaton the land had remained largely agricultural until after World War II with just sporadic development taking place on various sites in the district. The land had remained in the ownership of the Beaumont family until 1937 when it passed to the Beaumont heiress who had married Lord Howard of Glossop. Their son Miles Francis Fitzalan Howard inherited the estate on the death of his mother in 1971 and himself became 17th Duke of Norfolk in 1975. When Miles Francis came of age in 1936 his grandmother gave a lunch at the Doffcocker Hotel to which all the estate farm tenants and leaseholders were invited. There may well have been Heatons amongst them.

The Twentieth Century

The Clough, Chorley New Road. A large detached house built around 1870, very possibly on the site of the Clough Farm which the Heatons occupied in the 18th century.
(Photograph by courtesy of Bolton Environment Dept.)

Ladybridge, Chorley New Road. A grand mansion built about 1870 and now converted into a conference centre.
(Photograph by courtesy of Bolton Environment Dept.)

Beaumont tenants at a presentation to Miles Francis Fitzalan Howard, later 17th Duke of Norfolk, on his coming of age in 1936. There may well have been Heatons amongst this group.
(Photograph reproduced by courtesy of Mr Lance Taylor and Bolton Evening News)

When Baroness Beaumont died in 1937 a number of freehold ground rents secured on 430 various properties in Heaton let on 999-year leases were offered for sale to raise money for death duties.[3]

Lostock Junction Mills was one of the largest developments in the district, built close to the railway station and being expanded in 1900 and 1915. During the 1920s and 30s numbers of small estates of semi-detached houses were built and there was ribbon development of similar houses along the main roads. The area of agricultural land was further reduced by the creation of golfcourses, reservoirs and a municipal cemetery. After 1945 the pressure on land for house-building increased and many acres were sold to developers for this purpose, wherever planning permission could be obtained. In 1975 Lostock Junction Mills, which had closed in 1971, were demolished and the site made available for housing. Agriculture now remains a minority activity in the district with farmers having to contend with all the problems brought by farming on the urban fringe.

The Twentieth Century 167

Lostock Junction Mills and surroundings in the 1930s. (Photograph by courtesy of Bolton Evening News)

Food Production

At the turn of the century 90% of farmland was tenanted, but many large agricultural estates began to be broken up during the early years of the 20th century as the owners became disillusioned with the burden of death duties and poor investment returns from agricultural land. A substantial proportion of farmers were, somewhat reluctantly, obliged to give up their status as tenants and take on the responsibilities of owner-occupiers servicing a mortgage. They felt they were able to make more money by paying rent and using their capital for increasing and improving their "live and dead stock", or animals and equipment, rather than putting it into the purchase of land. In the area with which we are concerned most of the labour on the farm was provided by a farmer's family, usually for keep and pocket money, on the understanding that when a young man wanted to take a farm of his own he would receive a proportion of the live and dead stock from the family farm to get started.[4]

On the outbreak of the First World War food was rationed and in 1915 after the war had been under way for about twelve months, measures were brought forward to ensure that essential farm workers were not accepted for military service and were discouraged from volunteering. After 1916, when conscription was introduced, farmworkers over 25 were exempt and more women were employed on the land.[5] In 1917, at the height of the German submarine campaign against British shipping, compulsory ploughing up of permanent grassland was enforced by County War Agricultural Executive Committees set up for the purpose of ensuring good farming practice.

After the war County Councils bought up larger farms which were for sale and split them up into smallholdings of 20-40 acres, putting up houses and farm buildings and letting them to returning ex-servicemen. Although these holdings were intended to be the first step on the farming ladder many of the tenants never had the opportunity to take a tenancy of a larger farm and were still in occupation of their smallholdings decades later. Between the wars, farming, particularly in the arable sector, suffered from a severe recession and many farmworkers left the land for ever.

During the agricultural slump of the 1920s and 30s Lancashire fared rather better than other counties and the level of agricultural employment was generally maintained.[6] A large urban population living close by enabled farmers to sell retail direct to the domestic market. Potato growing was a profitable crop in East Lancashire, and the farmers on the farms above the milltowns maximised their numbers of dairy cows by grazing most of their land in the summer and buying in straw from lowland farms and cheap cattle cake from abroad to feed their cows during the winter. Many farms kept an increasing number of poultry in order to sell their eggs direct to the housewives.

It was not until the outbreak of war in 1939 again brought the need for a major effort to produce maximum quantities of food that the general situation improved. Similar measures to 1914-18 to bring about the maximisation of arable crop production were introduced with a stringent ploughing programme. Thousands of women joined the Womens Land Army to work on the land. Rationing of food was in force during and for a few years after the war and the emphasis on food production continued for another 40 years. In 1973 Britain's entry into the European Common Market with its Common Agricultural Policy brought farmers generous grants designed to promote greater efficiency. It was only in the late 1980s when surpluses of foodstuffs began to appear again that these grants were discontinued. The financial advantage swung towards the arable farmer at the expense of the livestock and milk producer and the situation at the end of the 20th century was a complete reversal of the position a century earlier, with the livestock farmer now very hard pressed as prices collapsed, and the cereals producer in a better position but still largely dependent on subsidies.

Although the Heatons' involvement in agriculture is now very much diminished, nevertheless in the earlier part of the 20th century they were certainly still farming in various parts of Lancashire, including the rural parts of the township of Heaton all of which were obviously in close proximity to the built-up areas of Bolton and Horwich. These afforded ready markets for the produce of these farms and "every day scores of milk floats trundled down into the urbanised valleys as the hill farms sought the higher prices for their milk and eggs in the retail market".[7]

The Twentieth Century

Heatons and the Cotton Industry

In 1914 William Heaton & Sons became a limited company. Mill no. 2 at Lostock Junction had been built in 1900 and in 1915 No.1 Mill was enlarged again. In addition the company also owned Delph Hill Mill at Doffcockers. By the end of World War I the total floorspace at all three mills was 660,000 sq.feet, housing 263,000 spindles and the firm was noted for the production of superfine Egyptian and Sea Island cotton yarn, in particular their fine "Aero" yarn for the manufacture of aircraft fabric. 1920, the year in which William Heaton died, saw the peak of production in the Lancashire cotton industry. Thereafter the mills spinning coarser yarn began to go into decline in the face of competition from Japanese exports and home cotton industries set up by countries such as India which had previously been major markets for Lancashire products. The producers of finer cotton products were insulated from this recession for a few years but then began to be affected themselves. Rationalisation and restructuring became the order of the day with mergers and closures commonplace.

After William Heaton died in January 1920 his children, who had inherited his shares in William Heaton & Sons Ltd., decided to take the opportunity to sell their interest to enable the merger to take place in March 1920 which created the combine of Crosses and Winkworth Consolidated Mills Ltd, initially controlling 27 mills in Bolton and district.. In consideration for the sale of their shares they took a debenture secured against the assets of the new merged company which was intended to provide them with a substantial income.

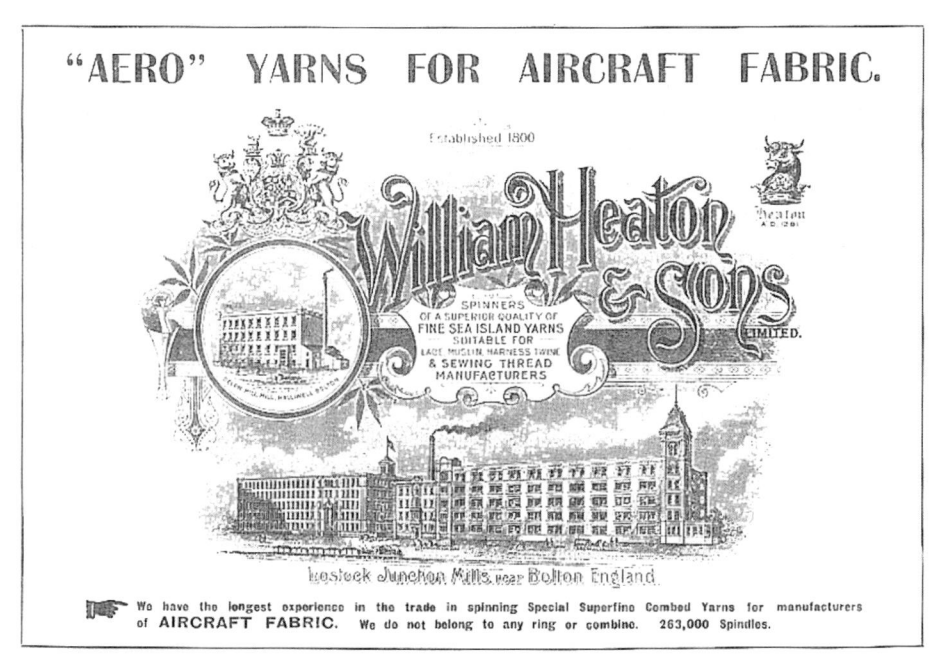

Advertising Poster of William Heaton & Sons. 1919.

During the 1920s four sons of William Heaton senior, John, Joseph, Benjamin and William junior were all directors of the company and in 1931 the trustees of the Heaton Debenture took a controlling interest in the firm. The company continued to trade throughout the depression and WWII but by 1944 the asset value had fallen considerably and the interest on the debenture was years in arrear. A reconstruction took place in August 1944 when the name of the company was changed to Crosses & Heatons Ltd. and Joseph Heaton became chairman and managing director, to be followed by Benjamin in 1948. Further company reconstructions took place but production finally ceased in 1971 when the Lostock Junction mill, at that time employing 250 people, was the only one remaining in the group, all the others having closed through streamlining and economic changes.[8] In 1973 the company was sold as a "shell" which became the parent company of a Lancashire hotel group.[9] At the close there were no Heatons involved in the management of the company.

Those male members of William Heaton's family who were not involved in actual cotton manufacture became cotton brokers and merchants, buying raw cotton from America, Egypt, the Sudan and the Carribean Islands where the fine longstaple cotton was grown and selling it on to the Lancashire spinners.

Notwithstanding the gradual decline in the cotton industry, William Heaton's immediate descendants appear to have been able to maintain adequate incomes with which to pursue their interests, mainly relating to the countryside. Most of them seem to have purchased country houses and land which enabled them to follow a rural lifestyle including hunting, point-to-point racing and livestock breeding for showing - a leaning towards the land and farming from which their grandfather Thomas had earned his livelihood and which their father had left to make his fortune in industry.

In 1969 Delph Hill Mill was closed and then demolished, the site being used for development as a public house. John Heaton's first mill at Picton Street had been converted into housing at the end of the 19th century, and in the 1940s the building was demolished and the site subsequently redeveloped with houses. Lostock Junction Mills having closed in 1971, were demolished in 1975 and redeveloped for housing in 1985. Thus might have ended the Heaton's association with the cotton industry which had lasted for the greater part of the 150 years during which King Cotton had reigned in Lancashire.

However, there was one surviving link between the Heaton family and textiles, which continued on a fairly substantial scale. In 1928 John Heaton, son of William of Lostock bought the firm of William Lawrence & Son Ltd, a cotton weaving company with which William Heaton & Sons had been associated in its heyday. This firm was managed initially by John Heaton and then in the early 1960s he was succeeded by his sons Martin, born 1915, and Richard, born 1918, together with their cousin Roger, son of Benjamin Heaton, himself a son of William of Lostock. The current senior management consists of Richard's son James Heaton and Peter Heaton, Roger's son. The company is currently based in Chorley and also has a mill at Halton in north Lancashire,

The Twentieth Century

very close to where the Heton family first emerged 800 years before. Until about 1965 the firm concentrated on weaving synthetic yarns but then branched out into processing yarn as well as weaving. They employ about 75 people and use the most modern machinery. By their policy of reinvesting in the latest technology they have maintained their business in the face of keen competition in the UK and abroad.

A Heaton Family outside Lancashire

The author's own branch of the family is just one of many who are now located outside Lancashire and Greater Manchester. Two generation spans are very long due to the size of his grandfather's family and the fact that his mother was his father's second wife. Edmund Heaton, originally baptised Edward, but who called himself Edmund for most of his life, was born to William and Alice Heaton in 1820. His wife Hannah, nee Spence, had 10 children over a period of 25 years, the author's father being the youngest, born in 1873. He too used the name Edmund all his life although it was not the name he was given at birth. The fact that he died when the author was aged only seven means that there was no first-hand information available as to the lives of himself and his brothers and sisters.

We have seen in chapter 10 how Edmund Heaton senior was able to establish a cotton waste bleaching business which enabled him to give his children a better start in life than he had himself. In the case of the author's father, Edmund Heaton II, he had a grammar school education and was then apprenticed to the electrical manufacturing firm of Ferranti who opened a

Lancashire mill girls in 1842.
(By courtesy of National Library of Wales)

Operative at William Lawrence & Son Ltd., 1999.

new factory at Oldham in 1879. After he qualified he obtained a job with a London firm of electrical engineers with whom he was responsible for contracts being carried out in various parts of the UK and in the USA. Thus he became one of a small number of members of his family who travelled outside the confines of south Lancashire and explains why the author and his siblings were not born and have never lived in the county. One of his contracts took him to the USA where he visited his brother Edward in Boston, Massachusetts, the city to which Edward had emigrated in the late 19th century. Unfortunately contact with Edward was subsequently lost and despite enquiries it has not been possible to track down any of the descendants of the author's close relatives who went to America in the late 19th century.

Edmund Heaton II met and married his first wife, Ethel Maria Dawe, of Yarmouth, Isle of Wight, when he was actually living in Newport, Monmouthshire but was engaged on a contract on the Isle of Wight where he met his wife-to-be. They were married at Yarmouth parish church on 27 December 1899. He was 27 and she was 25 and neither had been married before. Her father was William J. Dawe, the owner of a successful dairy business in Yarmouth.

Edmund and Ethel Maria moved around the country and as well as continuing his work as an electrical engineer he also established himself as a part-time farmer on tenanted farms in the years prior to the First World War. He took dairy farms in Monmouthshire and Godstone, Surrey and by 1913 he had established himself at Harleyford Home Farm, on the banks of the River Thames near Marlow, Buckinghamshire and was busy building up a herd of pedigree Ayrshire dairy cattle. The Ayrshire Cattle Society herd book for 1913 shows him as owning 31 pedigree animals. In 1914 he was 41 years of age and therefore not liable for military service but together with a number of his colleagues in the electrical industry he volunteered for a special unit which was being set up to man searchlight batteries on the east coast of England. Named the London Electrical Engineers and forming part of the Corps of Royal Engineers it accepted men with special knowledge and skills but over the age for normal military service. He served with this unit right through the war until he was demobilised in 1918.

Edmund and Ethel Maria had a total of six children but two girls died in infancy and those reaching adulthood were Gladys Ethel, born 26 Jan. 1902; Hilda May born 22 May 1908; Dora Olive, born 2 Oct. 1910; Reginald Edmund William, born 17 Oct. 1913. These are the author's half-brothers and sisters. Reg followed in his father's footsteps and himself became an electrical engineer. He married Marie Liggins and they had two children, Robert and Ann; Gladys never married; Hilda married Cecil Forcey, who eventually set up his own bakery and catering business on the South Coast, and their children were John, Anthony and Elizabeth who all married and had children of their own. Dora became a schoolteacher and married another teacher, Dennis Woods. Dennis became a headmaster and he and Dora worked together at schools mainly in Northamptonshire, Dora working and looking after their two sons Michael and Roger whilst Dennis was away in the forces in the Middle East through most of the war. All the children of Edmund's first marriage and their spouses have now died, except Dora.

When Edmund was released from the army in 1918 a slump began in farming which prompted him to give up agriculture and turn to his other profession of electrical engineering as a livelihood. The whole family went to live on the Isle of Wight near Ethel's parents whilst Edmund resumed his work on the mainland. Sadly, Ethel died there in 1924, aged only 50.

The younger children continued to live with their grandparents when their father was working away from home but in 1926, whilst working as resident engineer at Alders Papermill in Tamworth, Staffordshire, Edmund met and married Elizabeth Georgina Robinson. On 11 April 1928 Edmund Ronald Heaton, the author of this book, was born in the house at the Alders which went with his father's job, and on 5 July 1930 his brother Raymond Peter was born there also.

Mills for the manufacture of paper had existed on the Alders site alongside the River Tame since the 16th century and during the 19th century were owned by the Peel family, prosperous cotton spinners from Lancashire. Paper manufacture finally ceased in 1997 when the 29-acre site was sold for housing and all the buildings demolished, including the house in which the author and his brother were born.

In 1933, due to a change in policy with regard to power generation, Edmund lost his job at Alders and the house which went with it. The whole family, including Reg and Dora moved to Birmingham but the depths of the depression was not a good time for a man aged 60 to find a job and the family was maintained by the retail catering business which Elizabeth started, drawing on her previous experience as manageress of a number of such shops.

On 17 February 1936 Edmund died in Selly Oak Hospital, Birmingham and Elizabeth was left alone to bring up two boys aged 7 and 5. The eldest, Edmund Ronald, attended the Royal Masonic School, Bushey, Hertfordshire as a boarder from 1937 - 1944. His brother Raymond Peter eventually went to Kings Norton Grammar School, Birmingham where he stayed until he was 18, becoming head boy. Their mother carried on her business throughout the war under very difficult circumstances. The family's experiences were typical of many during World War II. Raymond was evacuated to a country area for some years, Edmund came home during the school holidays when he and his mother experienced some heavy air-raids on Birmingham. In September 1944 he left school to live at home and start work as a trainee chartered surveyor at a firm to which he was articled in Birmingham.

In April 1946, when he reached the age of 18, the author was called up for service in the army and joined the Royal Engineers as 14161179 Sapper Heaton E.R... His brother joined the RAF a few years later. Both brothers, with no particular social advantages, and whose father died when they were very young,

2nd Lieut. E.R.Heaton,
Royal Engineers.
Age 19 in 1947.

Flying Officer R.P. Heaton.
Age 24 in 1954.

were commissioned in the Army and the RAF respectively and both received a university education and became successful in their respective professions; achievements which, 50 years earlier, would have been regarded as highly unlikely. Thus had social conditions changed since the start of the century.

Elizabeth died in 1954, both brothers married and had children, and there are now male and female grandchildren. One of the author's sons has made his career in agriculture, so the occupation which maintained the Heatons for centuries is still followed in this family, at least for the present, and this branch of the Heatons seems assured of survival for a few generations yet.

Diversification

With the decline in the cotton industry, central government, local authorities and other bodies in south Lancashire tried very hard to attract new industries into the area and to bring about the expansion of alternative industries already located there, to try and minimise the effect of job losses in textiles on the general economy of the region. Between and after the two World Wars the hardest-hit parts of the county were given Development Area status and various incentives made available to industrial concerns. The retraining of a workforce largely experienced in the cotton industry was undertaken to equip them for other types of jobs, advance factories were built to be immediately available to rent, and market research and other initiatives were carried out.

The Twentieth Century

Over the years and particularly since 1945 there has been a quite considerable measure of success and firms engaged in chemicals production, aerospace technology, mechanical engineering, manmade fibres, paper, brick, and glass manufacture, as well as service industries, have been persuaded to locate themselves or expand in the area. Probably the most notable home-grown success was the tremendous advance made in glass technology by Pilkingtons of St. Helens through their invention of the float glass process in 1960, after years of research. This revolutionary method of glass manufacture was subsequently licensed all over the world and greatly increased the number of people employed by the company in Lancashire so that it became one of the largest employers in the region.

As Lancashire became far less dependent on the textile industry Heatons dispersed into most of the towns in the region, seeking the new jobs which were being created. The current telephone directories for Blackburn, Bolton, Liverpool, Manchester, St. Helens, Wigan and the adjacent districts contain nearly 600 households all bearing the Heaton name. The probability exists that a high proportion of those who come from this area of Lancashire and bear the name of Heaton are, in some way, connected with the family which is the subject of this book.

Notes and References

1. "Chorley New Road Conservation Area", pub. Bolton Borough Council, 1999.
2. Ibid.
3. Bolton Evening News, 21 Jan 1997.
4. "Agricultural History of England & Wales", vol.8, 1914-1939, p.58. Ed. J. Thirsk.
5. Ibid. p. 79.
6. Ibid. p. 239.
7. Ibid. p. 304.
8. Bolton Evening News, 14 Aug 1971; 28 Jan 1972.
9. Ibid. 10 May 1973.

Chapter Twelve

Heatons Elsewhere

One of the principal factors in our ability to trace the Heaton family back over many centuries is their apparent reluctance to move far from their ancestral home in south-east Lancashire. However some of them did undoubtedly move away and this chapter gives accounts of those who settled in three locations. Two moves were at very early dates, hence the connection with the family in Lancashire is dependent on a certain degree of hypothesis, but in the other case considerable research on both sides of the Atlantic has enabled rather more facts to be discovered.

Heatons in North America

It is likely that, from the 17th century onwards, numbers of Heatons emigrated across the Atlantic to seek their fortunes in the New World. The bulk of those who left probably did so in the later 19th century, including members of the author's own family, and of these we know surprisingly little, but it has been possible to trace a branch of the family who emigrated early in the 19th century, both back to a common ancestor in Lancashire in the late 16th century and forwards to their descendants living in the USA at the present time.

English Ancestry

William Heaton was baptised at Westhoughton, Lancashire, England, on 23 September 1781, son of James and Elizabeth Heaton, nee Nuttall, and he emigrated to the USA with his family in 1818, at the age of 37. His ancestry can be traced back to the slightly mysterious Ralph Heaton of Heaton (1589-1652), whom we have deduced, on the balance of probabilities, was the son of Ferdinando and hence connected to a line of Heatons extending back into the 12th century.

This branch of the Heatons had lived in Westhoughton for several generations. James, father of William, was baptised there on 12 June 1759 and married Elizabeth Nuttall at Bury on 16 February 1779. James' father was Atherton Heaton, baptised at Westhoughton on 7 April 1723 and buried there on 8 July 1778. He married Betty Magnall on 19 January 1746 at St. Mary's, Deane. The name Atherton occurs several times as a first name among the Heatons in the 17th and 18th centuries and derives from the surname of Philadelphia Atherton who married the Ralph Heaton mentioned above on 5 January 1613.

Atherton's father was John, born 1685 in Westhoughton and his mother was Jane Green, married to John on 11 June 1709 at Deane church. In previous generations the names in this line alternated between John and Atherton and we do not always know who the wives were. John's father was another Atherton, born 1664; before him came John, baptised 3 December 1645 and married to Jane; then Atherton, the eldest son of Ralph and Philadelphia, baptised 1 May 1617 at Leigh and buried at Blackrod 9 June 1662.[1]

William married Ann Mather at Wigan on 13 October 1805 and they had eight children in total who were: Jeffrey, born 22 August 1806; Amos, 24 November 1807; Elizabeth, 20 October 1809; John, born 1810; William, 20 January 1812; Ann, 17 April 1814, and Hannah 18 July 1819. Therefore all except the youngest daughter were born in England and emigrated to America with their parents in 1818. William was a master handloom weaver, no doubt assisted in this craft by his wife and older children, as was customary. Like most others in his trade in Lancashire he had found his earnings very severely reduced by the growing competition from the steam- and water-powered mills which were forcing prices for the finished product down below a level at which the family could reasonably exist. It is very likely that this difficulty in earning a living was what finally persuaded William and his wife that they should try to make a better life for themselves in the USA.

On 16 August 1819, the year after they left, there occurred the notorious "Peterloo Massacre". A large assembly of desperate handloom weavers and other workers with their wives and children, estimated at 60,000 in total, were holding a peaceful meeting to listen to speakers air their grievances, in St. Peters Fields, Manchester when the Manchester & Salford Yeomanry, the local mounted militia, on the orders of the magistrates, charged the crowd in an attempt to disperse it. This action resulted in the deaths of eleven civilians and injuries to some 400 others.[2] The plight of the handloom weavers continued to worsen as the powerlooms in the factories increased production and prices fell further. Within the next 30 years the ancient craft of handloom weaving virtually disappeared in England.

Arrival in the USA

When William and his family arrived in America[3] they settled in Lower Makefield township, Bucks County, Pennsylvania where the youngest daughter Hannah was born in 1819. Presumably William found the situation there more to his liking as the United States was not as industrialised as Lancashire at that time and it was still possible for a handloom weaver to earn a reasonable living. The prospects looked good enough for some of the sons to take up the weavers' trade like their father and others became blacksmiths. It seems that William's wife Ann probably died before the 1830 census in which she does not appear. William Heaton is recorded as marrying Deborah Carter in Philadelphia on 15 June 1834 but it seems he did not survive his second marriage long as on 3 November 1836 Mrs Deborah Heaton married William Anderson in Bucks County.

On 10 October 1828 Jeffrey, the eldest son, married Sarah Ann Winner, born in Bucks County. A somewhat unusual combination of marriages took place amongst the younger Heatons. It seems that the Heaton family from England made contact with a family of Heatons who had lived in America for some time, possibly since the 17th century. Four of the young people decided that their future lay together and that they would marry. Elizabeth Heaton, then aged 23, born in Lancashire, England, married Abner Heaton on 29 October 1832 and her brother Amos Heaton, aged 30 and also born in England, married Abner's sister Sarah on 29 October 1837. William, therefore, did not survive to see his second son married.

The Trek to the West

In 1837, for reasons which are not entirely clear but which may have been connected with the fact that many deaths were occurring through cholera in Bucks County, the families of Jeffrey, Amos, William junior, and Abner took the decision to move further to the west, where they knew that land would be available to them in Ohio. All the families sold or gave away whatever they could not take with them and equipped themselves with horses and carts which they required for the journey, and cattle needed to establish themselves on the new land. Men, women and children set out on a journey of several hundred miles, all their household goods loaded into carts, together with the smallest children, and the rest walked, leading the horses and driving the cattle. It is probable that all the wives were pregnant at that stage as they all gave birth a few months after arriving at their destinations. Their route of nearly 400 miles lay over mountains, across rivers, and along rough forest tracks where, although the Indians were not a threat, there was always the risk of attack by the dangerous bears, mountain lions, and other wild animals of this region. It was necessary to take this hazardous route to avoid the more populated river valleys where cholera was still rife. Eventually they arrived safely in Jefferson County, Ohio where some settled permanently but others moved on further west after a few years.

Weavers, Blacksmiths & Farmers

Jeffrey had followed the same craft as his father, William, and was initially a weaver but after moving to Ohio he changed his occupation to farming, first in Jefferson County and then, in 1849, moving on to Fulton County, Illinois where he purchased an 80-acre holding where he lived for the rest of his life. He died in 1858, leaving a widow, Sarah Ann, who lived on until at least 1889. Jeffrey and his wife had seven sons and three daughters. Simon, their third son, enlisted in the Union army and died from wounds on 29 November 1864, aged 30.

Jeffrey's eldest son, Henry Winner Heaton, born 9 March 1830, was also a weaver like his father and grandfather and he married Rebecca Ruth Patterson in Ohio on 17 May 1855. They lived in Fulton County, Illinois until 1862 when they moved to Schuyler Co. in the same state where they purchased 140 acres and apparently Henry turned his attention to farming.

Pioners migrating westwards, with carts very possibly similar to those used by the Heaton trekkers in 1837.
(Reproduced by courtesy of the National Library of Wales)

Henry and Rebecca had eleven children during the 1850s and 60s, eight sons and three daughters. The third son Sanford W. Heaton whose wife was Maria had seven children, all boys. We cannot trace them any further in detail but it would be fairly safe to assume, with all these male children in two generations, that many Heatons in this line are still living, direct descendants from William and hence from earlier Heatons in England.

Amos the second son of William, was a shoemaker by trade and when they arrived in Ohio he seems to have prospered as he is recorded as owning a considerable property adjoining the Quaker meetinghouse and graveyard in Smithfield, Jefferson County where still stands an old house in which Amos and Sarah may have lived in the 1870s. Amos established Heaton's Shoe Shop on Water Street in Sardis, Monroe County, Ohio and spent a considerable time there.

Amos and Sarah had seven children, three sons and four daughters, and the descendants of some can be traced through several generations and one right up to the present time through the female line Their eldest daughter Amanda

Jane, born 10 August 1840, living in Pleasant township, Jefferson Co., married Joshua Fisher on 1 February 1865 and they had 12 children between 1866 and 1884, 3 sons and 9 daughters. The youngest was Bertha Nana Fisher, born 7 August 1884 and married to Edward M. Wilkinson on 2 August 1903. Her daughter Pauline Cecelia Wilkinson, born 1 November 1912, married Gerard A. Robichaud on 19 March 1912 and became the mother of Judie Robichaud, presently married and living in California.

Other sons of William and Ann, who emigrated to the USA with their parents, were John and William junior. John, a weaver, married Sarah Brookes and had a son named William after his grandfather. William, son of William senior, apparently became a prominent citizen of Trenton, (now Emerson) Ohio, owning considerable property in the town. He married Rachel Stradling, had a daughter, Mercy Jane, and two sons, John W. and William A., and died in 1881. John W., it is believed, served in the Civil War, and married Hannah Furbey. William junior died in mysterious circumstances at the early age of 21. Nothing more is known of either of these two men or of any children they may have had.. Mercy married Joseph Philpott and had 4 daughters and 2 sons.

Elizabeth retained her Heaton surname when she married Abner Heaton, a blacksmith who practised his craft in Madison township, Guernsey Co. after the family arrived in Ohio. They later moved to Mount Pleasant, Jefferson Co.. Abner and Elizabeth had 2 sons and 5 daughters between 1835 and 1853 and their descendants can be traced for several generations. The eldest boy, Samuel was born 2 December 1842 and became a blacksmith, working in his father's shop from the age of 11. Samuel served in the Union Army under General Sherman from 1862-64. He had no children from his first wife Belle but his second wife Kate Alice nee Stewart, whom he married on 13 September 1877, bore him 4 sons and 1 daughter. Shortly after his first marriage he opened a blacksmith shop at Martins Ferry, Belmont Co., Ohio where he lived until he died on 12 May 1915, being survived by his wife. Their eldest son, Ralph, became a blacksmith also; the second son, Ross, was a draughtsman but we know little more about them. The third son Roy is said to have had a wife Helen and a daughter Geraldine, born 1919, but nothing more is known.

The Underground Rail Road

For several decades before the Civil War, slaves who had managed to escape from their masters in the Southern states were making their way northwards in attempts to reach Canada, the only place where they would be really free and safe from recapture. Even if they were able to leave the dangers of the slave-owning states and reach the North they were still subject to a law which said that they could be detained and possibly evntually returned to their masters. In the South they were dependent on their own ingenuity and help from free blacks and sympathetic whites but when they reached the Northern states they could be helped on their way by a system which grew up particularly in the states of Ohio, Indiana and Pennsylvania amongst the Quaker, Methodist and Mennonite communities. This became known as the Underground Rail Road and was designed to pass on escapees from one safe house to another until they reached the Canadian border. The descriptions used in relation to this process were all reminiscent of railroad practice. Escaped slaves were called "freight", the routes they took were "lines", stopping places were "stations" and their helpers were "conductors".

The village of Mount Pleasant where Elizabeth and Abner Heaton lived with some of their children was a principal station on the UGRR. The town, which was noted for its milling industry, had been founded in 1803 and incorporated in 1814 and had a strong population of Quakers. As members of the Quaker community in the town it is almost certain that Abner and Elizabeth were active in helping escapees on their way. It is estimated that between 40,000 and 100,000 escaped slaves used the UGRR to reach Canada.

More Blacksmiths

Abner and Elizabeth's younger son, John Cornelius Heaton, was born in Emerson, Jefferson Co. on 18 June 1848 and he too became a blacksmith. He married Martha Jane Wilson (1853-1908) in Mount Pleasant, Jefferson Co. on 2 August 1871, and it seems they lived there all their lives, becoming members of the Quaker community there. The year after Martha died he married Cassander Bell Rowland but he himself only lived another 12 months, dying on 23 May 1910. John Cornelius and Martha had 6 sons and 1 daughter, several of whose descendants can be traced.

Their eldest son, Frederick Clifton was born 11 July 1872 and followed in the family tradition by becoming a blacksmith in his turn, and living in Jefferson Co.. On the 7 October 1896 he married Elizabeth May Brashear from Belmont Co., Ohio. They had a total of nine children but one daughter died in infancy, and another at the age of 20; 5 sons and 2 daughters survived to adulthood. Their eldest son Harland married and had a son who served in the US coastguard in WWII but there were no grandchildren. The second son Lester also married and had sons and daughters and there were several grandchildren. Another son Brice married and had

An American Heaton. Frederick Clifton Heaton, aged about 20 in 1892. (Photograph kindly supplied by Mrs Julia Heaton Krutilla)

male children and grandchildren so the Heaton name continues with several members of this family. The other sons of John Cornelius and Martha married and produced several sons in their turn, and with this family the dispersal of Heatons to other parts of the United States really begins.

The youngest son David Medill Heaton was born on 9 May 1907, and lived in Jefferson County, Ohio and later in Weirton, Hancock Co., West Virginia. He was an automobile enthusiast and made it not only his hobby but also his living. He was still, therefore, working in a trade which might be said to be a 20th century successor to the craft of blacksmith which so many of his ancestors had practised. On 16 August 1941 he married Margaret Ellis and they had three children. Their eldest son David Paul was married twice but has no children. The younger son Craig was also married twice and has a son and daughter.

David and Margaret's only daughter was Julia Ann Heaton, married to David William Krutilla on 29 April 1972. Julia Heaton Krutilla has become a dedicated genealogist collaborating closely with Judie Robichaud in relation to the Heaton family in the USA. She is also a prominent member of several civic and genealogical organisations in Ohio, West Virginia and Pennsylvania. David and Julia have two children, Kendra Anne born 15 April 1979 and Garrett Reid, born 6 May 1985. They live currently in Weirton, West Virginia.

War Veterans

Several members of this Heaton family have fought in wars which have taken place since William, Ann and their children emigrated to America. Amongst those known to us as serving with the Union forces in the Civil War was John W. Heaton, 15th Regt. Ohio Volunteer Infantry, son of William and grandson of William senior. Another was Francis M. Heaton, 13th Ohio Volunteers, wounded at the battle of Chickamauga. He was the son of Amos and grandson of William. John P. Heaton,, his brother, was a corporal in the 3rd Ohio Regt.; captured at Stone River he was exchanged and returned to his unit in June 1863. Samuel H. Heaton, served in the 98th Regt. Ohio Volunteer Infantry under General Sherman from 1862-1864 and was discharged in June 1865 after seeing much hard fighting in Kentucky, Georgia and North Carolina. He was a son of Abner and Elizabeth and grandson of William and Ann. The only known Heaton fatality in the war was Simon, son of Jeffrey, William's eldest son. He was serving with the 36th Brigade of the 3rd Army Corps when he received wounds from which he died on 29 November 1864.

There are not believed to have been any Heatons from this family serving in the American forces in World War I but there were a number who enlisted in World War II. These include John Lee Heaton, son of Charles Ross Heaton, senior, and a descendant of Amos and Sarah. Robert E. Heaton served in the US Coastguard throughout WWII. He was a son of Harland and Helen Mae and a descendant of Abner and Elizabeth. William R. Heaton, son of Lester M. Heaton and descendant of Abner and Elizabeth, served as a Sergeant in the

1865 Discharge Certificates of Heatons who served in the Union Army, entered in the records of Jefferson County Courthouse, Ohio.
(Obtained by Mrs Julia Heaton Krutilla).

US Army Air Corps both in North Africa and Italy. He was hospitalised in N. Africa following a plane crash and when he recovered he was posted to a bomber base in Italy from where he undertook a number of missions. When his plane was shot down over Austria he survived but was taken prisoner and released when the war ended. His brother Lester also served in the US Army Air Corps and another brother Ramon was a seaman with the US fleet in the South Pacific. As far as is known there were no Heaton fatalities in World War II in this family.

At the Present Time

Seven generations of this family have now been in America for 182 years. They first used their traditional skills to earn themselves a living in a new country and have adapted these skills to meet fresh challenges as technology has changed. They survived the hardship of an ocean crossing and a long trek overland in order to establish themselves in a new location where they thought their prospects would be better and this belief has been justified. As was the case for their cousins left behind in England their living conditions, educational opportunities and economic position have greatly improved. Although the majority of them are still settled in the states of Ohio and West Virginia others have begun to spread further afield and descendants of William and Ann Heaton can now be found right across the continent from New York to California.

This has been the story of one single Heaton family from Lancashire and their descendants. Over the centuries there is no doubt that other members of the family of the Heatons of Deane have emigrated to America, both before and after the formation of the United States as a separate nation. Some may have gone to the South and indeed may have fought for the Confederacy in the Civil War. They all however have the same background in one small area of England and it is this, and the fact that some of them are so very keen on establishing their family history in as much detail as possible, which has enabled this history of this one family to be written and linked with their English ancestors of several centuries ago.

Heatons in North Wales

A probable branch of the Hetons from Lonsdale and Horwich has been settled in Denbighshire in North Wales for over 700 years and are generally known as the Heatons of Plas Heaton after the name of their house and small estate near Henllan, about 2 miles from Denbigh.

When King Edward I decided to invade Gwynedd in North Wales and make war on its Prince Llewelyn, one of the first of his tenants-in-chief to answer the call to arms was Henry de Lacy, Earl of Lincoln, and superior lord of extensive parts of Lancashire, including the Heton manors. De Lacy actively supported the king in the war of 1276-77 and when fighting broke out afresh in 1282 he again brought a contingent of men-at-arms and foot soldiers from Lancashire. It is believed that members of the Heton family, related to those established at Heton-in-Lonsdale and shortly to be at Heton-under-Horwich, were amongst a group of reinforcements sent to de Lacy in 1286 and that after marching from Chester to Rhuddlan they reached Denbigh on 16th October[4]. De Lacy had been granted the lordship of Denbigh in 1282 and proceeded to build his castle there, where Hetons formed part of the garrison.

There was a serious revolt by the Welsh in North Wales in 1294 during which the Earl of Lincoln was caught with too few men at Denbigh and was driven out on 11 November. It was not until the king arrived on the scene with a larger force about a month later that it was possible to recapture Denbigh and re-establish the garrison in the castle.[5] No doubt the Hetons in Denbigh were involved in much of the fighting at this time and eventually resumed their duties at the castle.

The First 500 Years

It seems likely that Hetons were principally engaged in garrison duties at Denbigh for nearly 50 years and it is not until a Survey of the Honour of Denbigh was carried out in 1334 that the name Heton first appears as holders of land in the area.[6] Service in the "Castleguard" of 40 days in wartime was most valued and all eleven English tenants at Lleweni had performed this service.[7] The parish of Llewenni contained 4559 acres and 4316 acres were allocated to English settlers when the Crown had taken possession after the Welsh revolt of 1294. This was by far the greatest percentage of escheated land in any parish and elsewhere the percentage of land made available to settlers was much smaller.[8] In the 1334 Survey the following entries appear:-

Henricus de Heton holds 4 acres in Lleweny for a rent of 3s.4d.
Willelmus de Heton holds 3 acres in Prees, formerly held by Ior ap Eden, rent 18d.
Johannes de Heton holds 3 acres in Grugor, rent 12d.
Ricardus de Heton holds 11 acres in Quilbreye, rent 5s.9d.
Ricardus de Heton holds 2 acres in Arquedell, rent 15d.[9]

To what extent these Hetons were related and which of them was to found the family which was eventually to become the Heatons of Plas Heaton we do not know but by far the commonest name in succeeding generations of Hetons here was Henry or Harri. According to the pedigree of the Heatons of The Green, Lleweni, included in Sir Samuel Rush Meyrick's edited version of "Heraldic Visitations of Wales (1586-1613)"[10] transcribed by Llewys Dwnn, Deputy Herald-at-Arms, and obtained originally by heralds from the family in residence at Plas Heaton; the founder of their line was Alexander, "lord of Heton", succeeded by Sir Charles Heton. However, there is no evidence that the first Hetons to settle in this area were persons of rank and succeeding heads of the family were not so designated by Meyrick. The only knight with a Heton name at this time was Sir William de Heton, son and heir of Roger de

Heton, holding lands at Heton and Urswick.[11] Therefore Alexander and Charles, or at least their respective social positions, have to be accepted as somewhat mythical.

The present family at Plas Heaton have in their possession a large tome compiled in manuscript by Reginald C. Heaton and completed in about 1924 which gives innumerable details of the Heatons of Denbighshire and Lancashire and also other families with which the Heatons have been connected over the centuries. The author has been able to refer to this book through the kindness of Mr Richard Heaton of Plas Heaton and the contents, in many respects, confirm and amplify the writings of Meyrick, Fletcher and J.H. Partington (q.v.).

After "Sir Charles" and starting, perhaps, at the time the Hetons gave up garrison duties circa 1325, Meyrick recorded, as heads of the family, four generations of Harri, then a Jenkin in the reign of Edward IV (1461-1483). Jenkin's son Harri is said to have married Anne, a daughter of David Myddleton of Chirk Castle. After this Harri there followed another four generations of Harri, then a Richard who is on record as marrying Elizabeth, daughter of Cadwaladr Wynne of Voelas. Over the centuries the Hetons formed unions by marriage with a number of ancient Welsh families. Up to this point Meyrick and R. C. Heaton are in agreement but afterwards Heaton has a more complex situation than Meyrick and is perhaps to be preferred, writing as he was 80 years later and with specific family knowledge.

He states that Richard son of Richard, born 1613, married twice. His first wife, Jane Lloyd of Foxhall had a son Hugh who himself married twice, his second wife Lucy, daughter of David Jones, a merchant of Denbigh, bearing him four sons, John, born 1653; Richard, 1658; Henry, 1661; Foulke, 1668. Meyrick states that Richard III married Margaret, daughter and co-heiress of Edward Davies of Denbigh in 1693, but they apparently had no children that survived to adulthood.

The eldest son John succeeded his father and married Mary Moyle, his first cousin, by whom he had 12 sons and 6 daughters. Several of the children died young and John was actually succeeded in 1718 by his fifth son Hugh, born 1687, only four years before Hugh himself died, leaving no children. A succession of Hugh's brothers then followed as heads of the family; firstly Richard, the 7th son, then John the 11th son and finally Benjamin, the youngest son, born 1700, who inherited in 1775 and died in 1776.

Benjamin, it seems was something of a wastrel who accumulated substantial debts and had to be rescued by his cousin, John Heaton, a lawyer and ships' cargoes broker in Hatton Court, Threadneedle Street, London, who agreed to pay off his debts totalling £857 and meet various annual pensions and payments for which he was liable. In return John was enabled to buy from Benjamin for a nominal sum of one guinea certain of his properties to keep them in the family. None of these four brothers had any male children who survived them and when Benjamin died the remainder of the Plas

Heaton estate in Denbighshire was inherited by the above John Heaton his cousin, who from his marriage to Martha Adamson in 1733 had also come into possession of the manors of Wereham in Norfolk, Bryncaeredig in Denbighshire, and certain properties in Warwickshire. Their son Richard was born in 1738 and died in 1791 and from this date on there are more details of the Heaton succession available through the researches of Mr Alan Fletcher[12].

This Richard married Sarah Venables and they were the parents of John Heaton of Plas Heaton (1787-1855), head of the family when Meyrick was compiling the contents of his book, which was published in 1846. When Richard died his son John was only four and the management of the estate fell to his mother until he attained his majority.

The Estate

From the small beginnings noted in the 1334 Survey it seems that additional land was gradually acquired, presumably by grant, purchase or marriage, until an estate of 1,342 acres had been built up[13] by the end of the 18th century. The first house the Hetons built on their land was of the small hallhouse type of two bays and this still survives as a farm building. In the early 17th century another house was built nearby which is now used as a farmhouse with traces of a moat and was recently described as "originally of central chimney and lobby entry plan with a small well staircase and an ex situ date of 1680"[14]. This is the date when the house underwent an extensive restoration by John and Mary Heaton whose initials J M H are carved on the beam over the entrance doorway.

In 1807 Sarah, widow of Richard Heaton, took the enterprising step of purchasing from Robert Williams Wynn an adjoining property known as Plas Newydd, comprising a substantial house of 5 reception rooms and 16 bedrooms plus servants quarters and with extensive outbuildings and 330 acres of land providing 28 acres of house and garden, 103 acres of woodland, 161 acres of pasture and 37 acres of arable.[15] This property, with additional land, was first offered for sale by auction in London in 1805 but was not sold. It was offered again the following year in Denbigh but apparently was still not sold and Mrs Sarah Heaton agreed to rent it for 12 months at the end of which time she bought it privately.[16]

The house was renamed Plas Heaton to perpetuate the name of the earlier houses the Hetons had occupied. Shortly before its purchase by the Heatons this 18th century house had been extensively remodelled and enlarged, involving the addition of one completely new wing whilst the older house consisting of the centre and the other wing was refaced.[17] The additional area of land brought the size of the estate up to 1,672 acres; not a large domain but sufficient to ensure that the family played a modest but significant part in local government and county society.

Family pictures in the house portray a number of 17th, 18th and 19th century members of the family including:-

Plas Heaton from the southwest, showing a side and the front elevation. (Crown Copyright. Reproduced by permission of the RCAHMW).

John Heaton, born 1696, a broker of ship's cargoes; his wife Martha nee Adamson; Robert Salusbury Heaton, Secretary to the Admiralty in William Pitt's government; and his brother Richard. The Salusburys are a prominent local family and the use of their name would appear to indicate a union between them and the Heatons at some stage. Other pictures are of John Heaton, son of Richard and Sarah, Recorder in 1811, High Sherriff in 1837; Rev Hugh Edward Heaton and his wife Catherine Maria; Lt.Colonel Wilfred Heaton in the uniform of the South Wales Borderers; his wife Florence nee Church.

Heraldry

In the Middle Ages, when the Heton family became of sufficient substance, coupled with their ancient lineage, to be accepted as gentry in Denbighshire, it is significant that the design they adopted for their coat of arms resembles very closely that of the Hetons of Heton-under-Horwich. Essentially the only difference is that the device on the bend of the Lancashire Hetons is "three bulls heads" whereas on the Denbighshire Hetons it is "three bucks heads". The introduction of this requisite difference on an otherwise identical shield is a feature which serves to strengthen the evidence of a connection between these Lancashire and North Wales families.

Estate Management

Records of the Plas Heaton estate at the end of the 19th century have been analysed by Mr Allan Fletcher and from these it is possible to determine the general pattern of management which was applied to the estate. The land was purely agricultural with a few urban properties owned in Denbigh and its most noticeable feature is the size of the farms into which the land was split. The average size of farm in Wales was rather less than 100 acres[18] and even in the more fertile parts such as the Vale of Clwyd only 40% of farms were from 100-300 acres. At Plas Heaton over 90% of the farms exceeded 100 acres in area and the average was 120 acres. The largest farm, of 183 acres, was the home farm, named Plas Heaton Farm and was let in 1892 at £220 p.a. representing £1.4s.(£1.20p) per acre. As the farms became smaller so the rent per acre increased, up to £2.8s.4d (£2.42p) for Tyddyn y Cerrig a holding of 12 acres only, where the rent of the house formed a greater proportion of the total. A quarry was let at £50 p.a. plus a royalty of 2d (1p) per ton (tonne) on the minerals extracted.

At later dates it seems that some of the land was taken in hand and farmed by the owners, and the present owner and his wife have farmed approximately 360 acres with sheep. The author is advised that the present area of the estate is some 1,400 acres. The opportunity has been taken to sell off small plots on the perimeter when planning permission can be obtained for housebuilding but no major development of any kind has taken place, contrary to the situation at the former Heaton lands near Bolton where large areas have been developed for building.

The Nineteenth & Twentieth Centuries

Whilst the purchase of Plas Heaton was proceeding John Heaton, the then owner, was a teenager at school at Eton where he shone as a bowler in the school cricket team, playing a prominent part in the Eton victory against Harrow in 1805 where he bowled out five Harrow batsmen and caught two others.[19] After he left school there is no record of John attending university; presumably he came home and managed the family estate and engaged in other local activities with which the Heatons concerned themselves. He attained his majority in 1808 and in 1814 he married Elizabeth Jones of Cefn Coch. She died eight years later having given birth to one daughter and five sons during that time. They were Sarah Elizabeth, born 1815; the eldest son, John Richard, 1816; Wilson Henry 1817; William Henry, 1818; Charles Wilson, 1820; and Hugh Edward born 1821.

Two years after his first wife died John Heaton married again to Anne Elizabeth Henniker, the eldest daughter of John, 3rd Baron Henniker of Thornham Hall, Suffolk, and she bore her husband another eleven children.

John Heaton was an active member of Denbighshire society and played a prominent part in local government in the county. He served on Denbigh Town Council, he was a magistrate for over 40 years and for half that time he was Chairman of Denbighshire Quarter Sessions[20]. He took up and pursued an unpopular cause which was the establishment of a mental hospital in the county. He persuaded his friend Joseph Ablett to donate land as a site and himself gave money and raised large sums from others to help meet the cost of erection of the building .

In 1837, as High Sheriff of Denbighshire he published the proclamation of the accession of Queen Victoria to the throne having previously, as Captain of the Denbighshire Yeomanry escorted the then Princess Victoria through the county on her way from Ireland to Windsor. For his long service to Denbighshire in various capacities he was offered a knighthood but he declined to accept.. He died in 1855, aged 67, and was succeeded by his eldest son John Richard who was 39 when he inherited the estate.

John Richard had made a career in the Army which he joined at 19 years of age and was commissioned as an ensign in the 1st Regt. of Foot. By 1835 he was adjutant of the regiment and two years later he transferred to the 7th Dragoon Guards as a Lieutenant, becoming a Captain in 1844 and Acting Major in 1845 when he was serving in South Africa with the 2nd Dragoon Guards. He was hurt during a skirmish that year and his injuries were so severe that he was invalided out of the Army on half-pay. He was at home in England for several years and during that time his father died, but he did not really take to life at Plas Heaton and he resumed his army career, being promoted to full Major in 1865 and to Lieut. Colonel in the following year. During 1864 he had been appointed Deputy Lieutenant of Denbighshire and over the succeeding twenty years he served the county in several capacities. In 1870 he became Sheriff and he subsequently was appointed Treasurer of the County in addition to serving on the Denbigh High School Board. He died in 1885.

John Richard had no children and two younger brothers had died before him. He was, therefore succeeded by his youngest brother Hugh Edward. He was a clergyman, a graduate of Jesus College, Oxford and an extremely erudite person. After a number of appointments in the Church he became vicar of Bettws-yn-Rhos in 1859 and later Rural Dean of Denbigh. During the American Civil War he made impassioned pleas from the pulpit for his congregation to give financial help to the desperate Lancashire cotton workers thrown out of work by the lack of raw cotton caused by the North's blockade of Southern ports. Did he know that some of those affected, both management and operatives, stemmed from the same family origins as himself some hundreds of years earlier?

Hugh had married Catherine Maria Craven and they had twelve children over a period of fifteen years between 1854 and 1869, the eldest son being Wilfred to whom the estate passed on the death of his father in 1891. The descendants of the other children were active in many professions and occupations including medicine and architecture.

Domestic Arrangements

The dependence by upper- and middle-class Victorians on the availability of servants to run houses of any size is shown by the arrangements which we know existed at Plas Heaton during a large part of the 19th century. Records from 1851[21] show that at that time the living-in staff included a butler, a footman, a lady's maid, a cook, a laundry maid, a dairymaid, and a handyman. Ten years later in 1861 the staff had increased to a butler, a governess, a housekeeper, a children's nurse, a lady's maid, a cook, a footman, a general maid, a scullery maid, a laundry maid and a dairymaid. In addition there would certainly have been a number of staff who arrived daily, including gardeners.

A parlour maid's duties kept her busy from 7 a.m. to perhaps 9p.m., with an afternoon break, and the other servants' hours were probably similar. Although the staff worked long hours they were well paid in comparison with rates in other similar households. In 1893 the rates paid were £40 p.a. for a parlourmaid, housemaid £36 p.a., the head gardener £54 p.a., and the two assistant gardeners 18s.(90p) and 13s. (65p) per week.

The 19th century Heatons at Plas Heaton were typical of their time. Paternalism was the essence of the relationship between themselves and their staff and discipline was strict. Democracy was not expected to play any part in the household, either by the family or the staff, although by the end of the century slightly more liberal views were creeping in.

Smaller Families

Wilfred Heaton was a professional soldier, commissioned in the South Wales Borderers in 1874. During the Zulu War in 1879 he was part of Lord Chelmsford's column which tried in vain to relieve the 1500 British soldiers who were massacred by the Zulus at Isandhlwana on 21 January, the day before 4000 Zulus attacked a small force from Wilfred's regiment in the famous action at Rorke's Drift. At the age of 24 he was a Captain and had been mentioned in despatches. He served for a number of years in India and in the army in Burma during the war of 1885/6 by which the British annexed Burma. It was in India that he met and married Florence Church, daughter of an Indian civil servant. This took place in 1889 by which time he was a Major. Wilfred and Florence had only three children, Wilfred John, the eldest, Hugh Edward, named after his grandfather, and Florence Catherine.

The Rev. Hugh Heaton died in 1891 and the family came home from abroad. Wilfred retired from the army in 1896 with the rank of Lieut. Colonel but re-enlisted on the outbreak of the Boer War in 1899. He was first sent to Ireland to raise a battalion for the Irish Reserve Fusiliers and then raised a battalion of the Garrison Regiment which he took to Malta and then to South Africa.. Back home in Wales as a Colonel in 1900 he devoted himself to estate management and various local activities. He was a Justice of the Peace, a Deputy Lieutenant, a school governor, and a member of the Denbighshire Infirmary Committee which his grandfather had been responsible for founding. During the 1914-18 war he had a job as a military censor. He died in 1921 and was succeeded by his son Wilfred John.

Wilfred John was born with a curvature of the spine and was dogged by ill-health, a matter of considerable concern to his family. The advice of a medical specialist in 1909 was that he should not attempt to play football, could play tennis or golf but should not study too hard. He was unable to follow his father into the Army and was prevented by ill-health from active service in the First World War. He never married and he was succeeded by his nephew Richard John in the ownership of Plas Heaton estate.

Hugh Edward served in the submarine service of the Royal Navy in World War I and after the war he continued his naval service, serving in Alexandria, Malta and other Mediterranean stations, accompanied by his wife, until he retired as a Commander RN in 1932 when he started a fruit farm at Rhual.[22] On 12 January 1921 Hugh Edward had married Gwenllian Margaret, only daughter and heiress of Lt. Col. Basil Edwin Philips of Rhual, Mold, thereby uniting the ancient estates of Plas Heaton and Rhual with its magnificent early 17th century mansion. Hugh Edward and Gwenllian Margaret had two sons, Basil, born in 1923 and Richard, born in 1926.

In 1938, with war looming, Hugh Edward resumed his naval service ashore on the Staff of Western Approaches, based at Liverpool. His wife played an active role in the Women's Auxiliary Territorial Service (the A.T.S.) and at the end of the war in 1945 she held the rank of Controller, equivalent to Colonel in the Army. She was awarded the CBE for her wartime services. Basil joined the Royal Artillery in 1942 and after the war stayed in the Army until he

Rhual near Mold, Flintshire. (Crown Copyright. Reproduced by permission of the RCAHMW)

retired as a Major after 22 years service, spending several years in the Far East, where he was awarded the MBE for his service in the Korean War. Richard served in the Royal Navy at the end of the war. Commander Hugh Heaton undertook much public work on his retirement from the Navy. He was a Deputy Lieutenant, a County Councillor (being Chairman in 1958/9), and a Justice of the Peace, as well as being a churchwarden of Gwernaffield church.

Rhual belonged to Gwenllian Heaton, heiress to the old Welsh family of Philips and when Basil married in 1955 she gave him the property. Richard inherited Plas Heaton from his uncle in 1956. The fact that Basil and Richard have both fathered only daughters raises the probability that in due course, after 700 years, a family named Heaton will no longer occupy Plas Heaton and also that the Heaton tenure of Rhual will have lasted only two generations.

Heatons in Yorkshire

The author has been made aware of the extensive research carried out by the late John Heaton of Keighley, Yorkshire, in relation to branches of the Heaton family in south Yorkshire, and which he completed only a few months before his death in 1993. However, his working papers have not yet been thoroughly examined and released by his family for further scrutiny so it is not possible, at the present time, to quote the various sources upon which Mr Heaton relied in reaching his conclusions.

These basically are that our first positively identifiable ancestor Waldef had a brother Adam who was the founder of a line of Hetons who, in the 12th century, established themselves at what is now Kirkheaton at the junction of the Calder and Colne valleys in Yorkshire. Their father Orm was, therefore, the common ancestor of the Lancashire and Yorkshire Hetons After several generations spent at Kirkheaton a younger son acquired land at Oxenhope and eventually at Oldsnap in the parish of Haworth, in the last half of the 14th century. Another branch of the family were responsible for founding Chillingham castle in Northumberland in the early 13th century. After a few generations Heton heiresses married into the de Grey family by whom Chillingham has been owned ever since. The Hetons at Kirkheaton eventually died out through lack of male heirs.

During the Wars of the Roses the Heatons of Oldsnap spent 25 years in Scotland to escape their Yorkist enemies and only returned in 1485 when the Tudor King Henry VII gained the throne. The late John Heaton tells how the Heatons lived on at Oldsnap and adjacent properties for generation after generation, through the death of Elizabeth the last Tudor monarch, and the accession of James I, the Civil War of 1642-49, the Commonwealth under Cromwell, the Restoration of Charles I in 1660, the "Glorious Revolution" of 1688 which brought William and Mary to the throne, and the 1715 and 1745 Rebellions by supporters of the Stuart dynasty.

In the 16th century a younger Heaton son took over Ponden Hall estate nearby and a succession of eight Robert Heatons occupied that house. In the middle of the 18th century the Heatons finally relinquished their house at Oldsnap and moved to a farmhouse nearby, at which date all the Heaton papers and records were moved to Ponden Hall. The late John Heaton traces his own descent from this time through six more generations to his birth at Bradford in 1922.

The Heatons at Ponden Hall were undoubtedly the best-known of the Heaton families in Yorkshire, principally because of their connections with the Bronte sisters and their father and brother at Haworth parsonage nearby and also because of their involvement with the burgeoning cotton industry in Yorkshire. Dr George Ingle's recently-published "Yorkshire Cotton" [23] gives details about the Heaton's cotton spinning and weaving interests, the mills which they owned, and the eventual fate of their businesses. Further material is available in Bradford Archives Dept. including an unpublished paper of 1924 by Mr William Shackleton.

The purpose of this brief section has been to show the link which is purported to exist between the Heatons of Lancashire and those of Yorkshire, and to demonstrate that to find this it is necessary to go back to the very earliest period which has been covered in the story of the Hetons of Heton-in-Lonsdale in this book. If the necessary evidence is eventually produced to show that the late John Heaton's hypothesis is correct and that Waldef did indeed have a brother Adam and that the two diverged to opposite sides of the Pennines then a further interesting development in the history of this Heaton family will have been opened up.

Notes & References

[1] Information supplied by Mr Ron Smith of Bolton, Lancs. and obtained from parish registers, Wills and other documents.
[2] " Oxford Illus.History of the British Army" OUP 1994, p.410. Assoc. Ed. Ian Beckett.
[3] Information for this section comes from Mrs Julia Heaton Krutilla of Weirton, West Virginia, USA, a meticulous genealogist with a comprehensive knowledge of her Heaton family history in the United States and to whom the author is greatly indebted.
[4] Information supplied by Mr Richard Heaton of Plas Heaton.
[5] J E Morris " The Welsh Wars of Edward I ", 1901, pp. 253/4.
[6] " Survey of the Honour of Denbigh ", P. Vinogradoff & F. Morgan, 1914.
[7] " The Englishry of Denbigh" D Huw Owen. Trans. of Cymmyrodorion Society, 1974/5, p. 75.
[8] Ibid.
"English Element in Perfeddwlad". T P Ellis, Y Cymmrodor, 1925, vol. xxxv, pp. 187-199.
[9] Vinogradoff & Morgan, op. cit.
[10] "Heraldic Visitations of Wales", ed. by Sir Samuel Rush Meyrick, pub. for the Welsh MSS Society, 1846. Vol II, p.349.

11 C. Moor "Knights of Edward I", Harleian Society, 1929.
12 Allan Fletcher. " Plas Heaton and the Heatons in the 19th century". Transactions of Denbighshire Hist. Soc., vol. 45. Largely derived from Plas Heaton papers at Denbighshire Record Office.
13 Ibid.
14 Edward Hubbard "Buildings of Wales - Clwyd". Penguin, pp. 180/1.
15 Allan Fletcher, op.cit.
16 Information supplied by Mr Richard Heaton of Plas Heaton
17 E. Hubbard, op.cit.
18 Allan Fletcher, op. cit. p. 29
19 Allan Fletcher, op. cit.
20 Ibid.
21 Ibid.
22 "A Short History of Rhual" by Major Basil Heaton and privately published by him, 1987.
23 Dr George Ingle "Yorkshire Cotton". Carnegie Publishing, 1997

Conclusions

This has been a story spanning 850 years and 28 generations. We have seen a family emerge from a period which marked the very beginnings of the English nation, in large part an amalgam of immigrant races. Throughout their history many members of the Heton/Heaton family have shown a degree of enterprise which has enabled them to overcome periodic variations and decline in their fortunes. On occasions it was this same entrepreneurship which failed and brought about a setback but such rewards and penalties are inherent in any enterprise involving risk.

In its early days this Saxon family probably suffered severely from the confiscations of land and destructive depredations of the Norman conquerors but they were eventually able to consolidate and expand their position in Lonsdale where their principal manor was turned into an exceptionally fertile holding, noted for its cereal crop production.

Their contacts and apparently good relations with their overlords enabled some of them, at the beginning of the 14th century, to establish themselves further to the south in Lancashire so that when the Hetons in Lonsdale died out through lack of male heirs at the end of the 14th century the Hetons near Horwich were able to continue and thrive. The very modest knight-service required by their overlords for the land both in Lonsdale and at Horwich appears to indicate that it required very considerable improvement and lengthy cultivation before it could be farmed efficiently, and several generations were to elapse before this work was completed.

A scheme of estate management had to be devised which would provide the head of the family with an income commensurate with his status whilst at the same time giving other members of the family security of tenure in relation to lands which they leased, farmed and sublet. It involved the creation of enclosed fields and small farms well in advance of the Parliamentary enclosures of the 18th and 19th centuries. The system of tenancies and subtenancies which achieved this, whilst perhaps frustrating to junior members of the family, deprived of the ownership of freehold land, nevertheless was ultimately to the benefit of many of them when that freehold land passed out of the control of the Heton family in the later 16th century.

Although one fortunate marriage to an heiress brought the manor of Birchley into Heton ownership, they were never able to make the sort of marriages which would have taken them into a rather bigger league of landowning families. In the 16th century when they needed good luck and a boost to their fortunes they could not call on the patronage of powerful people nor were members of the family at the time astute or rich enough to take advantage of the opportunities available in the land market following the dissolution of the monasteries. As with present-day small commercial companies they remained vulnerable to takeover and not of sufficient size to provide a springboard for expansion.

However, this is by no means the story of the few senior members of an elite landowning family who were able to achieve high social status until it all disintegrated around them with the loss of their land. Members of the family prospered as yeomen farmers in the 17th and 18th centuries on the land which they leased from their new landlords. The entrepreneurial spirit showed itself in the combination of farming with small textile businesses, initially on a domestic scale, but gradually increasing in size until the end of the 18th century saw the establishment by Heaton entrepreneurs and their contemporaries of cotton mills and factories which heralded the start in Britain of the world's first Industrial Revolution.

As the 19th century advanced some of these early small businesses became major cotton enterprises but others failed, causing hardship to their founders and those who had invested in them. All the time a proportion of the family continued in farming although the numbers fell as more and more moved into the new industries, attracted by the higher earnings available there.

There had been emigration to North America by a small number of family members since the 17th century but comparatively little movement otherwise out of Lancashire except by those who had made their way, from the earliest times, to London to seek their fortunes as merchants, lawyers, clergy and servants of the monarch. However, in the 19th century we saw, almost for the first time, family members making their way into other parts of Britain and pursuing more diverse occupations. This situation intensified during the 20th century, particularly when the cotton industry in Lancashire began to decline after 1920. The wars of the British Empire in the 19th century and two World Wars in the 20th century found Heatons caught up in these conflicts, as volunteers and conscripts, and serving throughout the world.

In the 1930s and particularly after World War II, diversification became the order of the day as government and local authorities strove to attract alternative sources of employment to the rapidly declining textile industry, and many people moved home in consequence. Nevertheless many Heaton names are still concentrated in south-east Lancashire and particularly around that area of Bolton where they were first established 700 years ago. This tendency for some families to concentrate and multiply in one fairly limited location is termed "ramification" and has been the subject of an intensive study which is reproduced in part in Appendix I.

Whilst to some, the loss of their ancestral freehold lands in the 16th century might be seen as the precursor to an overall decline in the status and fortunes of the Heaton family, this is to take only a limited view of the situation. Only a few senior members of the family were directly affected by the change in circumstances and even they remained substantial leaseholders, regarded as gentlemen, for the rest of their lives. Their junior contemporaries and descendants had never known anything but life as leaseholders and, with very few exceptions, appeared quite content to pursue their farming and business activities on that basis. Indeed, many yeomen preferred not to have to sink capital into the ownership of land, but to use it to increase their livestock and equipment.

It is true that in the 19th and 20th centuries the freehold owners were able to benefit economically from the expansion of Bolton and the demand for building land in the district of Heaton but the extent to which such good fortune would have benefitted the great majority of members of the family if the Heatons had still owned the land is impossible to tell. Obviously a small tightly-knit family owning such an estate might be expected to all enjoy the social and economic benefits accruing from it, but there are few precedents for the distribution of such wealth amongst hundreds of family members. Even when some industrialist members of the Heaton family were enjoying great prosperity, unknown to them other members were dying as paupers.

Probably the most notable feature of this Heaton family over the centuries has been their prolificacy and the rate at which their numbers have multiplied. Although the numbers involved have made it impracticable to try and trace all branches of the family through the 19th and 20th centuries the main line of descent of this Heaton family has been followed in as much detail as possible and it is hoped that this can form a basis for those who wish to investigate further. There is a strong probability that a high proportion of those living in or associated with south-east Lancashire and bearing this name has some connection with the family which is the subject of this book and with due diligence and a degree of good luck it is possible that they, if so interested, could establish this connection.

Whereas several of those families who succeeded the Heatons as owners of the manor and township of Heaton died out because of lack of male heirs, that has never been a problem with our Heaton family. They were there first, and they are there still, and likely to be for a long time to come.

Appendix 1

Ramification

Reprinted from " A History of British Surnames " by R. A. McKinley, 1990, by permission of the publishers Addison Wesley Longman Ltd.

A characteristic of locative surnames in some parts of England is a tendency for individual names to ramify and to increase greatly in numbers within a limited district, with only occasional individuals occurring elsewhere. It is the case generally in all parts of Britain, and with surnames in all categories, that instances can be found where one family has, over a period of several generations or even over several centuries, developed a succession of branches and increased considerably in numbers to the extent that the surname borne by the family has become locally quite common, while remaining scarce, or totally absent, in other parts of the country. Examples of surnames which have ramified locally to a moderate degree can be found in most counties from the sixteenth century onwards, and even before 1500 the beginnings of such developments can be observed in the c ase of a smaller number of surnames.

However, in some parts of Britain, especially in the north of England, there are areas where some locative surnames have proliferated very greatly, to a much larger extent than is usual when families ramify in the way just described. Such developments have been an important feature of surname history in such areas as south east Lancashire, the dales region of West Yorkshire, or the Yorkshire woollen district. In these areas many locative surnames have increased greatly in numbers, and continue to be very numerous there to the present day. Seventeenth-century sources, such as the Protestation Returns of 1641-42 for Lancashire, show that the process was already well advanced at that period. The locative surnames which proliferated are nearly all ones which originated in the parts where they expanded, and most were derived from the names of small inhabited localities, either detached farms or hamlets. The surnames from the names of towns or larger villages very rarely increased in numbers to anything like the same extent. Although the genealogical evidence for the Middle Ages, and even for the sixteenth century, is generally inadequate to enable pedigrees to be traced for families which were not those of large landowners, it must nevertheless be suspected that each such surname began as the name of a single family, whose surname was derived from the name of a farm or hamlet where the family in question were at first the only, or perhaps the principal, inhabitants. The evidence is hardly ever sufficient to provide conclusive proof of this, but it is often possible to establish that relationships existed in the sixteenth and seventeenth centuries between a number of families all with the same surname, and this suggests that at those periods all the bearers of any one of the locative names under discussion are likely to have had a common descent. These circumstances, and the way in which many locative surnames remained for a long period in one small area, centring in each case around the point of origin, creates a strong presumption that many of the locative surnames in question were at first each the surname of one family, even if the genealogical evidence to prove this does not exist.

It is probable that in these circumstances all the people bearing any one of the locative surnames in question were all descended from one common ancestor, living perhaps in the thirteenth or fourteenth century (the periods when most of the surnames concerned first appear). Many locative surnames which originated from place-names in south-east Lancashire, and proliferated there, are still among the more numerous in that region today, despite all the migrations and population shifts of the past two hundred years. Such surnames as Bardsley, Barlow, Butterworth, Clegg, Crompton, Heaton, Heywood, Lomas, Mellor or Wrigley continue to be very common names in what is now Greater Manchester, but are found much less frequently in other parts of the country. It is likely that each of these surnames originated with a single family, which gradually increased in numbers over a period of centuries. Similarly in parts of West Yorkshire there are locative surnames which have ramified there over a long time, and which are still very numerous there to the present day, while remaining much less common elsewhere. Examples of such Yorkshire surnames are Ackroyd, Armitage, Horsfall, Illingworth, Lockwood, Murgatroyd, and Sutcliffe. A fair number of other locative surnames could be cited as instances of names which have increased greatly in numbers.

The basic factor behind this development is the demographic history of the regions involved. Both south-east Lancashire and West Yorkshire are areas where there was a growth of population from the sixteenth century onwards. Over a long period the expansion was mainly the result of the natural increase of the existing population, with no more than a small amount of immigration from outside. To some extent the situation changed with the Industrial Revolution, so that Lancashire, for example, underwent large-scale immigration from Wales and Ireland. During the nineteenth century, however, despite the continued movement into the county of people from outside, many already well-established surnames derived from place in south-east Lancashire, continued to increase greatly in that area, with only a relatively small number of instances to be found anywhere else.

The ramification of some locative surnames in Lancashire and Yorkshire appears very striking to anyone who examines the history of surnames in either county, all the more so because the proliferation of surnames, whether locative or in other categories, did not take place on the same scale in most parts of England (and the processes which made some surnames very common in Wales, and in the Gaelic speaking parts of Scotland, seem to have been different). The process of ramification is especially obvious because there are many locative surnames which are derived from unique place-names, and which can have only one point of origin, even though there are some surnames of the type which could be derived from more than one place, and indeed often are...

... In these circumstances it is obviously pertinent to ask if the surnames which have become relatively numerous as a result of individual families ramifying share any common characteristics. Though the limitations of the existing sources of information and especially the gaps in the genealogical evidence, make it difficult to be certain of the position in respect of some surnames, it seems that most of the names in question did have some common factors in their history. Hardly any were the names of major landowning families, and few seem to have been the names of peasant families in origin. Most of them, where the facts can be discovered, seem to have been the names of either landowners of moderate wealth, belonging to what at a later date would be called the lesser gentry, or the names of substantial free tenants of the franklin or yeoman class. Families so placed would be in a better economic position than bondmen, minor free tenants, or landless labourers, and would be rather more likely to have numbers of children who survived into adult life. Another common characteristic of families with surnames which ramified is that most of them had already begun to develop into several different branches by about 1400. Families whose names ramified greatly in the sixteenth and seventeenth centuries were already showing signs of such a development considerably earlier. Besides this, it is likely that genetic factors had some influence, though it is impossible to be certain about that now.

Whatever the precise causes, and the evidence is not sufficient to enable any unqualified assertions to be made on the subject, there is over a long period a marked contrast between a minority of surnames, many of them locative, which have proliferated considerably, often in the areas where they originated, and the much larger number of names which have not multiplied significantly at all. Many locative surnames which are rare in most parts of Britain, and which appear in most regions as the names of perhaps one or two families, are still today quite numerous at and around their points of origin. For this reason alone it is important to locate, if at all possible, the place from which any locative surnames under invetigation have been derived. If this can be done, it will often be found that the surname, however scarce nationally, is fairly common in the district where it originated.

Appendix 2

Heaton Heraldry

The device on the coat of arms adopted by the Hetons of Heton-in-Lonsdale is essentially a symbol of the best known product of the land which they owned. Such unadorned symbols would seem to indicate an especially early origin for this coat of arms, later heraldic symbolism becoming rather more complex. There seems little doubt that this coat of arms was in use from the first half of the 13th century or possibly earlier and is described in heraldic terms simply as "vert three garbs or".[1] This is known as a blazon and in modern English the equivalent description is three golden wheatsheaves on a green ground, as illustrated on the front cover of this book. The manor of Heton-in-Lonsdale was noted for its production of cereal crops on its fertile alluvial soil and it seems very likely that this prompted the first Heton lord of the manor to adopt this design on his coat of arms. This same coat of arms was used by his male descendants until the main line of this family of Hetons in Lonsdale died out through lack of male heirs towards the end of the 14th century.

The branch of the Heton family which settled in Heton-under-Horwich towards the beginning of the 14th century adopted a completely different coat of arms. Their blazon was "argent on a bend engrailed sable three bulls heads erased of the field",[2] and was recorded as such during a Herald's Visitation of Lancashire in 1531 when Richard Heton was lord of the manor. This device was in black (sable) and white or silver (argent) only with no colours and it has been suggested[3] that this colour scheme and diagonal bends on a shield

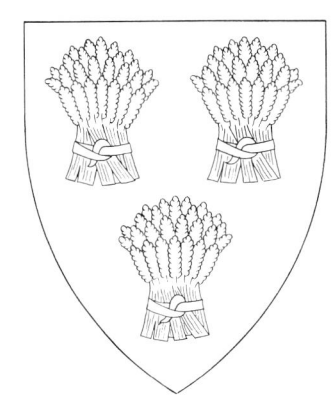

*Arms of Heton of
Heton-in-Lonsdale*

*Arms of Heton of
Heton-under-Horwich*

Arms of Heton of Chillingham.   *Arms of Heaton of Plas Heaton.*

were used by a number of gentry families in this part of Lancashire following a tradition set by the Grelleys, Barons of Manchester, and the most prominent family in the area in the early Middle Ages. Any male descendants who can trace their ancestry directly back to Richard Heton or one of his sons and who can satisfy the College of Arms of this, beyond reasonable doubt, are entitled to display this coat of arms.

The Hetons who established themselves at Chillingham in Northumberland fortified their original manorhouse and subsequently built the formidable border castle, largely in its present form, in 1345. It remained in their hands until 1426 when a lack of male heirs meant that the marriages of heiresses transferred the castle to the de Grey family.[4] The Chillingham Hetons' coat of arms was described as "vert a lion rampant argent and a border engrailed argent"[5] Another version was described without the border and could be earlier.[6] When the de Greys gained possession of Chillingham they adopted an almost identical coat of arms, the only difference being a change of ground colour, their blazon being "gules (red) a lion rampant argent within a border engrailed argent" [7]

The Heatons of Plas Heaton in North Wales, as has been stated earlier, chose a coat of arms which differed in only one respect from that of Heaton of Heaton-under-Horwich, with which family they believed themselves to be connected. The difference was that on the diagonal bend across the shield were portrayed three bucks heads instead of the three bulls heads of the Heaton-under-Horwich family, their blazon being " argent on a bend engrailed sable three bucks heads of the field"[8].

Even after the Heaton lands at Heaton-under-Horwich were sold to the Andertons several succeeding generations of male Heatons, descended from Richard of Heton and Birchley would, no doubt have had detailed knowledge of their ancestry and would presumably have displayed the arms to which they were entitled. The only physical example we still have of this is on the tomb of Bishop Martin Heton in Ely Cathedral, erected by his daughters in 1609. As time went by it seems the display of these arms fell out of use and the detailed evidence of the Heaton pedigree necessary to gain acceptance by the College of Arms was lost, although a knowledge of the blazon was retained by later members of the family.

The attempt in 1814 by a group of Heatons to revive their claim to the original estate (described in chapter 5) included investigation of the arms borne by earlier male members of the family but nothing came of this and it appears that no-one pursued officially their right to bear the arms at that time. It was not until the end of the 19th century that William Heaton of Lostock, encouraged by the research of John Heaton Partington, unofficially adapted the old Heaton arms and crest as the corporate arms of his company, William Heaton and Sons.

After William's death his son John bought a property at Prizet, near Kendal, then in Westmorland, now in Cumbria. At the end of the war in 1945 John Heaton of Prizet wished to erect a memorial to his father, William, and knew that it had been his father's wish to establish his entitlement to bear the Heaton's ancient coat-of-arms. This was never possible as he had not been able to produce evidence to satisfy the College of Arms of his direct succession from Richard Heton (1460-1535), the last Heaton to have had his pedigree recorded by a Heralds' Visitation of Lancashire in 1531. The problem was the ambiguity in the parentage of Richard's great-great-grandson Lambert Heaton (1619-1676), referred to in Chapter Seven and where we surmised, " on the balance of probabilities", that Lambert was the son of Ralph, and the grandson of Ferdinando. However, the College of Arms requires proof " beyond reasonable doubt" and this no-one has so far been able to provide. As Lambert's descendants appear to have been one of the most prolific branches of the family this is a disability which currently affects a large number of people.

John's only solution, therefore, was to apply to the College for a grant of arms, based on the ancient Heaton device, but with differences. The arms attributed to Richard Heton by the Heralds in 1531 were described in heraldic terms as " argent on a bend engrailed sable three bulls heads erased argent". The new arms granted to John Heaton on 17 August 1945 were "argent on a bend indented sable three bulls heads erased of the field " (i.e. argent)[9]. All direct male descendants of William Heaton of Lostock are entitled to display these arms. The search continues for the necessary evidence to establish beyond doubt the relationships of Ralph and Lambert.

Notes & References

1. Victoria County History of Lancs. 1914, vol.8, p.71.
2. VCH Lancs.,1911,vol.5, p.10
3. "The Pilkington Story", Elizabeth Williams-Ellis, 1997. Heraldry contributor Malcolm S. Howe.
4. Victoria County History of Northumberland, vol. xiv.
5. Ibid. vol. xiv, p. 327.
6. Burkes Armory 1843.
7. Ibid.
8. Ibid.
9. Richmond Herald, College of Arms, 1997.

Appendix 3

Heaton Burials at St. Mary's Church, Deane

Members of the Heton/Heaton family had been buried inside St. Mary's Church for many generations but eventually there came a time when no more burials could be accommodated there and graves were provided in the churchyard outside. The first Heaton memorial in the churchyard is dated 1709 and there are no memorials in the church itself. A meeting of the churchwardens held on 28 May 1807 resolved that the floor of the church should be levelled and reflagged and anyone who made a claim to burial ground in the church should arrange to lay stone slabs over the same. Records of many graves inside the church were presumably lost at that time as descendants failed to mark them and pay the annual fees required for their upkeep.

The memorials in this churchyard have been transcribed by Bolton members of Manchester & Lancs. Family History Society and supplemented by Mr Frank Stirrup and the reference numbers given below are on the microfiche which the Society has published for sale. In an abbreviated form the transcriptions are:-

199a Lambert Heaton died 21 Dec. 1850 aged 44 years.

504 Edmund Heaton of Haigh died 27 July 1819 aged 80.
     Elizabeth wife of the above died 9 Dec. 1813 aged 83.
     Elizabeth dau. of the above died 8 Aug. 1770 aged 2.
     William son of the above died 15 May 1772 aged 1.
     Elizabeth dau. of the above died 11 Feb. 1800 aged 25.

505 Lambert Heaton of Middle Hulton died 11 March 1866 aged 84.
     Betty Heaton his wife died 26 Feb 1875 aged 84.
     Elizabeth dau. of the above died 9 July 1828 aged 1y 10m.
     Elizabeth dau. of the above died 22 May 1833 aged 4.
     Nancy dau. of the above died 7 June 1846 aged 22.

506 Ellen Heaton of Heaton died 20 April 1850 aged 61.
     Isaac Heaton of Heaton died 21 Sept 1870 aged 79.

507 James Heaton buried 1 Feb. 1709.
     Elizabeth his wife bur. 6 Oct 1729.

Conclusion and Appendices 207

    John Heaton buried 18 July 1766.
    Elizabeth his wife bur. 30 Nov. 1779 aged 75.
    Rachel their dau. bur. 23 Jan. 1765.
    James Heaton buried 3 Oct. 1793.
    Ellen his wife bur. 15 April 1807.

508 One son and 8 daughters of James Heaton, yeoman of Heaton.
    Betty bur. 18 May 1752. Margery 23 Dec. 1758. Betty 28 June 1760.
    Ellen 5 July 1760. Margery 15 July 1760. Betty 30 May 1770.
    Rachel 10 Nov. 1770. Margaret 2 May 1771. William 8 May 1771.
    Jeremiah Heaton died 16 - 1796 aged 45 yrs. Mary his wife died 16 Mar 1832 aged 74 yrs. James their son died 13 July 1848 aged 71.

509 In memory of James Heaton died 11 July 1828 aged 32.
    also Alice Ainsworth died 8 Feb. 1867 aged 68.

510 Joseph Heaton, Over Hulton, died 19 July 1850 aged 74.
    Mary his wife died 5 Oct 1862 aged 81.
    Joseph their son buried 5 June 1804 aged 4 mths.
    Maria their daughter bur. 19 Oct 1806 aged 4.
    Jane his daughter died 10 July 1840 aged 27.
    John their son died 5 Oct. 1864 aged 57.
    Martha their daughter died 15 Feb. 1881 aged 65.
    James their son of Over Hulton died 30 April 1883 aged 78.
    Mary widow of John Partington and dau. of Joseph & Mary died 18 June 1891 aged 82.
    Maria daughter of Joseph & Mary died 14 June 1898 aged 73.

511 Lambert Heaton of Heaton died 2 June 1829 aged 77 yrs.
    Anne his wife died 7 September 1829 aged 81 yrs.
    William his son died 16 September 1857 aged 78 yrs.
    Sarah wife of William died 6 Jan. 1835 aged 48 yrs.

512 Peter Heaton of Halliwell died 15 Feb. 1822 aged 64.
    Betty his wife died 4 Nov. 1824 aged 64.
    Benjamin their son died 6 March 1824 aged 24.
    Peter Heaton died 2 Nov. 1856 aged 69.
    Mary his wife died 9 Mar 1853 aged 70.
    Benjamin their son died 9 May 1821 aged 1yr 10mths.
    homas their son died 7 Oct 1877 aged 63.
    Joseph Rowland their son died 26 Dec. 1884 aged 68.
    Elizabeth dau. of Peter and Mary died 10 Jan 1895 aged 74.
    John Pickering Heaton died 16 June 1833 aged 33.
    Robert Heaton died 14 September 1842 aged 34.

James Heaton died 9 February 1870 aged 46.

850 Elizabeth Heaton nee Millington died 27 Feb. 1925 aged 68.

990 Thomas Jones Heaton son of Peter & Annie Heaton of Willows Farm, Bolton died 18 Dec. 1903 aged 1yr 3m.

John Heaton of Over Hulton buried 4 June 1811 aged 72 yrs.
Mary wife of John Heaton buried 14 June 1803 aged 65.
Elizabeth their daughter died 1 May 1774.
James their son died 12 March 1776.
Mary their beloved daughter died 1 Aug. 1802 aged 35.
Ellen wife of John Heaton Partington and dau. of James & Annie Taylor of Twiston in this county bur. 12 Aug 1912 aged 74 yrs.
John Heaton Partington of Bridgewater Place, Middle Hulton
bur. 30 Aug. 1915 aged 76 yrs.

Appendix 4

Did they come with Canute?

A further extension of the research carried out by the late John Heaton, referred to in chapter 12 and which is known to the author, relates to the very earliest origins of the family which became the Heatons in Lancashire, and also in Yorkshire, North Wales and perhaps elsewhere in England. Based on his research John Heaton's contention is that this family is Scandinavian in origin but again there has been no action taken, as yet, to investigate the sources upon which he relied.

As already stated, he maintained that the father of Waldef, our first identifiable ancestor, was Orm and from him he goes back two generations of father and son to the time of King Canute in the early 11th century. He says that Orm's father Gamel was the first of the line to live permanently in England, Orm's grandfather Eilif having been awarded land in Yorkshire and Lancashire by the king when he arrived in England in 1016.

Prior to that date the earlier generations of the family lived in Norway, their names being Eilif's father Ulf, son of Rognvald son of Skogul Toste son of Rane whom John Heaton states was the earliest historical character in this line who can be identified and who was living in the last half of the 9th century.

Women named by John Heaton were Etheldritha, wife of Orm, Ragnhild, married to Eilif, and Ingibjorg, wife of Rognvald.

The probable effect of the Norman Conquest would have been, at the least, to replace Saxon overlords by Normans and the confiscation of land throughout England as King William and his tenants-in-chief proceeded to reward their followers by granting them possession of manors and evicting the former Saxon owners.. This process, coupled with the devastation of the North by William the Conqueror, very probably resulted in a substantial loss of assets to this family. So when Augustine first began to acquire land in Lonsdale there was a good deal of lost ground to make up.

Index

Entries in **bold** are illustrations

"Aero" yarns, **169**
A-frame houses, 20
Aberffraw, Anglesey, 43
active service, 23
Adam, brother of Waldef, 193
Adam, son of Roger, 20
Adam, son of Waldef, 9
Agincourt, battle of, 57
Agnes Hulton, wife of Richard Heton, 60
Agnes, wife of Roger, 22
agricultural depression, 142
agricultural productivity, 23
agriculture, 45
Alders Papermill, Tamworth, 173
Anderton Christopher II, 85
Anderton family, 72, 84, 85, 86,119
Anderton, James, 78, 79, 85, 100
Anderton, Christopher III, 85, 91
Anderton, Christopher, 72 - 78, 80, 84, 85, 95
Anderton, Fr Lawrence, SJ, 88
Anderton, Roger, 87
Anderton, Sir Charles, 2nd Bart., 86, 92, 112
Anderton, Sir Charles, 3rd Bart., 92
Anderton, Sir Francis, 1st Bart., 85, 91
Anderton, Sir Francis, 5th Bart., 92
Anderton, Sir James, 4th Bart., 92, 116, 117
Anderton, Sir Lawrence, 92
Anderton, Thurstan, 78
Anilla, wife of William IV, 31
animal prices, 14
anti-social behaviour , 45
Aquitaine, 49
arable farming, 142
Assessors for Hundred, 32
Atherton, first name, 176
Atherton, Philadelphia, 110
Augustine, 9,11,14,16,18,20,22

Banastre, Thomas, son of Roger, 45
Bannockburn, 32

Index

Beaumont tenants, **166**
Beaumont, Lady Mary Ethel, 87
Beaumont, Mona Josephine, Baroness, 87, 164
Billinge, Johan de, 51
Birchley Hall, 79, 85, **86**, 87
Birchley, 42, 43, 67, 102, 104, 196
Black Death, 32, 46
Black Prince, 48
Blacksmiths, 177, 178, 181
Bleaching, **151**, 152
Blundell, Elizabeth, 86, 87
Blundell, Henry, 86, 93, 121, 122, 134
Blundell, Robert, 86, 93, 94, 121
Bolde, Elizabeth, 70, 71, 75
Bolde, John, 70, 71
Bolton Borough Council, 164
Bolton Central Library, 4, 137, 160
Bolton Chronicle, 156
Bolton, 7, 46, 87, 141, 144, 152, 156, 164, 168, 169, 198
Bolton, Simon de, 28
Bolton, St. Georges Rd., 156
Bolton-le-Sands, 22, 27, 28, 29
Boroughbridge, battle of, 40
Boston, Mass., 172
Bosworth, battle of, 57, 59
Bradshaw, Elizabeth of Ravenhurst, 131
Brereton, Geoffrey, 73
Bretagh, Richard, attorney, 120
Brockholes, John, 33, 34
Bronte family, 194
Brune (Bourn), 11, 13, 20, 28, 29, 38
bubonic plague, 32, 46
building repairs, 46
Building works, 103
Burnt Edge farm, 138, 139
byre, 20

Calais, seige of, 43, 48
Canute, King, 209
carucate, fiscal measurement, 11, 14
Castles, Welsh, 27
Catholic press, Birchley, 88
Caton, William de, 31
cattle murrain, 120
chamfering & carving, 19

Chapel, St. Cuthbert's, Heton, 27
Charles II, King, 91
charters, 13th cent., 16, **26**
Chetham Library, 4
Chillingham, 193, **203**
Chorley New Road, 127, 163, 164,
Chorley, 170
Civil War, 88 - 91
Clitheroe, Honor of, 27
Clough Farm, 112, 121, 122, 127
Clough, The, Chorley New Road, **165**
coalmining, 151
Common Law, 73
company directors, 170
Conclusions, 196
Conservation Area, 164
Corn Laws, 140
corn, 24
Corrody, 51
Cosyn, Edward, 72, 73
cottage industry, 144, 169, 174, 197
cotton brokers, 170
cotton imports, 144
cotton spinning, 125, 144, 145, 194
cotton, longstaple, 170
County Palatine, 49
County War Agricultural Executive Committee (1917), 168
Coupmanwra, Thomas de, 27
Cow Hey farm, 138
Cranmer, Archbishop, 60
Crecy, battle of, 43, 47
Cressingham, Sir Henry de, 29
croft, village, 17
crofter, 152
Crompton, Samuel, 144, 146
Crosses & Heatons Ltd., 170
Crosses & Winkworths, 169
crucks, 19
customary acres, 117

dairy farms, 172
Dawe, Ethel Maria, 172
Deane Moorside farm, 136, 137
Deane Parish Church, St. Mary's, 61, **62**, 124, 127, 149
Deane, 6

Index 213

Deane, map of, **44**
Death sentence commuted, 129
Debenture, 170
deer, 36
Delph Hill Mill, 130, 147, 148, 158, 159, 163, 169, 170
demesne, 17
Denbigh, 27, 28, 184, 189, 190
Derby St. Mill, Bolton, 161
Derby, Earldom of, 59
Devastation by William I, 12
Development Area status, 174
Dieulacresse, Abbot of, 21, 22
Discharge Certificates, 183
Dispensation to marry (1398), 52
Diversification, 174, 197
Dixon, Janet Anne, 127, 159
Dixon, John, 127
Dixon, Rose, 127
Dobhill farm, 134
Dobson & Barlow, Bolton, 146
Doffcocker Hotel, 164
Domesday Book, 12, **13**
Domestic staff, Plas Heaton, 191
doomsman, 28

Edward I, King, 27, 37, 184
Edward II, King, 32, 37
Edward III, King, 31, 32
Egyptian and Sudan cotton, 159
Egyptian Mills, Bolton, 161
Elmar, Edward, 71, 72
Ely Cathedral, 96
emigration, 154
Entail, 66
Entwissle, Elys de, 53
Equity, 73
escaped slaves, USA, 181
estovers, 17
Estuary, River Lune, 14, 16
Etwall manor, 109
European Common Market, 168
Evesham, battle of, 25, 26

Family Tree 1, c.1140 - 1387, 30
Family Tree 2, c.1300 - 1500, 53

Family Tree 3, Richard Heton, 68
Family Tree 4, Martin Heton, 97
Family Tree 5, c.1534 - present, 118
Family Tree 6, Ravenhurst branch, 133
Farington of Farington, 58
Farington, Jane, 67, 69
farm buildings, 18th cent., 121
Farmers, USA, 178
farming, **18**, 103, 115
Farming, 19th cent., 140
Farnworth Workhouse, 163
Fashionable suburb, 164
Fealty, 13
Ferranti, Oldham, 154, 171
Feudal system, 12
Field names, Clough farm, 121
Filmer, Sir Robert, 97
Fire at Delph Hill Mill, 159
First World war, 167
fishing, 14, 17, 18,
Fletcher, Alice, 149
Food production, 167
forest clearance, 39
Forest Laws, 36
Forest of Horwich, 36
foresters, 38
Fosset, 69
freehold ground rents sold, 166
Furness, 27, 38
furniture, 20

Game Laws, 122
Garstang, Margaret, 60, 67
Gascony, 45
Gaunt, John of, 49
Gaveston, Piers, 40
Gerard, Jane nee Heton, 67, 70
Gerard, Miles, 67, 70
Gerard, Sir William, 109
Gerard, Thomas, 67
glebe lands, 17
Glyndwr, Owain, 56, 57
Great Council, 25, 31
Great Exhibition, 1851, 158
Grelley family, 36

Index 215

Grelley, Robert de, 37
Grelley, Thomas de, 37
Grimsargh, 11, 20
Gwynedd, 27

Halidon Hill, battle of, 43, 47
hallhouse, 18, 19, **21**
Halliwell, 59
Halton, 12, 31, 170
handloom weavers, 150, 177, 178
Hardwick manor, 109
Hardy & Page, 4
Harold, King, 12
Harwood Common, 101
Hawise, 23
Haymaking, 18th cent., 126
hazards, 32
Heaton & Brimelow, 160
Heaton burials at St. Mary's Church, Deane, 206
Heaton Hall, 18th cent., 16
Heaton hamlet, 12
Heaton Heraldry, 202
Heaton Old Hall, 54, 55, 95, 108, 124
Heaton township, 102, 105, 164
Heaton, Abner, USA, 178
Heaton, Alexander & Alice, 112
Heaton, Amos, USA, 178
Heaton, Ann Maria nee Taylor, 155, 156
Heaton, Ann, wife of Robert Filmer, 97
Heaton, Atherton, 110
Heaton, Basil, Rhual, 192
Heaton, Benjamin, chairman 1948, 170
Heaton, Charles & Alfred John, 161
Heaton, Charles, Great Lever, 161
Heaton, Edmund Moses, 153, 154, 171
Heaton, Edmund Ronald, 173, **174**
Heaton, Edmund, (b. 1740), tanner, 137
Heaton, Edmund, (b.1765) of New Field farm, 138, 151
Heaton, Edmund, farm labourer, 163
Heaton, Edward/Edmund, 150, 171
Heaton, Elizabeth, petitioner, 106
Heaton, Elizabeth, USA, 178
Heaton, Ffardinando, (b.1645-), 112, 113
Heaton, Gwenllian Margaret, Rhual, 192
Heaton, Hannah nee Spence, 154, 171

Heaton, Hugh Edward, Plas Heaton, 190-192
Heaton, Isaac of Ravenhurst, 135
Heaton, James of Ravenhurst, 131
Heaton, James, (b.1730), 132, 134
Heaton, James, (b.1950), 170
Heaton, James, printer, 156
Heaton, Jeffrey, USA, 177
Heaton, Jeremiah, (b.1753), 134
Heaton, Jeremy, (b.1779), 139
Heaton, John & Thomas Wood, 161
Heaton, John Cornelius, USA, **181**
Heaton, John of Blackrod, (b.1738), 136
Heaton, John of Ravenhurst, (b.1704), 131, 132
Heaton, John of Rylstone, (b.1769), 136, 145
Heaton, John Richard, Plas Heaton, 190
Heaton, John, (1735-1819), **124**
Heaton, John, (b. 1784), 160
Heaton, John, of Keighley, 193
Heaton, John, of Prizet, 170
Heaton, John, Plas Heaton, 186, 187
Heaton, Joseph, chairman 1944, 170
Heaton, Lambert (1619-1676), 110, **111**, 163
Heaton, Lambert son of John, 125, 146, 148
Heaton, Lambert, (b.1714), 119-122, 124
Heaton, Lambert, (b.1751), 121, 122, 127, 128
Heaton, Lambert, (d.1736), 119
Heaton, Margery, 116
Heaton, Martha, wife of Lambert, 117
Heaton, Martin, (b.1915), 170
Heaton, Mary nee Crompton, 136
Heaton, Mary of Ravenhurst, 135
Heaton, Mary, of New Field farm, 141
Heaton, Nancy nee Howarth, 145, 146, 149
Heaton, Peter & Sons, 158
Heaton, Peter (b.1788), 128, 158
Heaton, Peter Roger, 170
Heaton, Ralph, (1589-1652), 109
Heaton, Raymond Peter, 173, **174**
Heaton, Richard, (b.1918), 170
Heaton, Richard, (d.1647), 107
Heaton, Richard, of Plas Heaton, 186, 192
Heaton, Roger son of Richard, 105
Heaton, Sarah, Plas Heaton, 187
Heaton, Sarah, USA, 178
Heaton, Thomas & Joseph, 158, 160

Index 217

Heaton, Thomas, inventor, 157, 158
Heaton, Thomas, Liverpool, 149
Heaton, Thomas, printer, 155
Heaton, Wilfred John, Plas Heaton, 192
Heaton, Wilfred, Plas Heaton, 191
Heaton, William & Alice, 139, 149, 150, 171
Heaton, William of Lostock, 4, 127, 159, **160**, 163, 169, 204
Heaton, William of Westhoughton, 176, 177
Heaton-with-Oxcliffe, 24
Heatons in Yorkshire, 193
Henniker, Anne Elizabeth, 189
Henry III, King, 25
Henry IV, King, 49, 57
Henry V, King, 57
Henry VI, King, 57
Henry VIII, King, 66
Heton Chapel, St. Mary's Church, 61
Heton Edmund de, 33
Heton, 12, 20, 27, 67
Heton, Adam de, 29, 34
Heton, Adrey, (1556-), 74
Heton, Anne, (1557-), 74
Heton, Bishop Martin, 96
Heton, Bryan, 96, 106
Heton, Catharine de, 33, 34
Heton, Catharine, wife of Lambert, 95
Heton, Christiana de, 28
Heton, Elizabeth nee Aghton, 69, 70
Heton, Ferdinando, 95, 108
Heton, Harri, 186
Heton, John de (1462 -), 58
Heton, John I de, 28, 31, 34, 37,
Heton, John II de, 37, 38, 40, 42, 45
Heton, John III de, 42, 43, 50
Heton, Lambert, 95, 108
Heton, Margaret de, 33, 34
Heton, Nicholas de, (1436), 56
Heton, Ralph, 74, 75, 76, 78-81, 95
Heton, Richard of Heton & Birchley (1460 - 1535), 58, 59, 60, 67
Heton, Richard de (1361), 50
Heton, Richard, (1559), 74, 79, 105
Heton, Roger de, Kings Surgeon, 43
Heton, Roger, lawyer (1473 -), 73
Heton, Sir Roger de, 13, 22, 23, 25
Heton, Sir William de, 25 - 28, 31, 34

Heton, William de, (1398), 51, 58
Heton, William II de, 28, 29, 31
Heton, William II, (1445), 58
Heton, William II, daughters, 58
Heton, William III de, 28, 29, 31
Heton, William IIII de, 31, 32, 33
Heton, William of Birchley, 67, 69
Heton, William V de, 31, 33
Heton, William, son of Rauffe,(1549), 70, 71, 74, 76
Heton, William, the Merchant, 74-77, 95, 98
Heton-in-Lonsdale, 6, **8**, 11, 12, 14, 15, 16, 18, 23, 26, 28, 29, 36, **202**
Heton-under-Horwich, 28, 36, 37, 38, 43, **202**
Hietune, 12, **13**
Higher Derbyshires farm, 152
Higher House farm, 117, 119
hill country, 16
Hodgkinsons farm, Heaton, 125, 147
Hoghton, Adam de, 11, 21
Hoghton, Christiana de, 26
Hoghton, Hamo de, 26
Hoghton, Sir Richard de, 29, 33
Hole, Ralph de, 20
Holts farm, Lees, **153**, 154
Holyn (Hollin) Hey farm, 106, 158
Homage, 13
Horton Arms, Chadderton, 152
Horwich New Chapel, 149
Horwich, 7, 67, 69, 168, 184
houses, 17, 20
Howard, Miles Francis Fitzalan, 87, 164
Hulton, Richard de, 38, 44
Hulton, Robert, 59
Hulton, William de, (1369), 50
Hundred Court, 28
Hundred Years War, 32, 47
Hundreds map, **10**
"Hungry Forties", 152
husbandmen, 98
Huyton, Robert de, 42

Ince Blundell, 86, 94
Industrial Revolution, 7, 124, 197
Inflation, 99, 103
Inventions, 157
Isabel, wife of Roger the Kings Surgeon, 43

Isabella the recluse, 56
Isabella, Queen, 32
Isolda, wife of Richard de Heton, 50

Jesuits & Jacobites, 91
Joan of Arc, 57
John, King, 11, 20
John, Prince, 9
Justices of the Peace, 31, 51, 54

Keepers of the Peace, 31
Kellett, Robert, 117
Kendal, 3rd Baron, 22
Kings Coroner, 27
Kings Escheator, 29
Kings Surgeon, 43
Kirkheaton, 193
Kirkman, Joseph, 139
Knighthood, 23
Krutilla, Julia Heaton, 182

Lacy, Alice de, 40
Lacy, Henry de, 27, 37, 40, 184
Ladybridge, Chorley New Road, **165**
Lancashire & Yorkshire Railway Co., 163
Lancashire, 6 - **9**, 11, 17
Lancashire, Sheriff of, 22, 31
Lancaster Assizes, 22
Lancaster Castle, 16, 32
Lancaster, 6, 11, 12, 20, 27, 29, 33
Lancaster, Duke of, 49
Lancaster, Thomas, Earl of, 40
Lancaster, William de, 11, 22
Land drainage, 141
Leases, 103
Lewes, battle of, 25, 26
"Lieutenants" in Halliwell, 158
Lincoln, Earl of, 27, 28, 37, 40, 184
Lineage, 160
Linen, 144
Liverpool, 149
Livestock, 115
Llewelyn ap Gruffudd, Prince of Gwynedd, 27, 184
Llewenni, Denbighshire, 185
London Electrical Engineers, 172

Longshaw Fold farm, 120, 129
Lonsdale Hundred, 29
Lonsdale, 7, 9, 20, 184
Looms, 132
Lostock Hall, 55, 67, 69, 84
Lostock Junction Mills, 159, 160, 166, **167**, 169, 170
Lostock, Baronetcy of, 91
Lower House farm, 116
Lune, River, 6, 9, 18, 27

Magna Carta, 25
Manchester (Mamecestre), 37
Manchester Grammar School, 63
Manchester, Barony of, 27
manor, lord of the, 14, 23
manorhouse, 18
manorial rolls, 14
markets, 24, 46
Markland, Mary, of Westhoughton, 136
Markland, Ralph & Elizabeth, 135
Mather, Ann, 177
Matilda, Empress, 9
menial services, 17
Meyrick, Sir Samuel Rush, 185
Middleton, 102
Mill Cottage, 17
mill girls (1832), **171**
mill, 17, 22, 24
Montfort, Simon de, 25, 26, 31
Morris, Betty, 125, 147
Mortimer, Roger, 32
Mosley, Sir Edward, 109
Moulebreck, 31
Mount Pleasant, Ohio, USA, 181
Murder! , 128
muslin manufacture, 148

Napoleonic Wars, 140
Nevilles Cross, battle of, 48
Nevy Fold farm, 145
New Field farm, 138, 139
Nicholson, Anne, 124
Norfolk, 17th Duke of, 164
Norman Conquest, 9, 12
North America , 176

Index 221

North Meoles, 71
North Wales, 28
Northumberland, 9
Northumbria, 9
Nuttall, Thomas, esq, 148

Old Hall Farm, 124, 127
Oldsnap, Yorks., 193
Orleans, siege of, 57
Overton Church, 17
Oxcliffe, John de, 27
Oxford Council (1258), 25, 31
Oxgang, 11, 22

pannage, 13
Parliament, 25, 31
Partington, John Heaton, 4, 137, 160
Partington, Mary nee Heaton, 137
Patents, 157
payment of relief, 31
Penanllu, North Wales, 43
Pendlebury, James, 120
Penwortham, Barons of, 11
Penwortham, Lordship of, 27
Perwich - , 72, 73
Peterloo, 177
Picton Street Mill, 124, 130, **147**, 170
Piggott & Dean's Directory, 160
Pilgrimage of Grace, 63
Pilkington, Ann, 110, 163
Pilkington, Betty, 125, 129
Pilkington, Richard de, 42
Pilkington, Robert, 129
Pirates, 16
Plas Heaton Heraldry, 188, **203**
Plas Heaton, 185, 187-**189**, 193
Poitiers, battle of, 48
Ponden hall, 194
Pool Fold farm, 129
Population explosion, Bolton, 141
potato growing, 168
Poulton, 13
Prescott family, 136
Printer & stationer, 155

rack rents, 120
Radcliffe, William, 44
railway network, 140
Ramification, 163, 199
Ravenhurst branch of the Heatons, 131
Ravenhurst farm, 112, 131, 132, 134
Receivership, 93
recusants, 87
Redman, Agnes de, 21
Redman, Henry de, 9, 21
Redman, Norman de, 9
Reinfred, Gilbert fitz, 9, 23
Rhual, **192**, 193
Richard I, King, 9, 144
Richard II, King, 49
Richard III, King, 59
Robert the Bruce, King, 32
Robichaud, Judie, 182
Robinson, Elizabeth Georgina, 173
Roger de Heton, son of Roger, 20, 21
Roger of Poitou, 9, 12
Roger, son of Augustine, 11, 20
Roger, son of Sir William de Heton, 28
Roos connection, 52
Rorkes Drift, 191
Rossal, 22
Rosset, 29, 38
Rothwell, Anne, 119
Rumworth, 67, 69
Runymede, 25
Ryley, Edmund, 131
Ryley, Elizabeth, 131
Rylstone Mill, 145, 146

Sabina, 20
Salford Hundred, 28, 36, 44
saltmarshes, 16, **19**
Savoy Hospital, 72, 73
Scandinavian origin ?, 209
Scotland, border with, 27
Scots, 16, 26, 32
Second World War, 168, 182, 184
seisin, livery of, 13
Settlements (1529, 1530), 67
sheep rearing, 24

Index 223

Sheepcote farm, 138, 139
shell company, 170
Simpson, Mary, of Halliwell, 158
Skipton, 87, 145
Slack Hall farm, **138**, 139, 150
Sluys, naval battle, 43, 47
Social classes, 98
solar, 19
South Wales Borderers, 191
Spence, Anthony & Esther, 152
Spence, Hannah, of Chadderton, 152, 171
Spring Gardens, Bolton, 123, 125, 149
St. Helena Mill, Bolton, 144
St. Mary's Church, Deane, 62, 117, 206
Stamford Bridge, battle of, 12
Stanley, Thomas, Lord, 57, 59
Stapleton, Miles, Baron Beaumont, 87
Statute of Uses (1536), 66
Statute of Wills (1540), 66
Stephen, King, 6, 9
steward, 16
suit of mill, 22
Sunderland, 69
surnames, 13

Tar Hall farm, 138, 151
Tempest, Henry, 87, 148
Tempest, Mary Ethel, 87
Tempest, Sir Charles, of Heaton, 87
Tempest, Stephen, 87
Textiles, 116, 144
Thornton, 11
Thurland, Thomas, 72, 73
Torver, 11, 20, 22, 29
Tostig, Earl, 12
Townleys, farm, 159
Township of Heaton, 163
Trade & Industry, 144
"trappers", 157
Trek to the West, 178, **179**
Tudor, Henry, 57, 59
turbary, 17

U S War veterans, 182
Ulverston, 9, 11, 14, 20, 22, 26, 29, 38, 67, 69

Underground Rail Road, USA, 180
upland farms, 138, 141, 163
Urswick (Great), 20, 38
US Civil War, 182

Victoria County History, 24
villeins, 16

wages, 33
Waldef, 9, 22, 193
Wales, 27
wardship, 20, 21
Warin, Bussel 2nd, 11
Warper operative (1999), **171**
Warre, Thomas de la, (1420), 54
Warres, de la, Barons of Manchester, 37
Wars against French & Scots, 47
Wars of the Roses, 57, 193
wattle & daub, 18, 19
Welsh wars, 23, 37
Wesham, 11, 20, 29
Westby, Richard, 33, 34
Wetherheld, Roger, moneylender, 71-74
Whalley Abbey (1536), 64
Whalley hermitage (1438), 56
wildfowling, 14, 17
William Heaton & Sons Ltd., 169
William I, King, 9, 12, 14, 16
William Lawrence & Son Ltd., 170
William, son of Waldef, 9
window shutters, 19
Winstanley, Humphrey, 69, 78
Womens Land Army, 168
Woodward, Ellen, 134
yeoman farmers, 33, 98, 134, 197
Yorkshire, 9, 193